The Road
A Study of John Bunyan's Pilgrim's Progress

VIEW FROM
THE FRONT OF
HOUGHTON HOUSE
Supposed to be
The House Beautiful

The Road

A Study of
John Bunyan's Pilgrim's Progress

By
John Kelman, D.D.

Volume I.

With Eight Illustrations from Photographs
by the Author

KENNIKAT PRESS
Port Washington, N. Y./London

THE ROAD

First published in 1912
Reissued in 1970 by Kennikat Press
Library of Congress Catalog Card No: 77-113339
ISBN 0-8046-1025-8

Manufactured by Taylor Publishing Company   Dallas, Texas

TO

MY MOTHER

WHO FIRST LED ME TO THE BOOK

AND TO THE ROAD

PREFACE

The Pilgrim's Progress *is one of the everlasting books. Each new generation repeats the miracle of finding strength and consolation for its altered thoughts and needs, in the work of an author upon whom his times had branded a peculiar mark, both in respect of his theological convictions and his suffering of persecution. The reason for this is, of course, the essential humanness of the man and his allegory. It is this human quality, this unswerving truth to experience rather than to theory, which forms the link between him and such great humanists as Chaucer, Dante, Shakspeare, and Goethe. His claim to rank among them on the supremest heights of genius may be disputed: his claim to match them for humanity, pure and unerring in its delineations, is beyond dispute.*

The present series of studies is built up from notes of addresses given to classes in Peterculter and in Edinburgh, and subsequently printed in shorter form in the pages of the Expository Times. *The writer hopes to follow this first volume with two others, the second continuing the commentary through the remainder of the First Part and (more briefly) the whole of the Second Part of the* Pilgrim's Progress, *and the third consisting of essays on various biographical and literary subjects connected with John Bunyan and his work.*

The first two volumes are intended as a commentary or textbook upon the Pilgrim's Progress, *to be read point by point along with the original. In them are gathered notes from existing commentaries old and new, and references to cognate thoughts and passages in other literature. At the same time an endeavour has been made to construct a continuous exposition,*

THE ROAD

which (again in virtue of the human interest of John Bunyan's mind) may have a certain independent value for the thought of the present day.

We are warned, in Bunyan's rhymed conclusion of Part I. :—

> *"Take heed also, that thou be not extreme*
> *In playing with the outside of my Dream."*

It is a very necessary warning, when the outside is so full of charm and interest. Yet there is no reason why the most powerful preaching should be made less effective by the discovery that it is also very perfect art. Religion and Literature are both of them rare gifts of God to man, and we shall only wonder the more at the lavishness of His generosity as we see how variously gifted this tinker of Bedford was.

The story of Christian is on the one hand an allegory of the spiritual life, and on the other hand a romance in which the unity of the leading character is sustained throughout, as in an actual biography. Yet it is to be remembered that the Pilgrim is not presented as the only type of Christian life and character. Theologians generally, and especially those who wrote in an age which tended to define its faith with extreme precision of detail, have been apt to demand too much uniformity in religious experience. Bunyan was too close an observer of life to fall into that mistake. Christian, Hopeful, and Faithful arrive at the Celestial City each in his own way, though for a longer or shorter distance they may travel together. And this breadth and catholicity of portraiture is another reason for the perennial vitality of the Pilgrim's Progress.

CONTENTS

CHAP.		PAGE
I.	THE BEGINNING OF THE PILGRIMAGE	1
II.	OBSTINATE AND PLIABLE	11
III.	THE SLOUGH OF DESPOND	20
IV.	MR WORLDLY WISEMAN	26
V.	RIVAL GUIDES	33
VI.	THE WICKET GATE	40
VII.	THE INTERPRETER'S HOUSE	49
VIII.	THE INTERPRETER'S HOUSE—THE SCENES IN DETAIL	55
IX.	THE WAY OF THE CROSS	69
X.	FORMALIST AND HYPOCRISY	77
XI.	THE HILL DIFFICULTY	83
XII.	THE HOUSE BEAUTIFUL	93
XIII.	THE HOUSE BEAUTIFUL—(*continued*)	103
XIV.	THE STUDY AND THE ARMOURY	113
XV.	THE BATTLE WITH APOLLYON	124
XVI.	THE VALLEY OF THE SHADOW OF DEATH	142
XVII.	POPE AND PAGAN	153
XVIII.	FAITHFUL	159
XIX.	FAITHFUL'S TEMPTATIONS	167
XX.	TALKATIVE	180
XXI.	WILDERNESS AND CITY	198
XXII.	VANITY FAIR	203
XXIII.	VANITY FAIR—THE PERSECUTION	216
INDEX		231

ILLUSTRATIONS

VIEW FROM THE FRONT OF THE HOUGHTON HOUSE .	*Frontispiece*
	PAGE
SLOUGH OF DESPOND, ELSTOW	20
THE WICKET GATE, ELSTOW	40
SIR THOMAS HILLERSDON'S MANSION, ELSTOW . . .	62
THE CROSS, ELSTOW	70
HOUGHTON HOUSE	94
PULPIT, ELSTOW CHURCH	177
THE MOOT HALL, ELSTOW	203

CHAPTER I

THE BEGINNING OF THE PILGRIMAGE

THE opening words of the *Pilgrim's Progress*, telling of the WILDERNESS and the DEN, introduce the book with a sigh. John Bunyan, too, was a footsore pilgrim. The den is Bedford Jail—the traditional jail on the bridge, in which he spent his last term of imprisonment in the year 1676,[1]— so that it was from prison that this book also came, like so many great books. John in Patmos, Cervantes in Spain, Ayala in England,[2] Luther in the Wartburg, Rutherford in Aberdeen—these are a few of Bunyan's fellows in this respect.

THE DREAM has a double significance and interest.

1. Dreams were by the Puritans regarded in the solemn and, indeed, fearful aspect of the normal means by which the supernatural world broke through upon the soul, in revelations which were generally ominous. A sensitive and brilliant imagination like Bunyan's was peculiarly subject to such conceptions. 'Even in my childhood,' he tells us 'the Lord did scare and affright me with such fearful dreams, and did terrify me with fearful visions.' It is interesting to compare this with the dream-lore of Shakespeare, and with such weird ' year and a day ' premonitions as that of Boyle of the famous Hell-fire Club. A similar

---

[1] For proof of this statement see Dr Brown's *John Bunyan*, chapters viii. and xi.; *cf.* Froude's *Bunyan*, p. 73: also *John Bunyan*, by the author of *Mark Rutherford*, pp. 50-52.

[2] *Cf.* Snell's *The Fourteenth Century*, p. 371.

1

uncanny character appears frequently in the present book, which breaks into many portentous terrors.[1]

2. The dream was the conventional form of the older English literature of the imagination. The early French romances regularly take this form, and retain it in their English translations. Chaucer's introduction to his *Romaunt of the Rose* gives the mediæval point of view concerning dreams very fully. One of the best known and finest instances is Langland's, beginning—

> 'In a somer seson whan soft was the sonne . . .
> I was wery forwandred, and went me to reste
> Under a brode banke bi a bornes side,
> And as I lay and lened and looked in the wateres
> I slombred in a slepyng, it sweyued so merye.'

De Guileville's *Pèlerinage de l'Homme*, which is in some ways the prototype of Bunyan's book, begins similarly, as also the other thirteenth-century epics of the *trouvères*, such as *La Voie de Paradis* and *Le Songe d'Enfer*, of which latter, it is said, the influence is strongly marked in Dante's *Inferno*. It is worthy of remark, however, that Dante's vision is not a dream.[2] He was wide awake (in this, as in so much else, an exception and a protest), when—

> 'In the midway of this our mortal life
> I found me in a gloomy wood,'

THE MAN is suddenly introduced—a typical figure, like *Everyman* in the old Morality Play. The rags in which he is clad are borrowed from Isaiah lxiv. 6. And the first thing noticeable about this ragged man is that his face is turned away from his own house. There are many things that set men's faces from their own house—tempting sins, the craving for excitement and company, a roving fancy.

---

[1] *Cf.* Cheever, p. 17, and Froude's *Bunyan*, ch. i.

[2] Compare the interesting and suggestive contrast between Dante and Petrarch as travellers in Snell's *The Fourteenth Century*, p. 242. For Dante's dream in the *Vita Nuova cf.* Rossetti's *Dante and his Circle*, pp. 33, 116.

THE BEGINNING OF THE PILGRIMAGE

But the only respectable one is Conscience, which is the cause of this man's attitude.

The central facts about this man are, that he is—

    1. *A man with a burden.*
    2. *A man with a book.*

The social problem has been summed up in the phrase: 'Two men, a woman, and a loaf.' The Christian problem is similarly summed up in ' A man, a burden, and a book.'

1. *A man with a burden.* Sin is often described by active and aggressive metaphors—it is a deceiver, a destroyer, an enemy, etc. This passive one is more dreadful, for it tells simply of the dead weight of fact. Facts are ' chiels that winna ding.' Sin is, to Paul, ' this dead body '; and the flaccid mass of inelastic flesh, at once soft and heavy, is horrible enough without the implied hint of decay. The worst thing about sin is just that it is there—an irrevocable fact which the sinner has put there. When he realises this he feels it as a burden : he cannot sleep, or eat, or work, or play as once he did. Yet that is a precious pain. The far deeper danger is that one should grow accustomed to it, as the Swiss peasant to the growing load of hay or Milo to his ox, until he is able complacently to ' draw iniquity with a cart rope.' The unblushed-for past—the dead weight of sinful facts faced deliberately and carried lightly—that is a doom far deeper than the most oppressive load.

2. *A man with a book.*[1] There are among us many ' whose life was moulded by a book.' We all of us possess several books, but there are some whom one book possesses. It is of vast importance to choose carefully what book that shall be. A man's one book will very likely become his tyrant. Doughty travelled in Arabia for three years with nothing but

---

[1] On the paramount influence of the Bible on John Bunyan's writings, see Stevenson's *Text-Book*, chap. i.

the Bible and Spenser's *Faerie Queene*. His *Arabia Deserta* is written as with the pen of Spenser. One of the most pathetic things in Nansen's *Farthest North* is the story of that dreary winter when the two men, cut off from all the world, had no literature but the *Nautical Almanac*. Here we have the Great Book doing its work. It has become the master of the man's imagination, the tyrant of his conscience. The Bible is the never antiquated text-book of Hebraism. Culture, in the form of Hellenic æstheticism and intellectualism, is also God's word to man. But it is the other word, spoken in the harsher tongue, which has deepened and kept deep the conscience of the generations.

The burden was not the fear of punishment, although indeed there was the prophecy that 'this our city will be burned with fire from heaven.'[1] It was his sense of the fact of sin. Burns' scornful lines are familiar—

> 'The fear of hell's a hangman's whip
> To keep the wretch in order.'

Yet the fear of punishment is also a factor in the event, and we need not be too dainty about this. The prodigal son came back to his father only when the fear of perishing came upon him; it was not a noble, but a very mean motive for coming, yet the main thing is the fact that he came.

The Pilgrim's treatment by his family was an appeal to every form of human weakness. *Deriding* appealed to his self-esteem; *chiding* to his anger and his cowardice; *neglect* to his loneliness and need of friends. Some are mocked out of their highest destiny, others scolded out of it, others, who would have resisted active opposition, miss it through the humiliating experience of neglect. It is this that is hardest of all

---

[1] It is a striking fact that, although *Grace Abounding* was published in 1666, the year of the great fire of London, and the *Pilgrim's Progress* only ten years later, there is no allusion in either book to that event, unless indeed we may see one in this sentence, whose ultimate source, however, is of course to be found in the Bible.

THE BEGINNING OF THE PILGRIMAGE

to bear—the sense of one's utter insignificance, the quiet flow of the world past one. There is, indeed, one harder thing, and that is *pity*. Browning never described a nobler course than that of his *Grammarian*—

> 'He knew the signal, and stepped on with pride
> Over men's pity.'

But here the man turned the tables on them. *He began to pray for and pity them.* He takes the high ground of certainty, ' We are of God, and the whole world lieth in wickedness.' Doubtless they would not thank him, but they would feel it. Nothing is so impressive as a man who is absolutely sure. His pity was irritating at the time, but it brought them after him in the end.

This may seem to the reader a poor introduction to a hero.[1] First impressions are important, and neither tears nor fears are impressive. Yet Bunyan acted advisedly in this. To him, as to all Puritans, it was not the man, but the man's conscience that was the real hero. As in that wonderful poem, *The Hound of Heaven*, by Francis Thompson, it is not fear, but Heaven, that is pursuing the soul. The situation, when that is realised, becomes terrible indeed, but not pitiable. And further, there is here a very true heroism, in spite of fears and tears. Nothing in the world is so heroic, after all, as to cut one's way alone through conventions and habits and troops of friends, out into the open, where there is no company but conscience, and no property but the burden of one's own sin.

In the words which follow the start we are introduced to the new figure of Evangelist. Bunyan's ministers would form a rare gallery of portraits. Each is individual, clearly drawn, and characteristic. Of Evangelist there are in all three notices, but this is the only one found in the original edition.

[1] *Cf. Kerr Bain*, i. 48.

As the editions went on, Bunyan's conception of Evangelist was enriched and changed somewhat. In the tenth edition a verse was added here in which the words occur, ' Evangelist who lovingly him greets.' Experience mellowed Bunyan's conceptions, and love is the last word to life, which in this instance goes back and makes itself also the first.

The picture of the man is essentially that of a prophet. He is severe, austere, without those little human touches which make us feel in him a man, a brother. He is aloof and withdrawn. This air of authority and mastership is at once attractive and repellant, and in both ways it is liable to deterioration. When it repels it is apt to react in a kind of self-conscious isolation and imaginary sense of martyrdom very deadly to the prophet's influence. When it attracts it may become priestliness, or it may lapse into mere personal vanity and conceit. Evangelist-worship, with the excessive sense of the importance of the Evangelist's own spiritual experiences and exploits, and the neurotic personal relations which are apt to follow, is one of the perpetual dangers of this high office. Here, Bunyan is sane and healthy as usual. This prophet's authority rests on nothing but the sheer force of truth; his work is to send men away from himself to the light by which man must live.

Evangelist's way of dealing with this inquirer is instructive and significant by its extreme simplicity. There is no trick or machinery of any kind, but the simplest sort of fair and honest dealing. There is no haste nor ' indecent urging,' for the soul's processes cannot be forced. There is no play upon the feelings. From first to last the interview is an appeal to reason. Reason as an instrument of evangelism is generally undervalued among us, yet some of the most eminent Christians [1] have testified that they owed their conversion to a sermon or a book, not rational merely, but con-

[1] *E.g.* the late Rev. Professor Laidlaw of New College, Edinburgh.

THE BEGINNING OF THE PILGRIMAGE

troversial and argumentative. The most striking feature of Evangelist's work here is its reticence and reserve. He does not say more than is absolutely needed; and the mark of excellence in dealing with the souls of men is to have learned not to say too much.

The art of questioning is also well developed here. By swift advances he immediately gets beyond all possible shams to realities, beyond side-issues to the heart of the matter, beneath confused states of feeling to the actual facts of the case. Like an able lawyer, he is only interested in facts, and is determined above all else to reach perfect clearness.

What is revealed by this scrutiny? *A man, in utter bewilderment and abject fear,*—' he looked this way and that way as if he would run, and yet he stood still.' This sentence has been compared to the statue of a racer, petrified as it were in the act of starting. The reason of such an attitude is frequently spiritual inertia and paralysis of will. Thousands of men know but cannot go. When the Psalmist says, ' I will run in the way of thy commandments when Thou hast enlarged my heart,' he wishes his soul to be set free to do what it knows quite well. But *this* inactivity is different. The man does not know where he is nor what to do. What he wants is enlightenment and definite direction. 'The propeller,' as Dr Kerr Bain says, 'works close to the rudder,' and there will be no want of pace if the man knows where to go.

The first effect of Evangelist on the pilgrim is to bring out into clearness the truth about himself and his condition. Amidst all his bewilderment one thing grows perfectly plain. He is terribly afraid of death. There is a light-hearted way of discounting death, and mocking the fear of it, which passes for courage, and is really mere slightness of intellect and poverty of conscience and imagination. The awfulness of death remains, felt by ineradicable instinct, and it was meant to remain. The subject may be called crude, harsh, morbid, if you like; but the winding-sheet, the coffin, and the six feet of earth are facts that wait for us. We may change the colour of its livery, but the fact we cannot change. It has been supposed to be a religious thing to meditate on death, and forecast its circumstances, and in this way religion has grown morbid. A well-known passage in modern fiction illustrates the morbidness without the religion. Thinking of her birthdays 'she suddenly thought one afternoon, when looking in the glass at her fairness, that there was yet another date, of more importance to her than those; that of her own death, when all these charms would have disappeared; a day which lay sly and unseen among all the other days of the year, giving no sign or sound when she actually passed over it; but not the less surely there. When was it? Why did she not feel the chill of each yearly encounter with such a cold relation?'[1] The only use of such speculations is to force death back into the region of actual realities that we may reckon with it, and pass on to the true business of life. Lost in the mists of the future the event of death seems uncertain and life eternal. Did we know the hour, life, foreshortened by the exact sight of the end, would shrink to a very small appearance though the limit were at fivescore years.

Out of the mist the spectre of death has risen with appalling clearness upon this man, because death is but the second last of terrors. It is the depth 'lower than the grave,' the days after the day of death, that arm the fear. This, too, is a great human fact.[2]

What is the solution? The wicket gate stands for an incident in life that will destroy the fear of death. What it means we are not yet told. The man cannot see it, and he says so frankly. At this stage he can see nothing clearly, for

---

[1] *Tess of the d'Urbervilles*, ch. xv.
[2] *Cf. Hamlet's* soliloquy and Browning's *Christmas Eve*, iii.

THE BEGINNING OF THE PILGRIMAGE

the whole region of religious truth is confused and obscure. No directions mean anything to him. The redeeming feature is that he says so frankly ' No.' The exaggeration of experience, the too facile compliance with advice which one does not as yet understand, are the real dangers of this state. Evangelist is too wise to urge him. There is a shining light ahead, and he points him to that. Every soul of man can see at least *some* light of hope ahead, shining in the direction of the God or Christ or ideal which is as yet obscure. It may be but the light of some possible duty, some sense of honour, some belief in life, some vague trust in the future. Such an experience is splendidly sung by Longfellow in his *Light of Stars*. The point is, not that the light is full, or even comprehensible. If it be clear enough to flee towards, that is enough. For, here as elsewhere, *solvitur ambulando*. What is wanted is directed motion towards the light; the rest will follow. So it comes to pass that one may be on the road to Christ when one cannot as yet see Him.[1]

What follows is immediate action—Carlyle's great expedient in the 'Everlasting Yea' of *Sartor Resartus*. It is a rude beginning of Christian's journey, this breaking away from the people about him with his fingers in his ears, yet it is the only way to begin a decisive course. The future is so beset with uncertainties that the only safety lies in refusing to hear any voice but one, and refusing to dazzle with side-lights, even from kindly windows, the eyes that have caught the first faint gleam in the sky that calls them on.

The last words of the description are full of poetic and dramatic suggestion, ' he fled towards the middle of the plain.' We see the man going out into the open of the world, and we feel the vast loneliness of the second day of religious experience. That plain has to be crossed, though it be dreary and

[1] Many passages in Romanes' *Thoughts on Religion* afford fine illustrations of this.

dispiriting as the first stage of Childe Roland's adventure in Browning's similar allegory. There is always, however, the possibility of the visions of the plain.[1]

[1] *Cf.* Ezek. viii. 4: Ramsay's *Education of Christ*; Prologue, on 'The Power of the Great Plains.'

CHAPTER II

OBSTINATE AND PLIABLE

It is a curious fact this, of the neighbours meddling with a man's religious life. One would think it easy for people to mind their own business, but in such matters it never is. The sudden earnestness of a companion makes him a living conscience, irritating other consciences around him.

This is the first of those couples, or small groups, in the choice of which Bunyan shows himself so great a master of antithesis. Passion and Patience, Evangelist and Worldly Wiseman, Timorous and Mistrust, etc., are all significant and suggestive. Here as elsewhere the names are simple English words, in striking contrast with the fanciful names of the Euphuists, or even those of many religious writers.[1] Obstinate and Pliable are two opposite and common types. They appear in Lord and Lady Macbeth, and many other instances, for they stand for deep-seated elements in human nature and permanent factors in history. Here, therefore, we are at a point of peculiar interest and importance, watching Christianity touching these, and seeing the various effects produced, as a powerful chemical produces different reactions in different substances it encounters. It is to be noted that Obstinate and Pliable at first resolved to fetch Christian back by force, but that later on they changed their minds, Christian being the sort of man to make them think twice before attempting it.

OBSTINATE.—There was enough in Bunyan's own experience to let him know Obstinate from within. ' In these

[1] *Cf.* William Law's *Fulvius, Cœlia,* etc.

days I would find my heart to shut itself up against the Lord, and against His holy word; I have found my unbelief to set, as it were, the shoulder to the door, to keep Him out.' Here, however, we have the type full-drawn and unrelieved.

1. *A narrow man*, and therefore unintelligent. In the ' narrow forehead ' of this fool there is room for only one idea at a time. He knows not the width of the world nor the manifold height and depth of human experience. The only use that he makes of his mind is, as Dr Kerr Bain happily says, to make it up. He is all will and no thought, though indeed that is rather an animal habit of *staying put* than anything that ought to be called will. The object of this stupid persistency may be either some trifle which has chanced to become his hobby, or it may be a blind attachment to the present order, or a worship of consistency, according as the man is vain or servile or self-conscious.

2. *A self-conceited man*, for this Obstinate is of the vain class as well as of the worshippers of consistency. He cannot bear to confess that he ever made a mistake. He will not revise his course of conduct, but will carry it on after he sees it to be foolish or bad, simply because he has made it his. This is cleverly shown by his estimate of others. They are ' craz'd-headed coxcombs.' The twelfth juryman, alone in his opinion, finds the other eleven the most obstinate men he has ever met. It is a characteristic view of others, whether they are seen in books or persons. To advise him is to alienate him. Like a Brahmin, he finds the place on which your shadow has fallen defiled by it. He will oppose anything in which he has not had a hand, for, in every enterprise, he must be all or nothing.

3. *A bad-tempered man*. His arguments are interjections and bad names. He hates argument, because he cannot bear to be opposed. Any one who knows a subject well enough to

OBSTINATE AND PLIABLE

argue about it, seems to be doing him a personal injury. The silence of Christian towards Obstinate is wise, for this kind of temper shows him to be essentially a weak man. Obstinacy is mistaken for strength by shallow people, but really it is often a kind of instinctive trick of self-protection for the weakest characters, and its refusal to argue is an instinctive cover for the conscious ignorance of the most poorly equipped minds. Yet this man will persist in it with determination to the very last. He is 'obstinate in destruction.' Like the athlete who knows that the overstrain of his race is killing him, like the man of whom Professor Drummond used to speak, who deliberately sacrificed his eyesight to his vice, this man goes conscious to his doom. To put down your foot firmly is a good habit; but to put it down firmly on thin ice over deep water means death.

The chief reason for such fatal obstinacy lies in the region of conscience. To know the better and do the worse embitters a man. Misery of temper is the effect of rejected truth, and hardness of heart is the penalty of experience ignored or repudiated. There may be a hint of this in his reference to the 'company of these craz'd-headed coxcombs.' Had he, one wonders, been of that company himself? At all events, fewer people fall upon bitterness like this through native disposition than through turning their backs to the light. 'A little grain of conscience made him sour.'[1]

PLIABLE.—The excellently drawn character of Pliable is epitomised in the inimitable touch, ' I begin to come to a point'; just as Mr Blindman, the foreman of the Vanity Fair jury, says, 'I see clearly that this man is a heretic.' Bunyan knew Pliableness as well as Obstinacy by experience, for indeed the changes of mood in *Grace Abounding* become

[1] Tennyson, *Vision of Sin*.

almost monotonous. But Bunyan, like Peter, had his originally pliable nature tempered into fine steel.

It is the picture of a slight, impressionable, easily influenced character, of the sort which affords such sport in the plays of Shakespeare and Sheridan. He is a man without backbone, failing in will and decision, just as Obstinate fails in intelligence and feeling. He has neither conscience nor faith nor sense of duty of his own. He is one of those feeble fellows whom R. L. Stevenson describes as 'creatures made of putty and packthread, without steel or fire, anger or true joyfulness in their composition.'[1] A man like this has, properly speaking, no character at all. The spiritual vision of faith and the moral sense of duty are the secrets of a steadfast soul. They are the rudder of the ship in motion, and the anchor of the ship at rest. On the whole, Obstinate is a better and more hopeful man than Pliable. Perverse though he be, and boorish beside this other, yet there is character in him, and more can be made of him.

Pliable appears to be a gentleman, and rebukes Obstinate for reviling. Indeed, as Dr Whyte says, 'Obstinate's foul tongue has almost made Pliable a Christian.' What is the worth of gentlemanliness? Much every way, and Ruskin states a truth well worth attending to when he says that taste is morality. From the days of Chaucer's 'verray parfit gentil knight,' the ideal of the English gentleman has been one of God's greatest gifts to England. But morality is more than taste, and to be a Christian involves far more than even the highest human culture. It is not without significance that George Herbert introduces his great picture of the English gentleman, not in the Church but in the Church porch. Dr Whyte quotes Thomas Goodwin's saying that 'civil men are the world's saints,' and in truth a well-mannered man is forgiven almost anything. Pleasant

[1] *Crabbed Age and Youth.*

OBSTINATE AND PLIABLE

manners may cover very bad character, and it is character that counts.

1. What affects Pliable? Unlike Obstinate, the spiritually stupid man, he has a nimble imagination. But it is a wrong sort of imagination, a faculty of day-dreaming, which is the slave of a sensuous and pleasure-loving nature, while the will meekly follows it down the line of the least resistance. Here we see this imagination revelling in the purely spectacular. For British people, the spectacular is an acquired taste, and any branch of art is degenerate in which that is substituted for deeper and more serious sources of interest. There has, however, been one curious exception to this, in the conceptions which religious people of many sects have borrowed and materialized from the apocalyptic visions of heaven. It is such a spectacle that fascinates Pliable—a mere celestial show, thick with tinsel. What he takes for religious fervour is but a refined form of the lust of the eyes. What would this man have done if he had reached heaven? He had no character, no faith nor love, to give him enjoyment in its real joys. Imagine him talking for five minutes with one of the prophets, and you shall see the small soul of him shrivel up until like the greater Lippo Lippi,[1] 'mazed, motionless, and moonstruck,' he cries for 'a hole, a corner to escape.'

2. What persuades him? Persuasion is a very serious matter, for it means that a mind has given itself over to another's influence. When St Paul says *I am persuaded*, which he seldom does, we feel that we are looking on at a tragic crisis. One sentence will show us the quality of Pliable's persuasion. 'And do you think,' says he, 'that the words of your book are certainly true?' 'Yes, verily,' is the reply, 'for it was made by him that cannot lie.' There is no argument there but mere statement, and it is char-

[1] Robert Browning, *Men and Women*.

acteristic of the man that he is satisfied. In the main he listens, and his questions are not searching. He is the sort of man who is fond of confidential talk, who likes to whisper in a corner where 'there are none but us two here.' But he has nothing intelligent to add to the conversation. In fact, he has no more learned the use of his mind than Obstinate has. If Obstinate's mind was only there to be made up, Pliable's was only there to be handed over. The dangers of reason in religion have been often dwelt on. From the time of Newman onwards there has been a persistent modern fashion of setting up faith in a fallacious rivalry to it. But the want of reason is a greater danger to religion than reason ever can be. The refusal to think fosters a slim faith which is nothing more than the desire to believe, and the faith of Pliable is pilloried beside the faith of Obstinate as an equally dangerous example of a man who does not know the use of his mind.

Pliable's deepest fault was what Professor Drummond has called *Parasitism*. 'Trust thyself,' says Emerson, 'every heart vibrates to that iron string.' Not Pliable's heart! He leans on others and needs company. His characteristic question is, *And what company shall we have there?* Like all irresolute men he is bad company for himself and hates to be alone. The love of company is in some men simply the escape from ennui, the interest of life needing the stimulus of converse. But this is a worse case, where a man leans upon others not as a stimulus for his mind's action but as a substitute for it, that he may 'borrow their purposes.' It is a true commonplace that all the greatest acts of life have to be done alone and on our own responsibility. Matthew Arnold's great verses on *Self-dependence* are indeed but one side of the truth, yet they are a necessary counteractive to such a character as this which gives itself up in blind trust to every stranger at first sight.

OBSTINATE AND PLIABLE

It was a sure instinct that led Bunyan to make Pliable hurry Christian on, with his ' Come on, let us mend our pace.'[1] Nothing could better show the slightness of this restless creature. It is one of the youngest of temptations, this impertinent enthusiasm to put all the world right. In true pilgrims, indeed, life soon corrects the well-meaning folly; but Pliable is no true pilgrim.

It may be added that there is another kind of Pliable with whom one meets at times. Some men, in virtue of the very clearness of their vision and the vividness with which they see every detail of a situation, find much to attract them on both sides of most questions. Some of the great Trimmers of history are in this class. For them there is a very different verdict from Bunyan's on Pliable; but they do not concern us here.

In his intercourse with these two Christian does not show at his best. Bunyan has left room for his growth, and one of the chief marks of greatness in the allegory is the steady and sustained development in the character of Christian, as well as in his wisdom and tact. He hardly ever seems to miss a lesson of experience. One thing, however, he has already acquired, and that remains with him throughout. Here, as always, he is *a man with a book*. One remembers the story of Erskine, whose saying became historical for controversy, ' Moderator, rax me that Bible.' So every man that faces Christian has to face his Book also.

1. *Christian and Obstinate.* It seems that we have two Obstinates and one Pliable here, and Greek has met Greek. It is not quite so, however, for the general character of Christian shows us that such doggedness as his has to be fought for. The trial to such a man in meeting Obstinate is not his bad temper or his rude manners. The real trial is his certainty. To meet any man who is absolutely certain

[1] *Cf.* p. 69.

THE ROAD

of what you deny, or to read a book written by such a man, is a staggering difficulty for many minds. It is here met by an enforced doggedness which is a match for Obstinate's own. Both men are dogmatic, but this blessed obstinacy pronounces the other 'dogmatic and wrong,' as Matthew Arnold facetiously says of Ruskin.[1] Bunyan knew the secret well, and had resisted Satan for days together with a text that 'stood like a mill-post at my back.' This dogmatism recalls St John's frequently recurring 'We know' in his First Epistle, and Whittier's—

> Yet in the maddening maze of things
> And tossed by storm and flood,
> To one fixed stake my spirit clings,
> I know that God is good.'

What are we to say to this obstinacy of Christian's? Must a man be narrow-minded in order to succeed? It has been said of Petrarch that 'he who discerns is conquered by him who wills.' Yet he who both discerns and wills conquers him who only wills without discerning. It is true, as we have said, that wide discernment showing both sides of every question is apt to slacken will; but that is not necessary, and the combination is the secret of religious success.

Strength of will is evident in Christian throughout this passage. 'If we be truly willing to have it, He will bestow it upon us freely'—that is the keynote of all his thinking. The one question for each of the men is, Does he really want it? But behind this strong will lies a vision clearly discerned. 'Had even Obstinate himself but felt what I have felt,' he says. In his speech to Obstinate there are no daydreams, but a strong man's view of facts, both of glory and of fear. Thus the obstinacy with which he meets Obstinate is of the right sort. He does not say, You go your way and I mine; for a Christian in whom will and vision have met must proselytise.

[1] *Letters*, p. 63.

OBSTINATE AND PLIABLE

2. *Christian and Pliable.* His treatment of Pliable is distinctly inferior to his treatment of Obstinate, and Dr Kerr Bain is right in pronouncing him at this stage a poor evangelist. This may possibly be intentional on Bunyan's part, for his Christian is usually a good judge of character. Some of his arguments and appeals are poor, but perhaps they are given as good enough for Pliable. And what strikes us above all here again is his great power of vision. Much is spectacular, but a deeper vision lies behind, of things so great that he can ' better conceive of them with his mind than speak of them with his tongue.' He has been both in heaven and in hell, and the vision struggles in vain for adequate utterance. Discounting the spectacular element, that which appealed to him most in heaven was his thought of the holy dead, the victors in life's conflict, and the King. There is also a touch of deep pathos in the saying that there 'none of them are hurtful, but loving '—words that remind us of Bunyan's England with the many hurtful men of whom we read in *Grace Abounding*.

CHAPTER III

THE SLOUGH OF DESPOND

ONE of the greatest dangers to life, and especially to travel, in the England of old days, arose from those deep and treacherous morasses which it has taken centuries to drain. In every county of England there were many 'sloughs' in those days, and tradition has fixed upon one near Bedford for the suggestion of this picture.[1] A modern annotator quotes the striking lines—

> 'Where hardly a human foot could pass
> Or a human heart would dare;
> On the quaking turf of the green morass
> His all he had trusted there.'

What does THE SLOUGH OF DESPOND mean in the allegory? Christian himself answers, tracing his misadventure to fear. It is the despondency of reaction which, if it become permanent, may deepen into religious monomania. It is to some extent physical, the result of overstrained nerves, so that the *change of weather* mentioned may be taken quite literally. A clear air and a sunny day are great aids to faith, and there are many, like Robertson of Brighton, whose fight with depression is brought on by rainy seasons.[2] Thus it is not only sharp conviction of sin that we have here, but a state of hopelessness and weariness of spirit whose causes are very composite. All the evil side of life flows into it.

---

[1] The older bridges in the neighbourhood of Bedford have flood arches which suggest many such sloughs in rainy weather. One especially, which lay between Bunyan's cottage and Elstow Church, is described in Dr Brown's *John Bunyan*, chap. iii.

[2] *Life of Robertson of Brighton*, chap. vii.

SLOUGH OF
DESPOND,
ELSTOW

THE SLOUGH OF DESPOND

Every sinful memory and unbelieving thought increases it. Bunyan's reticence adds to his power here as elsewhere, for by not defining it more particularly he leaves each reader with a general symbol which he can fill in with the details of his own experience.

Dr Whyte reminds us that Christians are partly responsible for this slough. The Christian life is sometimes described in such a way as to make one think that there is no use trying; and there are many, like Widow Pascoe in *Dan'l Quorm*, who express a melancholy resignation in such phrases as ' trusting Him where they cannot trace Him.' These are the chronic folk of the slough, who dwell so near its banks as to be spiritually bronchitic with its exhalations. This is bad enough, but when despondency comes to be regarded as a virtue, and happy faith in God as presumption, then the slough has become a place of sin as well as of misery. Humility, doubtless, is derived from *humus*; but as the quality of a living soul it must mean *on* the ground, not *in* it. Nor does it mean grovelling either, but standing on the ground. The voice Ezekiel heard still calls to all men, ' Son of man, stand upon thy feet.'

The mending of the slough is a perpetual attempt, for human nature is permanent, and to a large extent generation after generation has to perform the same task. How many words of cheer have been spoken to the despondent, down all the centuries from Marcus Aurelius to Robert Browning! But the old *Weltschmerz* engulfs all such words, and Hawthorne's *Celestial Railroad* crosses the slough over a very rickety bridge built upon such foundations. And yet the work of two hundred years done by the King's labourers since Charles the Second's time has not been all in vain. The kindlier views of God and of life have done something to lessen the swamp for modern men.

Bunyan's stepping-stones are Scripture promises. There

are other stepping-stones. Tennyson speaks of making 'stepping-stones of our dead selves to higher things,' and many a man, learning self-respect through failure, has blessed God for these. Again, there are yet other stepping-stones. There is a certain valley in the North where a rude path, hardly distinguishable at the best of times, leads through dangerous moss-hags right across the centre of a morass. In rainy weather the track would be wholly obliterated but for the little footprints of a band of children who go to school that way. Many a traveller has found his path safely through the Slough of Despond by following in the children's footsteps. But after all there are no such stepping-stones as God's promises. A white boulder is a poor enough object until you see it shining in a morass; then it means life and safety. So the promises of God, that have often seemed but wayside facts of no particular interest, shine suddenly with the very light of salvation when we see them in the Slough of Despond. Only, the slime of the Slough has made the foothold upon some of them slippery. Misquotations and misunderstandings have rendered them useless to some pilgrims' feet. How many texts of Scripture, *e.g.*, have been hidden from discouraged souls by the slime of that misquoted text, 'The prayer of the wicked is an abomination to the Lord.' A walk through any cemetery will show, by the errors in the quotations, how inaccurately the letter of Scripture is generally known, and such inaccuracies spoil the stepping-stones.

It is hardly necessary to remind the reader that the whole of *Grace Abounding* is one long scramble through the Slough of Despond. 'I found myself as in a miry bog, that shook if I did but stir,' says Bunyan; and the whole book moves forward floundering from promise to promise.

This slough is bad enough for Christian, but it is the undoing of Pliable, and so becomes an ordeal for the testing of

THE SLOUGH OF DESPOND

pilgrims. 'Almost all men,' says Cheever, 'are at some time or other inclined to set out on pilgrimage,' and there would be crowds of Christians if it were quite easy to be one. But this great over-grown baby, Pliable, is the type of that large number who cannot stand discomfort. 'Where are you now?' he cries; and this is the worst of depending upon day-dreams, or impulses, or authority, without having thought out the situation for oneself. These may at any time vanish, and where are you then?

The tragic difference between the two pilgrims is that one of them gets out of the slough on the side nearest Destruction, and the other on the side nearest Heaven. Despondency is a temporary experience, and there is not much importance in merely getting out of it. The question is, When you arrive at the bank, are you farther away from your old sins or farther away from your new purposes than when you were in the midst? The one thing that remains possible, even in the deepest discouragement, is an unflinching determination for progress, which despises the recollection that the old way of life is so near and possible and pleasant.

> 'Not enjoyment and not sorrow
> Is our destined end and way,
> But to act that each to-morrow
> Find us farther than to-day.'

On the farther side another figure is introduced—that of Help. This lightly-touched incident reveals a breezy creation as light-hearted as he is strong of hand. The immersion is not taken very seriously; and indeed one can almost catch a suspicion of humour in the first question as to 'What he did there?' A man in Christian's condition can hardly look dignified, and there is a distinctly ludicrous side to his plight which must appeal to the sense of humour invariably found in Help. In fact, this is part of his helpfulness. If you can get a man to see the absurdity of his gloom you have won half your battle. There is, of course, also a more solemn meaning in the question. Help is but repeating the lesson which Elijah learned in the desert—that there is no necessity for the loss of hope.

Help, in clerical garments or in the garb of a layman, is one of those perennially blessed people whom men instinctively trust. There is a healthy sense of efficiency about them and a broad human nature. David Scott is happy in his picture of Help the Athlete. He is the natural successor to the Herakles of Euripides whom Browning transcribes so wonderfully in *Balaustion's Adventure*, and to Shakespeare's Henry V. on the night before Agincourt. He is the kind of man that Charles Kingsley was, whose 'nearest work' is that of helping 'lame dogs over stiles.' He is the type that Jerome describes for modern days in his chapter on *Evergreens* in *Idle Thoughts*, and Mrs Browning in her *My Kate*. And indeed Help is often a woman, and among all woman's new ideals of to-day there is none that will ever fulfil her nature so perfectly as the oldest of all—the helpmeet.

Help is an office which conventional piety may sometimes count secular. Yet what is called spirituality is to a certain extent a matter of temperament, and those who have a special aptitude for helping need ask for no higher office. Paul has included 'helps' among the great functions of Christian ministry, and the beautiful legend of Christoferus has proclaimed the essential Christianty of such service. Ruskin has said finely : 'There is no true potency, remember, but that of help, nor true ambition but the ambition to save.'

Two notes regarding Christian may end our consideration of this incident. (1) His confession that *fear had followed him so hard*. It was a frank avowal, and characteristic of the Puritan conscience. It reminds one of the 'black care' sitting behind Horace's horseman, or of the sound of invisible horses' feet which many an Australian rider has heard chasing

THE SLOUGH OF DESPOND

him through the silent and solitary bush. (2) Christian himself has to do half the work of his deliverance. The hand of Help is only a lever whereby the man may swing himself up to firm ground. No man can escape from despondency except by action.

CHAPTER IV

MR WORLDLY WISEMAN

WE have already seen how impossible it is for anyone to take a serious step in life without the intrusion of others with their advice. Obstinate and Pliable began this interference: now WORLDLY WISEMAN takes it up where they have left it. Christian, it seems, has yet to learn that some men are enemies of the soul. Like a child he takes it for granted that all are helpers or pilgrims. This seems a chance meeting; for while some enemies seek us out, most cross our path casually. Yet it is no chance meeting after all. The spirit of the world comes very often in hours of violent reaction after despondency. A singularly interesting parallel is to be found in Goethe's *Faust* where it is the *Erdgeist* and Wagner that come to Faust first after the *Weltschmerz*.

The type, and indeed the name, are familiar in English literature.[1] But every age has its own type of Worldly Wiseman. Perhaps the most conspicuous example is that eighteenth-century exponent of the 'paying virtues,' the diligent apprentice who becomes the wealthy merchant—of whose gospel Dick Whittington was so popular a precursor in the fourteenth century. In the nineteenth century Stevenson borrows from Bunyan the idea and the name, and actually continues the conversation of Worldly Wiseman in *An Apology for Idlers*.

Here again, as in the case of Pliable, we are apparently in the company of a gentleman. He is not vulgarly loud nor unduly confidential. He introduces himself patronisingly, and

---

[1] *Cf.* Kerr Bain, ii., note L.

MR WORLDLY WISEMAN

his friendliness is that of the superior person. There is no more trying patronage than that of the shrewd self-made man whose first conviction is that he has conquered the world and understands life. The reason for that conviction is that he has learned the art of falling on his feet—an art generally attainable with some attention. So his 'good fellow' is a dangerous beginning. Cowper has warned us of—

> 'The man who hails you Tom—or Jack,
> And proves by thumping on your back
> His sense of your great merit,'[1]

and Polonius gave excellent advice to Laertes on this matter.[2]

When he goes on to speak of the 'burdened manner,' we begin to wonder whether he is the perfect gentleman he takes himself to be. There is a lack of sympathy here which betrays the inherent coarseness of grain. Emphasis upon surface absurdities is a rude appeal to shame; and the earnest soul, more sensitive in virtue of his finer and deeper nature, is ever at a disadvantage in the company of the ready and complacent manners of the finished man of the world. The burden, as has been aptly said, was a fact before it was a manner, but Worldly Wiseman is not the man to realise that.

There is a deadly cleverness in the question about Christian's wife and family. It is noteworthy that the three chief references to his home occur not in the first but in the second edition of the *Pilgrim's Progress*. Bunyan has been accused of making his hero a selfish religionist deserting his home to save his soul. It is enough to answer that the conditions of allegory necessitate this form. In real life he would be winning their bread all the time, and the estrangement of pilgrimage would be but in heart and interests. The deeper question remains, whether such severing of earthly ties is necessarily involved in the Christian ideal. Maguire tells that

---
[1] Cowper *On Friendship*.
[2] *Hamlet*, Act i. sc. iii.

THE ROAD

Archbishop Leighton's sister said to him, '*You* may serve God very well who have no family to occupy your thoughts, nor children to call off your attention from religion'; to which he answered, 'And Enoch walked with God, and begat sons and daughters.' The fact is that a man in Christian's case feels himself not fit for love. Christian could neither give it nor receive it rightly, and he left them only in the hope of gaining them eventually in a love that was worth the name. George MacDonald, with bitter truth, has compared the godless loves of the world to the manna that was kept to the second day.

When Christian replies that he will accept Worldly Wiseman's counsel *if it be good*, he evidently thinks himself a shrewd and experienced person. He remembers how he refused Obstinate's advice, but here he is dealing with a different man. The advice he gets is subtler than it looks. 'Get rid of thy burden and enjoy God's blessings.' The obvious reply is that that is just what Christian is seeking to do. Yet there is deep subtlety in both parts of the advice. The first is wrong because it makes getting rid of the burden the main direct object. There are worse things than that burden; but Worldly Wiseman does not know what conscience is, nor revere its rights. The second is wrong, because it suggests that Worldly Wiseman has a religion too —an equally real one, and far more comfortable. His creed is that of 'God's good gifts.' No one is more bitter than he against atheism, which he regards as a kind of anarchy, a disturbing unconventionality. His comfort depends on the conventionality of his view of all highest and deepest things. God must be remote—the 'Providence,' which one of George Eliot's characters speaks of as 'them that's above.' In this view there is no trace of that conscience which keeps Christian in torment with the sense that he has forfeited God's good gifts.

MR WORLDLY WISEMAN

Worldly Wiseman's opinions are all founded upon that lower kind of common sense which looks at life solely from the commercial standpoint. In its own province common sense is a true guide ; in matters where heroism and spirituality are involved it can only betray.

1. *His opinion about Evangelist.* He protests against Christian's view of him as a great and honourable person. His standards of greatness and honour are not those of real worth and personal value, but merely of social standing and what he calls good manners. There is an element of active hatred in his attitude which makes one suspect an irritated conscience. Worldly Wiseman has had bad quarters of an hour when things that Evangelist has said have gone home. All effective evangelists may lay their account that they shall be taken by Mr Worldly Wiseman as a personal insult and resented. It is the old story of the counsel's advice to his junior, ' No case, abuse the plaintiff's attorney.'

2. *His opinion about the Christian life* is a catalogue of sorrows, unrelieved by any faintest appreciation of the chance of heroism which they offer. St Paul gives a catalogue of tribulations almost identical with this, but it leads on to the triumphal shout of the last words of Romans viii. In this one-sided view of Worldly Wiseman's we see the limits of his common sense. He speaks like a man who knows everything there is to know. This cynical knowledge of the world, in spite of its claim to omniscience, is really the most partial and shallow of views. There is another world of fact, including the whole region of spiritual help from above and lofty adventure within, about which such a man knows nothing whatever. One who knows only the world does not know half the facts even of the world itself. In regard to all the highest experiences of life ' the natural man is a born fool.'

3. *His opinion about the Bible* leads him into rudeness.

THE ROAD

This hard scorn of the worldling for all that concerns the Scriptures is a unique phenomenon. It brings out the inherent vulgarity of worldliness, to which none of the choicest souls can ever wholly lower themselves. It is to be noted, however, that it is not against the Bible that he speaks, but against the average man meddling with it. The Bible is meant to be understood, and Worldly Wiseman understands it too well to read much of it. If it has any meaning it condemns him, therefore he takes refuge in pretending not to understand it. He accordingly leaves it to those who will explain it away until no part of it means anything in particular. It is interesting to note that Mr Foster of Bedford told John Bunyan, in his examination, that he 'was ignorant and did not understand the Scriptures; for how,' said he, ' can you understand them when you know not the original Greek ? ' etc. At this point Worldly Wiseman quite loses his temper. His 'hadst thou but patience to hear me,' is worthy of Sir Anthony Absolute.[1] The explanation must be that Christian has confronted all these opinions of his with the most provoking of all words to Worldly Wiseman—' I know.'

Worldly Wiseman's advice follows. It is to go to the village of Morality, where he himself goes to church. It is suspicious that that village is so near—not quite a mile off—for there is no near cut in the matters of the soul. He who sets out in earnest to reach Morality finds himself facing the most elastic mile in all the world. 'Far off, like a perfect pearl, one can see the city of God. It is so wonderful that it seems as if a child could reach it in a summer's day. And so a child could. But with me and such as me it is different. One can realise a thing in a single moment, but one loses it in the long hours that follow with leaden feet.'[2]

[1] *The Rivals*, Act i. sc. i.   [2] *De Profundis*, p. 60.

MR WORLDLY WISEMAN

He sees the village shining ahead of him, but at nightfall it is no nearer than it was at daybreak. That was the length of the mile for Christian; for Worldly Wiseman it was indeed but a short distance. Morality meant for him a very different thing from what it meant for the other. It is astonishing how different are the moral ideals of different men. A very interesting list of favourite types of ideal manhood could be culled from the works of popular authors, and whatever else might be found, there can be no question of the abundant room for varieties within such a list. Worldly Wiseman's would be little more than a set of notes of commercial expediencies and social proprieties. There is nothing in all this, however, which in any way opposes a strong emphasis upon the ethical side of Christianity.[1] In a very real sense it is always true that character is salvation. The morality of the *Pilgrim's Progress* is severe throughout. The question is not one of morality as an alternative to conversion, but, on the contrary, of how a real and stable morality may be reached.

This view of Worldly Wiseman's morality is borne out by his two friends Legality and Civility. The letter of the law, and a polite sense of propriety whose exactness is prompted not by conscience but by fashion, offer as low a standard as any worldling could desire. There is no more favourite charter for the right of free living than the habit of asking, in connexion with each deed, whether polite society will admit

[1] Compare Mr Bernard Shaw's characteristic statement that the difference between the conclusions of Bunyan and Nietzsche is merely formal, and his illustration of it by 'Bunyan's perception that righteousness is but filthy rags, his scorn for Mr Legality in the Village of Morality.' The latter of these phrases is absolutely true, and the former absolutely the reverse. But then one remembers that in this author's view 'The whole allegory is a consistent attack on morality and respectability.' If John Bunyan had written a book about Bernard Shaw, we would have had some memorable reading (*Man and Superman*, Epistle Dedicatory, xxxii.).

or forbid it. That is Civility's code. Legality's is, if anything, subtler. It asks in connexion with each detail, Can this be pronounced positively wrong? All which does not come under that category is allowable. These are both standards of conduct unsanctioned by Heaven. They are unfit for honourable men, and are dear to the heart only of pedants and bargainmongers in morality. The chances are that those who dwell in this village, and make friends of these men, will end by giving hush-money to conscience, and adopting as their whole moral code the one great commandment, Thou shalt not be found out.

CHAPTER V

RIVAL GUIDES

IT is always easy for the conscienceless to give complacent advice to the conscience-stricken. The vacant houses, cheap living, and fashionable neighbours of the Town of Morality sound irresistible, but the conscience of Christian has to be reckoned with.

Mount Sinai, for all these thousands of years, has been the commanding metaphor for conscience and the law of God. Geographically, the mountain stands like an iron peak shot up by the desert, from its masses of hard and pitiless red rock. Historically, it has been the platform from which the world has received its laws. Disraeli introduces it into his *Tancred* as the mount of moral vision for the dreamer who is his hero. Bunyan's Pilgrim has it thrust upon his path, precipitous and overhanging, threatening him with its crushing rocks and its deadly flashes of fire. His burden, too, becomes heavier as he goes, but the reason for that seems to be that he is out of the way. This is not a universal experience. To some, as in the story of Christoferus, the weight of the burden appears to increase when they are in the direct and difficult line of their task. To these the increased heaviness is the forerunner and signal of a blessed vision of the full-grown Christ. To this man also, the heavier burden is a signal of something coming to him from God; but how different the vision shall be! It is perhaps true that an increased sense of burden may be taken as a precursor of spiritual crisis of one sort or another. The whole incident shows at least this, that Mr Worldly Wiseman is a comfortable friend only to those who can find their own devices for getting past Mount Sinai. There is a point in most lives when it needs an obstinate and perverse courage to silence conscience, by deliberately choosing the world and forsaking Christ. Those may thank God who find that attempt a failure, to whom Worldly Wiseman's promises are broken, and who find instead of ease, safety, and friendship, the increasing burden and terror, and the deepening loneliness which these promises bring.

Here Evangelist again appears upon the scene. This and the still later encounter with Evangelist were added after the first edition. John Gifford [1] had been John Bunyan's Evangelist, and it is an awful thing to evangelise a man whose conscience and imagination are 'taking notes' like his. Besides, Bunyan himself had done much evangelising. It may be noted that here, as elsewhere, there is neither word nor hint as to what denomination Evangelist belongs to; we are dealing with matters far above and far below all that.

Evangelist comes to meet him, drawing nearer and nearer. His coming is deliberate, for he has been watching the man growing worldly in his own pitiful fashion. His services are unsought, and in such cases they are often unwelcome, but that is none of his business. Erring Christians have been known to answer such approaches by resenting the intrusion and joining another church, but Christian is too far in among realities for that. The question is asked, ' What doest thou here ? '—the very question which Elijah heard on the road to the same mountain. But here, in a later edition, the word *Christian* is added, evidently for emphasis. A Christian should never be cowering under Mount Sinai.

As before, Evangelist is strong in questioning. He will not shoot his arrows in the dark, but must have clearness. The whole passage shows us the spiritual hunter stalking a human soul. When the case has been set in clear light, he begins his

[1] *Cf.* Brown's *John Bunyan*, chap. v.

terrible address. He has nothing personal to say, nor is there any resentment for Christian's treatment of himself. He thinks neither of possible offence, nor consequences, nor misjudged motives. He has the words of God to speak to the man, and so absorbing is that conviction that he seems to have lost consciousness of himself altogether. The first of these words are the terrible ones that echo through *Grace Abounding* from the deathbed of the apostate Francis Spira.[1] They are words from the Epistle to the Hebrews, which killed Spira and haunted Bunyan. They are followed by a quotation from the Prophet Nathan, ' Thou art the man.' This direct personal attack is characteristic. It reminds us of John Knox's words in his liturgy ;[2] the visitor ' may lift him up with the sweete promises of God's mercie through Christ if he perceive him to be much afraid of God's threatenings. Or, contrariwise, if the patient be not touched with the feeling of his sinnes, he must be beaten downe with God's justice.' Bengel, writing on the Rich Young Ruler, has the similar sentence, ' Christ sends the secure back to the Law ; the penitent He consoles with the Gospel.' This ' beating down ' is the process which R. L. Stevenson describes with such power in the *Celestial Surgeon*. It is like the beating of a man fallen asleep in the snow, or the blow of the rescuer which stuns the drowning man when he would cling to him and drown both. The one unpardonable sin with Bunyan is that of drawing back. Those who are treated most harshly in his whole allegory are all sinners of this sort. It is because Christian has begun this backward course that he is so sharply dealt with ; and here, in such a phrase as ' begun to reject,' we notice the exactness of Puritan speech. Every word is weighed and intended.

The authority of a man who can make another man fall down at his feet as dead is a dangerous gift. In a pre-

[1] *Cf.* v. 65.   [2] *Visitation of the Sicke*.

sumptuous man, or one of small nature, it is apt to be abused. The slightest touch of vanity or love of power renders it an evil influence; but here it is justified because the man is essentially the prophet—he is the mere voice in which words of God are spoken, the mouthpiece of truth and duty.

To that authority Christian capitulates without a struggle. Of all sound natures the words of Augusta Webster's *Circe* are true—

> 'Why am I given pride
> That yet longs to be broken ? . . . Why am I who I am ?
> But for the sake of him whom Fate will send
> One day to be my master utterly ? '

Those are happy over whom this mastery is effected, not by mere personal fascination, but, as in this case, by the recognition of the voice of conscience.

In the sequel Evangelist proceeds to explain Christian to himself. He severely criticises the Gospel of Morality,[1] but the heart of the accusation of Worldly Wiseman is his turning Christian *from the Cross*. ' The cross of Christ is foolishness unto them except to make signs with it, and put it on the roofs of their houses and the outsides of their churches.[2] As for Evangelist, ' where'er he goes there stands a cross.' The cross interprets life to him, and all views of life which omit the cross are merely shallow and deceitful imaginations. In this instance Evangelist sees one labouring to persuade a man that the means of Eternal Life will be his death. To believe that is to fall into the most hopeless of all conditions, described in Browning's *Death in the Desert*—

> ' For I say, this is death and the sole death,
> When a man's loss comes to him from his gain,
> Darkness from light, from knowledge ignorance,
> And lack of love from love made manifest.'

From this extreme danger he points him back to the Cross against which he had been warned. It is actually the less

[1] *Cf.* Butler, quoted by Dr Whyte, pp. 16, 17.
[2] *Cheever*, p. 158.

dangerous course; and now, like John Butterworth, Christian will go to Christ ' though He had a drawn sword in His hand to slay me.'

The wickedness of the Deceiver is concentrated in the words ' how unable.' To take the responsibility of handling a human soul and guiding its destiny is a crime for the unable. Efficiency is the test of everything that calls itself Salvation. Is it *able* to deliver, to keep, to save to the uttermost? One remembers Heine's bitter words about the Greek culture he had lived for; when he was dying the poor Venus he had loved could not save him—her arms were broken.[1]

Thus far Evangelist has been explaining the situation to Christian rather in a criticism of his tempter than of himself, but from the outset he has made the man responsible for it all, by his own *consenting thereto.* In such cases men blame everything but themselves—their friend, the devil, circumstances, temperament. And within these there lurk still subtler excuses. Here there was the argument of natural affection for his wife and family, and there was also the desire of greater liberty. All of these are cut through by this incisive Evangelist. The root of the evil had been his own consenting. As for natural affection, when it comes to a choice between that and conscience, a man must hate his father and mother, etc. As for liberty, Legality is the son of the bondwoman, and the mere attempt at morality unlit by the light of faith is but lifelong futile drudgery in the prison-house. Finally comes the curse pronounced upon every one

[1] In May 1848 Heine went out of doors for the last time. It was to see once more the Venus of Milo. His words are, "Only with pain, could I drag myself to the Louvre, and I was nearly exhausted when I entered the lofty Hall where the Blessed Goddess of Beauty, our dear Lady of Milo, stands on her Pedestal. At her feet I lay a long time, and I wept so passionately that a stone must have had compassion on me. Therefore the goddess looked down compassionately upon me, yet at the same time inconsolably, as though she would say, 'See you not that I have no arms, and that therefore I can give you no help?'" *Life of Heine*, vol. ii. chap. 13; *cf.* vol. i. chap. 8.

THE ROAD

that *continueth not*, reminding us once again of the great lesson of the book. It is a big contract to be a Christian—a matter in which men are working for the long result.

The effect upon Christian is immediate. ' Words and fire ' come out of the mountain. The phrase might seem impossible for artistic narrative, but Bunyan's art instinctively constructs so good a tale that it is able to bear many such violent strains. This is a fine example of that characteristic of the *Pilgrim's Progress* which R. L. Stevenson points out in his remarkable essay—the narrative losing itself in the spiritual significance. Nothing could more exactly describe the situation when conscience, that has been silent while we were tempted, speaks when we have fallen, and the story of our defections is told in words of flame.

The close of the incident is very beautiful. Christian's words, *Is there hope* ? remind us of the same question at the close of Tennyson's *Vision of Sin*. But the answer here is plainer. Tennyson's words are—

> ' At last I heard a voice upon the slope
> Cry to the summit, Is there any hope ?
> To which an answer peal'd from that high land.
> But in a tongue no man could understand ;
> And on the glimmering limit far withdrawn
> God made Himself an awful rose of dawn.'

Evangelist has more definite things to say than this. But the best thing recorded is that *one smile* he gave him. Worldly Wiseman has plenty of smiles : so, for that matter, sometimes has Help. But this is the ' tenderness of the austere man,' [1] the most inspiring smile on earth.

It is instructive to contrast the characters of Worldly Wiseman and Evangelist regarded as advisers. The first is hail-fellow-well-met, slight, and hypothetical ; the second dignified and even official, but thorough and imperative. The first has no horizons (the sure sign of a false kind of breadth), and in consequence there is no real clearness of

[1] Renan.

vision in him even for things near; the horizons of the second are Heaven and Hell, which he sees as tremendous ramparts of the Universe, and within the space between, his insight and his outlook are pitilessly clear. The first, with all his show of friendliness, is hard, cold, and untender; his comfort is a mere narcotic, and he lacks the manly virtues of chivalry and a sense of honour. The second is tender and compassionate; his healing is by surgery which wounds in order to cure, and his bearing is that of the soldier of Jesus Christ. Finally, the first is mistaken in his dealing with a burdened man; the second is correct. Both are there to help the man off with his burden, and they have at least this much in common, that neither of them attempts himself to take it off. The difference lies in the fact that the former sends him for relief to certain inconsiderable and helpless persons; the latter passes him over to God and the Christ of God.

The combination of manliness and tenderness in Evangelist makes him an excellent mirror for ministers. His *manliness* stands in contrast to Sydney Smith's famous saying that there are three sexes—the male, the female, and the clerical. Here there are no mannerisms or cheap sentiment, but that higher common sense which deals with facts and reasons, and leaves the impression that it is a stupid thing not to be a Christian. His *tenderness* appears in the gradual relenting to forgiveness, when severity has done its work. He has felt the misery of the hour as much as Christian, and he does not spare himself while he wounds the other. He knows the need to be extreme, and the moment to be critical. And yet he never lapses into brutality, as earnest men are apt to do. He is a man essentially kind, and not severe—which is perhaps the testing-point for good or bad Evangelists. In this it will be seen that he reflects the character of God, whose 'strange work' is severity, and whose heart is revealed in the tender promise that a bruised reed shall He not break.

CHAPTER VI

THE WICKET GATE

THE story of THE WICKET GATE is a masterpiece of power and simplicity, qualities which Bunyan learned from Christ's own metaphors, such as the ' Fold,' the ' Bread,' and indeed the ' Way ' and the ' Gate.' It is in strong contrast to the elaboration of the same scene in the spurious Third Part of the *Pilgrim's Progress*.[1] In that there is much detail of a shower of arrows, a certificate, and a magic crutch replacing a weak reed, and having the virtue to stay the bleeding of wounds, to give strength, and to refresh the spirits by emitting an odoriferous perfume. Bunyan's experience of God's grace was a far simpler matter.

The Wicket Gate is said to have been suggested by the old church door at Elstow. But in the story it is brought out into the open and stands across the way, a mere gate without either an enclosure or a house. Obviously such a gate is there to mark a boundary. It stands for a decisive choice, separating the course of the journey into two sections, one before and the other after it. It is, as Cheever has called it, ' a beginning and an end.'

[1] In 1692-93, four years after Bunyan's death, this Third Part was published by Joseph Blare, a London publisher, who signed the preface J. B., and professed that it was the fulfilment of the promise made in the last sentence of the Second Part. This preface is a model of audacity and cunning :—' It is a piece as rare and transcending what has hitherto been published of this kind, that I dare without any further apology, leave it to the censure of all mankind who are not partial or biassed : and so, not doubting but it will render comfort and delight, I subscribe myself as heretofore your soul's hearty well-wisher, J.B.' In the eighteenth and early nineteenth century editions it was usually bound up with the First and Second Parts. Compare Brown's *John Bunyan*, chap. xix.

THE
WICKET GATE,
ELSTOW

THE WICKET GATE

It stands for one aspect of conversion, its human aspect, as a decisive choice. The question has been asked why the gate stands so long before the Cross, and it is curious that Mr Stead omits all mention of it in his children's version of the allegory. Bunyan has a marginal note to the effect that 'there is no deliverance from the guilt and burden of sin but by the death and blood of Christ'; and no one need fear for his orthodoxy! Yet he knew human nature well enough to be aware that sometimes one aspect of the great crisis comes first to a man, and sometimes another. In this case Christian takes the critical step immediately upon a clear apprehension of God's *goodwill* in Christ. It is exactly the act which is described as repentance unto life in the answer to Question 87 of the Westminster Shorter Catechism. The full meaning of the Cross he will realise afterwards; meanwhile there is only the light shining on him through the archway—hope in God's goodwill seen in the framework of an active choice.

The illumination reminds us of the orientation of ancient temples, which were so built that on a certain day the light of the rising sun struck through the open door direct upon the statue of the god. The contrast is very significant. In the older case the light shone not to bless the man but to honour the God—here it is upon the worshipper that it shines, and the great truth is proclaimed that not only is man for God, but that God is for man also.

It is a clever touch in Hawthorne's *Celestial Railroad* which obliterates the wicket gate from fashionable modern religion as a narrow and inconvenient obstruction like Temple Bar in Fleet Street, and erects upon its site a railway station and ticket office, declining, however, to give an opinion as to whether the tickets will be received at the Celestial City. The difference between the two religions is that the one has within it a distinct act of choice and the other no such decision.

Whom does the figure of Goodwill stand for? One naturally thinks of the angels' word to the shepherds,[1] and there is from the first a suspicion of superhuman personality. This is distinctly developed in the Second Part, where Goodwill is spoken of as 'the Lord.' At this stage the author has hardly decided the point even with himself. It must have seemed a delicate and hazardous matter thus to represent the Saviour, and the indistinctness shows the modest reverence of Bunyan's spirit. In the famous Greek phrase, the figure is 'divine, or mortal, or both mingled.' It reminds one of Mr Hole's picture of Christ looking down upon Jerusalem, where the face gains its unique impressiveness by being shadowed to indistinctness against the setting sun. The simple soul of Bunyan finds the right way in this as in so much else, the child entering where the man cannot enter. If we contrast this Goodwill with Milton's Christ, we feel at once how much too strong the light is in the latter presentment. The fact that makes such blending of the human and the divine possible at all is the great event of the Incarnation, in which history and mystery are so marvellously mingled; and the remembrance of this may have encouraged Bunyan in his daring portraiture. It is significant that, by the time of the writing of Part Second, Bunyan had as it were grown accustomed to the figure, and we miss there the delicate and almost timid shyness which is seen here. It is like a picture spoiled by retouching, and Dr Kerr Bain justly notes how seldom an author may venture to introduce characters again in a second work. Abundant examples of sequels in fiction will occur to the reader.

He knocked more than once or twice, we are told. This reminds us of the folly and presumption of staking our religious destinies upon a single test, such as the answer to a specific prayer, as if we had a right to prescribe immediacy

[1] Luke ii. 14.

to the great Will that stands behind. This man was wiser. All he saw was a rough and heavy wooden gate studded with iron nails, if the suggestion of Elstow Church be correct. All a man may see may be the chair he kneels at, or whatever part of the solid material world confronts him as he makes his spiritual choice, but ever through the waiting time there are the words, 'Knock, and it shall be opened unto you,' written overhead. While these words are there his duty and his wisdom are to wait.

When Goodwill came to the gate it was a 'grave person' that Christian saw: the word *grave* retaining its older sense which the Latin *gravitas* expresses, rather than the modern sense, in which it would be the epitome of the legend that though Christ was often seen in tears no one ever heard Him laugh.

In contrast with such a view, and showing how cordial the grave man may be, are the first words of Goodwill explicitly reported, 'I am willing with all my heart.' These words are the refrain of some very beautiful verses, included in B. M.'s *Ezekiel*, under the title of *The Man at the Gate*. No words could better express the cordiality of Christ. They free Him from all ecclesiastical bonds of routine or mere form. Instead of being 'the head of the clerical party,' a functionary of the Church, He appears as a layman in all the freshness of Goodwill. Though pilgrims come to Him every day, yet each new soul is as interesting to Him as if it had been the first.

The little incident next told is deeply true to experience. Beelzebub has a castle near the gate, from which arrows are shot at those who would enter.[1] The demonology of Bunyan will have our attention later. The air in Puritan

---

[1] It has been supposed that this castle was suggested by the detached bell-tower which rises but a few feet distant from the wicket gate in Elstow Church.

times was full of devil-lore, and the stories regarding Luther had their parallel in the experience and imagination of all earnest men. The arrows of Beelzebub shot at souls near the wicket gate are those special temptations which come upon men while they stand reasoning and hesitating before the great decision of their lives. At such times the whole nature is excited and the nerves strung and tingling. Many examples might be quoted from Bunyan's own experience as related in *Grace Abounding*. In narratives of the more violent types of religious revival, such conditions frequently assume even physical aspects. But in any case it is a time of danger. By and by the man will have the shield of faith which comes after a strong output of the will in decision; as yet he is defenceless, and the one hope for safety is to flee quickly within. The *pull* given by Goodwill has much familiar Scripture behind it.[1] Here we have a very vivid description of God's act and man's free choice combined in the supreme event of conversion, as indeed they are combined in every act of life.

An extraordinary wealth of religious thought has gathered round the figure of the door open or shut. The words of Goodwill are from Rev. iii. 8, and they give an additional hint of the divineness of the personality. We may contrast this with the shut door which no man can open, the tragedy of opportunity for ever lost, of which Christ tells in His parable of the ten virgins. Another contrast may be suggested by the legend that before the destruction of Jerusalem the enormous brazen doors of the Temple swung open without the touch of hands for the exit of God. Again there are the two metaphors of Christ knocking and man knocking at a closed door, each of which has its own significance at life's hour of crisis. Here, the thought that is most impressive is the contrast between without and within. Out-

---

[1] *Cf.* Cant i. 4, Ps. xviii. 16, Jer. xxxi. 3, John vi. 44, xii. 32.

side all is danger, the uncertainty and the fear of life; inside, the loving Christ and His embrace. Before the opening of the door some wait, as has been suggestively said, looking through open spar-work, beyond which they can see but cannot penetrate; while others seem to be facing closely joined panels relentlessly opaque. In either case the tragic fact is that as yet there is a plank's breadth between them and their highest destiny. Perhaps the strangest phenomenon of the gate is that so many go on knocking as if it were closed and fail to see that it is wide open already. In any case, after whatever experience on the other side, the supreme issues of life are in these simple words, ' he opened the gate.' To hear that gate shut behind us, to be suddenly sure of God's acceptance—life has no experience comparable with that.

The first question which Goodwill asks is, How is it that Christian comes alone?—for, as we shall find at the Palace Beautiful, the Lord had said that He ' would not dwell in the mountain of Zion alone,' and He misses those who do not come.

In Christian's answer regarding Pliable we have the phrase repeated, ' that side next to his own house.' This vivid description of turning back has evidently caught the writer's imagination. Yet Christian turns quickly to the confession of his own failure. It is the mark of a really great soul that he does not dismiss the names of those who have disappointed him with a bitter last word. There is no boasting over Pliable, but only a sense of what might have been in his own case. In the initial verse he had called himself an undeserving rebel—an epithet that shows marks of the times in which the book was written. Here he describes himself in a poorer aspect. The incident reminds us of the words of another famous Christian, who, on seeing a criminal being led to execution, exclaimed, ' There, but for the grace of God, goes John Bradford.'

THE ROAD

All that Goodwill has to say about the dangerous mountain to which Christian had wandered is that it has been the death of many and will be the death of many more. One of the deepest mysteries in the whole tragedy of life is the refusal of Christ to coerce the wills of men, and His sorrowful contemplation of the fact that there are those who will not come unto Him and have life. The next words of Goodwill abound in graciousness and remind us of Knox's sentence in his Communion service, ' Our Lord keepeth not back any penitent person, how grievous soever his sins before have been, but only such as continue in sin without repentance.' Thus is the figure of Goodwill a wonderful combination of awfulness and pleasant tenderness. His welcome is gentle and hearty as a child's, yet ' His decision is final ; His will is fate.'

The figure of the Way, taken up and made eternal by Jesus Christ, may be traced back to Isaiah's grand conception of the Highway.[1] It was a figure in which were blended a magnificent realisation of past deliverance with an equally magnificent assurance for the future. The path, running high and straight across the desert, might be that which had led from Egypt or that which would yet lead from Babylon to the home-land of Israel. The narrowness of this way has been sometimes so understood as to teach that of two ways we must always choose the least pleasant if we are to be sure that it is the way of Christ.[2] This is certainly a wrong view. God may, and often does, lead men in ' ways of pleasantness and paths of peace,' as He did of old. It is straightness that is the real test. In choosing between two possible careers, it is wholly a mistake to decide upon one simply because it involves more self-sacrifice than the other. The right question to ask is, Which of the two lies most directly in the line of usefulness and service ? In which

---

[1] Isa. xix. 23; xxxv. 8; xl. 3.
[2] *Cf.* Fielding Hall, *The Soul of a People*, chap. xxiii.

THE WICKET GATE

shall I best be able to exercise my powers, to let my natural disposition and education tell, and so to find my special destiny? The path which meets these requirements will certainly be found at times narrow and difficult. There is the Cross, the need for some self-denial, in every day's journey.

It has been noticed already that Christian enters the Wicket Gate with his burden still upon him. To those who find that strange, the words of Montgomery may be quoted, that '*The Pilgrim's Progress* is the history of *one* man's experience in *full*, and the experience of many others in *part*.' In fact this was Bunyan's own experience, for he tells us that for two years he preached nothing but sin and hell. It will be observed that Christian does not take with him the love of sin, but only the weight of sin. There is in an old book of religious emblems a woodcut representing the covetous man struggling to get through the gate with an enormous bundle of wealth upon his back, but held from entering because the bundle was larger than the door, a lesson which John Bunyan would certainly have endorsed. But that is not the burden which Christian carries through the gate, and the general course of experience here described seems to be that of a man who first knows the wonderful welcome of Christ's love, although his conscience is not yet at peace, and who afterwards comes to understand the Cross and is assured of release from sin. The practical lesson of it is, in Dr Whyte's words, ' get into the right way and leave your burden to God.' It is thus that the labouring and heavy-laden find rest unto their souls. But this rest is not idleness. Christian immediately girds up his loins, and the strenuous phrase is characteristic of the whole book.

We can imagine the feelings with which Bunyan wrote the final words, ' Christian took leave of his friend.' At first he may have hesitated to use such a familiar title for the person who has been growing more and more manifestly divine. Yet on second thoughts it could seem no irreverence, since Christ Himself had said, 'I have called you friends,' and 'ye are My friends.' Indeed it is the tenderness and familiarity of Goodwill which are the note of all this passage. He is tenderer than Evangelist, tenderer than any man. His tenderness is that of the Shepherd whom Faber describes so feelingly in his hymn, 'Souls of men, why will ye scatter.' He is there to welcome pilgrims, and it is characteristic that He is described by Christian to the Interpreter as the 'man that *stands* at the gate.' It is Christ's typical attitude, as Stephen saw Him in his vision.[1]

The contrast is inevitable between the reception at this gate and the story of the other gate, the gate of Eden, when

> 'the hastening angel caught
> Our lingering parents, and to the eastern gate
> Led them direct.'[2]

---

[1] Acts vii. 55. [2] *Paradise Lost.* xii.

CHAPTER VII

THE INTERPRETER'S HOUSE

'It would be difficult,' says Cheever, ' to find twelve consecutive pages in the English language that contain such volumes of meaning . . . in so pure and sweet a style, and with so thrilling an appeal to the best affections of the heart, as these pages.' This is high praise, yet the imagination and conscience of Christendom has borne it out, and the passage describing the INTERPRETER'S HOUSE is one of the great Christian classics. The form which the allegory here takes is familiar in the earlier literature. Like the play within the play of *Hamlet*,[1] this shows a set of allegorical tableaux within the main allegory. An interesting parallel may be found in the complicated 'riddles' of the Child and Lion, etc., which, like some of these of Bunyan, stand for teaching regarding the Law and the Gospel, in the history of the *Holy Graal*.[2]

As the Interpreter is the Holy Spirit,[3] this house has often been identified with the Church, in which case this part of the allegory would be comparable with Herbert's *Temple*. The idea would of course be a true one. Even of the architecture of old English churches, Coventry Patmore's words are true, that it is ' as if the Spirit had builded its own house.' Here, too, this would be suitable, for the Church stands just where it ought to be, immediately on the other side of the Wicket

---

[1] Act iii. sc. 2.
[2] Dent's *High History of the Holy Graal*, branch 6.
[3] Mr Stevenson, in his *Text-Book on the Pilgrim's Progress*, points out the interesting parallel between Christ's promise of the Holy Spirit and Goodwill's words about the Interpreter.

Gate. Mr Worldly Wiseman's church in the village of Morality, standing on the other side of the gate, is doomed to failure and is indeed a fraud. To those who have never made the great choice represented by the Wicket Gate, the Interpreter's House might indeed be a place of many and fascinating interests for the intellect and the imagination, but it is a place of essential falsehood and consequently of spiritual danger. On the other hand, after the great choice has been made, the sooner Church membership follows the better. Additional arguments in favour of this view of the Interpreter's House are the figure of the minister at the beginning of the passage, and the treatment of the subject in Part II., where the Table, the Bath, and the Seal are introduced.

Yet in spite of all these considerations, it seems probable that the Church is not here meant. The Christian ministry is always a favourite subject with Bunyan, and frequently appears in his pages apart from the Church. Again, the House Beautiful is evidently meant for a formal and detailed picture of the Church, and to have introduced this less distinct picture of it would have involved a confusion of allegory which would be unlike Bunyan. Accordingly, it seems better to take this passage as an account of personal illumination by the Holy Spirit, apart from the services of the Church. We are presented with views of life regarding several of the fundamental religious experiences and thoughts, which may be taken as gathered from among his own memories. The earlier part of *Grace Abounding* contains striking accounts of private dealing of this sort between the Holy Spirit and John Bunyan. It will be remarked that all the views, given by the Interpreter in his seven scenes, are essentially views of life. The religious teaching of them is psychological or experimental, showing religious truths, not so much as they are in themselves, but from the man's point of view. They are

THE INTERPRETER'S HOUSE

the answers given by God to the deepest questions which life has suggested to man.[1]

The figure of a House of Interpretations is a peculiarly interesting one. Hawthorne may have been thinking of it when he wrote his *Hall of Fantasy*. But the finest parallel is D. G. Rossetti's master-conception of the *House of Life*. Of this famous poem, Pater writes one of his most suggestive and illuminative passages : ' The dwelling-place in which one finds oneself by chance or destiny, yet can partly fashion for oneself ; never properly one's own at all if it be changed too lightly, in which every object has its associations—the dim mirrors, the portraits, the lamps, the books, the hair-tresses of the dead and visionary magic crystals in the secret drawers, the names and words scratched on the windows,—windows open upon prospects the saddest or the sweetest ; the house one must quit, yet taking, perhaps, how much of its quietly active light and colour along with us ! '[2]

The Interpreter's House shows the Holy Spirit working upon memory, imagination, experience, and knowledge of life. Out of the complex of these, certain images or facts seem to arise and shine conspicuous for a lifetime as the master-truths and commanding inspirations of the soul. The vast importance of these, shows how critical is the time which a man passes immediately after his great decision. It is a time comparable with Christ's sojourn in the wilderness and St Paul's in Arabia, and they are happy who emerge from it under the power of such visions as those which Bunyan here describes.

Part III. introduces at this point also the healing of the pilgrim's wounds. At first this appears fantastic, but the idea is happier than most of the conceptions of Part III. For a great deal of healing comes by knowledge, and many of

---

[1] *Cf.* Walt Whitman's *Answerer*.
[2] *Appreciations*, p. 238.

THE ROAD

the wounds of the spirit are closed when a man attains clear views of God and life, men and things. This is that ' comfort of the truth ' of which Christ spoke.[1]

It is to be noted also that at this gate, as well as at the Wicket Gate, Christian has to knock over and over. Formerly it was knocking in order to travel, here it is knocking in order to see. Spiritual illumination does not by any means always come in intuitive flashes. Far oftener, as in this instance, it is the result of severe thought and determined meditation. Even in spiritual vision a man must knock over and over in order to see.

Whatever view may be taken of the Interpreter's House as such, there can be no question that the Interpreter stands for the Holy Spirit. The figure of the Interpreter is touched lightly and with great reverence in the allegory, like that of Goodwill in the previous passage. Indeed, we hardly ever get a full look of the Interpreter at all, and the spiritual impression is preserved by this reticence. It is characteristic of Bunyan that so little direct reference to the Holy Spirit is to be found in his allegory. Yet the presence of the Holy Spirit is felt throughout it. The pilgrim is under divine illumination, guidance, and comfort during the whole journey, and it is by a true instinct that Bunyan allows us to feel these mysterious factors in life rather than to see their origin.

Two things at least we learn from the Interpreter's House regarding the Spirit of the Lord. (i.) *His hiddenness.* ' The hiddenness of perfect things '[2] is a well-known phrase whose far-reaching insight experience is constantly confirming. Here, nothing could be homelier than the incidents of the narrative. There is no apparent magic, but merely the speech of what always seems a human voice—

[1] John xiv. 16, 17.
[2] Walter Pater, *Marius the Epicurean*, chap. vi.

THE INTERPRETER'S HOUSE

> '... that gentle voice we hear,
> Soft as the breath of even,
> That checks each fault, that calms each fear,
> And speaks of heaven.'

He seems to have identified Himself with the personality of the pilgrim, and the scenes which He shows him seem to be but the man's own hopes and fears written large—

> 'And every virtue we possess,
> And every victory won,
> And every thought of holiness,
> Are his alone.'

Above all, keeping Himself in the background, He takes of the things of Christ and shows them; yet these are shown by the agency of the very ordinary and homely facts of life—a man lights a candle and Christian follows him. The Holy Spirit is not the rival of human means of teaching. He quotes familiar words of Scripture which grow luminous as He uses them. The men around us, the common facts and objects that may be seen in any day's walk, are capable under His power of taking on the highest spiritual meaning.[1] (ii.) The *gentleness* of the Interpreter is noteworthy. He took Christian by the hand, and, as Gregory says, 'his touch is itself a teaching.' Nothing in the world is so delicate as this means of grace. The quiet voices of the Spirit have power both to shake and to strengthen the human soul, yet every experienced Christian knows how easily the Spirit can be 'grieved' and even 'quenched.' No figure in the whole book is at once so awful and so tender as this half-seen and suggested form of Him who has the 'world's secret trembling on his lip.'

While there is no attempt at systematic teaching in the successive scenes, they form a unity when taken as a whole. The minister, the human spiritual guide, is merely introductory, and naturally occurs first in Bunyan's thought of such matters as are here dealt with. Then there is, in the

---

[1] *Cf.* Robert Browning's *Francis Furini.*

THE ROAD

dusty room, a presentation of the fundamental conception of Law and Gospel, which shows these not in themselves, but as they affect the Christian. Then follow, still from the point of view of experience rather than of abstract doctrine, pictures of the supreme human and divine factors in the Christian life. The human factor is patience and the divine is grace. The next is the strenuous and victorious picture of the whole life, in which the entire *Pilgrim's Progress* may be said to be summarised. But to a soul like Bunyan's there is an inevitable and constant undertone of tragedy in the thought of life, and before the visions close we have to look upon two aspects of the underlying terror. The first is of that despair, which is the judgment of the careless on this side of death,—the other is of the judgment beyond the grave.

These scenes we shall examine more fully in the next chapter; meanwhile, a phrase in which the author epitomises them is worthy of remark. The scenes end in six lines of verse, which are, as poetry, below the level even of Bunyan's verses. But the first line tells us that we have here seen things 'rare and profitable.' There could not be a happier combination. To be interesting is one ideal of religious teaching; to be profitable is, alas, in many cases a quite different one. Human teaching which combines the two has come within sight of the ideal education; and the very note of the teaching of the Spirit of God, rightly understood, is just that combination. His is the most profitable teaching that is ever given, but while he teaches he also quickens all the vital interests of life, so that his scholars confess with full assent, that they have 'seen things rare and profitable.'

CHAPTER VIII

THE INTERPRETER'S HOUSE—THE SCENES IN DETAIL

I. THE CHRISTIAN MINISTER

FOR Bunyan, this introductory picture was inevitable in any passage concerning spiritual illumination. His own debt to Mr Gifford was so great as to ensure that, and there can be no doubt that the face which Bunyan saw in this picture was that of his old friend. His Evangelist and many other helpers represent various aspects of the ideal ministry; this is a general conception rather than a specific, telling us in a few words the main points which Bunyan considers essential in the Christian minister. With this conception may be compared Cowper's in *The Task*,[1] and also Herbert's in *The Temple*, and Keble's in *The Christian Year*. The words ' very grave person ' remind us that this is a minister of the Puritan times; yet it is not implied that his visage is so forbidding as those in the pictures of ministers on the walls of Hawthorne's *Old Manse*; rather must ' grave ' be understood, here as on page 43, in the richer sense of the Latin word *gravitas*.

Bunyan's respect for the office of the ministry is here stated with startling emphasis. This is the ' only man ' whom the Lord has authorised as guide—a strong statement, and one which would surprise us less if it came from the pen of one who believed in sacerdotalism and apostolic succession.[2] Yet so catholic is this minister that no hint enables

---

[1] *The Timepiece.*
[2] *Cf.* Stevenson's *Text-Book*, pp. 45, 46.

us to guess to what Church or denomination he belongs.[1] His only authority is truth which he knows, character which he has attained, and the urgency of an inner calling to proclaim his truth and to enforce his character.

1. *His eyes are lifted up to heaven.*[2] The first requisite for a Christian minister or man is that he be looking in the right direction. This is not a mere pose, as in some old-fashioned photograph or engraving. We are saved by what we see, and it is equally true that by what we see we are also saviours. This passage reminds us with curious frequency of Hawthorne's work, and here the *Great Stone Face* comes to mind. Compare also a very remarkable scene in Edna Lyall's *Knight Errant*, in which the robber, carving a crucifix, unconsciously reproduces the face of his prisoner. These are but various ways in which the old story of St Stephen is told again. Those grow like Christ who see Him as He is, and this must be the first task of every minister. The eyes of a fool are in the ends of the earth—on his salary, his ritual, politics, or the faces in the pews; this man 'looks beyond the world for truth and beauty.'[3]

2. *The best of books.* The Bible is and will be for ever the only thing that will permanently preach. The hunger and weariness of humanity will to the end of time refuse with indignation any other food and rest than this. It is true

---

[1] It is a striking fact that the principle upon which John Gifford and his congregation entered into fellowship with each other was 'ffaith in Christ and Holiness of life without respect to this or that circumstance or opinion in outward and circumstantiall things.' The congregation still retains the same openness, in regard, *e.g.*, to the practice of infant baptism. Concerning that, and other questions of denominational separation, Bunyan has expressed himself in no measured terms. *Cf.* Brown, *John Bunyan*, chaps. v. and x.: *John Bunyan*, by the author of *Mark Rutherford*, p. 97.

[2] This description of the Christian minister has, with a singularly touching and delicate appropriateness, been selected for the inscription on Boehm's great statue of Bunyan in Bedford, the panels on whose pedestal represent the burdened pilgrim's interview with Evangelist, and the angels at the Cross. [3] *Cf.* p. 9.

that there is an unintelligent way of preaching the Scriptures which is deadly dull, and to be uninteresting is the last vice of the pulpit, as Sydney Smith has it. Yet there is no need for this. Within the Bible the field is rich and varied, if one will only be at pains to study it intelligently. This, however, involves study in other fields, and Matthew Arnold is undoubtedly right when he says that ' No man, who knows nothing else, knows even his Bible.' [1]

3. *The law of truth upon his lips.* In the whole range of personal character nothing is so vital as this. Speech is the special instrument of the minister's service, and it is in regard to speech that the cleansing of character is most indispensable.[2] The minister must be a sincere man, which means not only fearless but accurate in speech. He will not as a rule be tempted to any deliberate statement which he knows to be false, but rather to the exaggeration of feeling and experience. Walter Pater, quoting Flaubert, urges that the essential element in style is not the forcible word, but the exact word.[3]

4. *The world was behind his back.* Hawthorne again interprets Bunyan's meaning in the happy phrase, ' not estranged from human life, and yet enveloped in the midst of it with a veil woven of intermingled gloom and brightness.'[4] The compromise has always been a difficult one to define, and the true definition will depend partly upon the conditions of the age, partly upon the circumstances of the individual. It is in the midst of the bright spectacle of life that the minister has to live and speak, and he will certainly do his work better if he feels its brightness. At the same time, he who has once gazed on the things beyond the world ought to be fascinated by them; and thenceforth, in comparison with them, the world will be behind his back. An

---

[1] *Culture and Anarchy*, chap. v. Compare the wider interpretation of the phrase ' word of God ' ably expounded in Horton's *Verbum Dei*.
[2] *Cf.* Isa. vi. 5-7.   [3] *Appreciations*, on *Style*.
[4] *Mosses from an Old Manse*, '*The Old Manse.*'

interesting contrast suggests itself between this and two other ways of contempt for the world—(*a*) that of Meredith's *Egoist*, to whom the world is but a foil for the selfish enjoyment of love, and (*b*) Leonardo da Vinci's *La Gioconda*,[1] who has been through all experience and whose smile expresses the cynical conclusion that she has found out the world (seen in the background of the picture), and, like the Preacher, pronounced it vanity.

5. *He pleaded with men.* There are many things that go to make up the work of the ministry, but its essential use is practical. More now than then, perhaps, a many-sided interest and a wide acquaintance with human affairs is involved in its work. All the more necessary is it to remember that the essential reason of this profession is to persuade people to do certain things, and especially one great thing. However wide may be the horizon of its interest, evangelism is at the heart and centre of the ministry.

II. The Dusty Room

Here again we have the Law and the Gospel, but this time under a new aspect and with a lighter touch. Formerly the Law kills, here it only irritates; producing that condition of confusion, turmoil, darkness, dirtiness, which is just the thing known as dustiness—a thing by itself. ' I have had enough,' as Cheever makes Christian say, ' of that fierce sweeper, the Law. The Lord deliver me from his besom ! ' The only thing which can remedy this morbidly irritated condition is the Gospel in its sweet, clean, and allaying power. When a man finds its peace, the mirrors of the soul are clear again, and reflect truly the face of God and the things of the world.

One may push the parable a very little farther and find in it yet another suggestion regarding the ' ethics of the dust.'

---

[1] *Cf.* Pater's *The Renaissance*, p. 131.

What is this dust of life, which the Law does not create but stirs up ? The answer is given by this very dusty world of ours, so full of the wreckage and debris of things. Upon everything under the sun falls constantly the deposit of everyday wear and tear. Silently and insensibly it settles, till bright things lose their brightness and clean things their cleanness. So, in the inner world, apart from deliberate acts of sin, the dust of life unconsciously falls. The fragments of broken attempts, the wear and tear of temper, the momentary desires and thoughts that are unworthy, form a kind of spiritual and moral debris, whose minute deposit has dulled the soul. We never know how much life is injuring us until conscience wakens to the fact that the finer purity of an earlier day is gone, and the room is covered with dust.

III. Passion and Patience

Dr Whyte's treatment of these is one of the most striking parts of his book, and as suggestive a piece of psychological analysis as could be found anywhere. This passage, one of the most familiar in the *Pilgrim's Progress*, is a child-piece ; and such sentences as ' where sat two little children, each one on his chair,' and ' first must give place to last,' etc., are perfect as parts of such a piece. The picture of Passion is extraordinarily vivid, considering the few words in which it is expressed. You feel that this little autocrat and egoist monopolises the whole room. Patience, on the other hand, is statuesque—' very quiet,' like Patience on a monument. Contrasting the fury of Passion with the stillness of Patience we might easily imagine that the former was the more forceful and energetic, while the latter, with its excessive repose, was a picturesque rather than a practical virtue. This, however, would be wrong, for in actual life the task that is set to men is that of combining activity with patience—perhaps the most difficult undertaking in the world.

The scene might be understood of individual passions, and it would be easy to point out what particular bag of treasure it is that each is raging for, and what the corresponding exercise of patience. But it is obvious that here we are dealing rather with general symbols which represent aspects of life as a whole. Passion is the selfish life, and the bag of treasure is life's opportunities of gratifying self. Passion thus understood is never satisfied. When it gets its treasure, you have the selfish rich man; when it fails to get it, you have the selfish poor man. But to both cases alike the closing words of *Vanity Fair* apply: ' Ah, Vanitas Vanitatum! which of us is happy in this world? which of us has his desire? or, having it, is satisfied?' These are the rags in which Passion is left—rags of respectability and a moral and spiritual nature in tatters. There, in the feebleness of reaction, and amid the ashes of Passion's burned-out fires, many a life discovers its folly only when too late. Often, too, there are others round about Passion who are left in rags—wives, children, or friends.

On the other hand, Patience is here understood as the comprehensive virtue in which are included all others which go to make a right life. It involves on the one hand self-discipline and the denial of indulgence in a thousand forms; on the other hand that faith which endures as seeing the invisible, and in consequence of that vision forms a proper estimate of the relative values of things here. There is indeed a way of canonising Patience as the one virtue, which is deadening to the higher energies of life, and sets for the ideal a merely passive and negative character.[1] Nothing could be farther from John Bunyan's view, and this picture must be taken along with that of the Fighter of the Palace.

[1] *Cf.* Chaucer, *The Clerke's Tale* and *The Tale of Melibœus*.

IV. The Fire at the Wall

Here life is seen in a new aspect, chosen in order to bring out the spiritual forces of good and evil which are at work upon it. The scientific definition of life as the 'sum total of the functions which resist death' is strikingly applicable here. This view, which Professor Henry Drummond expounds so eloquently in his *Natural Law in the Spiritual World*,[1] is exactly that of Bunyan's figure. Life is a wasting thing, a waning lamp, a dying fire. And just as, in the natural world, there are many diseases and accidents which threaten to hasten the decay and violently end the resistance to it, so there are in the spiritual world agencies such as temptation, discouragement, and many others, which tend to extinguish the inner fire. These are all summed up in the figure of Satan casting water upon the flame. Yet the wonderful fact is that the flame is not extinguished. There are lives known to us all which seem to have everything against their spiritual victory—heredity, disposition, circumstances, companions,—yet in spite of fate their flame burns on. The secret is that Christ is at the back of the wall, and there is no proof so wonderful as this of the reality of Jesus Christ as an agent in human life.[2]

Besides the two main agents there are plenty of human ones at work for both these ends. Some people are for ever throwing cold water upon the fires of the soul, devil's firemen whose trade seems to be that of discouraging. Others, and these are the blessed ones of the world, pour in upon the flagging spirit the oil of good cheer and hope

[1] P. 104.
[2] *Cf.* the passages from Bunyan's own experience quoted in Stevenson's *Text-Book*, p. 48.

THE ROAD

V. THE FIGHTER FOR THE PALACE [1]

This passage is a masterpiece of compression and vividness, told in the spirit and with something of the atmosphere of the old French romances, which, in Bunyan's day, were still popular and familiar to the general public through the medium of chap-books. First of all, one is struck by the great company round the door, the hesitating crowd of would-be heroes. All the open doors of life have this crowd around them, because at each there are enemies making entrance dangerous. We have already seen that this is so at the Wicket Gate, and here again we find, as Peyton says, that 'God is hard upon man.' [2] Every opportunity in life demands some courage to enter it. Bunyan himself knew well from experience both the hesitation and the sense of enemies, and others before and since have similarly hesitated. Two instances, of very different types of men, may illustrate the situation in various aspects :—Professor Romanes tells us that ' Even the simplest act of will in regard to religion—that of prayer—has not been performed by me for at least a quarter of a century, simply because it has seemed so impossible to pray, as it were, hypothetically, that much as I have always desired to be able to pray, I cannot will the attempt.' [3] Mr Snell writes of Petrarch : ' Only his capacity for religious emotion is allied with moral infirmity, and that is one of the reasons why his character is apparently so complex. This, however, is a familiar experience. St

---

[1] Mr Foster finds the original of this palace in the very beautiful ruin, supposed to be the work of Inigo Jones, which immediately adjoins Elstow Church. (*Bunyan's Country*, p. 63.) The spectacle of 'certain persons walking on the top' of the palace may have been suggested by statues which may be seen on the battlements of such ancient castles as Alnwick and Chepstow. Such figures on castles were common in England.

[2] *Memorabilia of Jesus*, p. 233.

[3] *Thoughts on Religion*, p. 133.

SIR THOMAS HILLERSDON'S
MANSION, ELSTOW
*Supposed to be the
work of Inigo Jones*

THE INTERPRETER'S HOUSE

Paul himself confesses, " That which I do, I allow not " ; and Ovid observes in a similar strain : " Video meliora proboque, Deteriora sequor." Petrarch shares their inconsistency. Pitying himself, he would gladly flee from his earthly prison-house to the arms of the Crucified, but doubts and fears hold him back. The desire for fame which has clung to him from boyhood, he cannot give it up.' [1] The saddest figures to be seen about such gates are those who have allowed their hesitation to run on until the gate is closed, and who now stand like the foolish virgins, willing when it is too late.

Nothing could exceed the effectiveness of the clear image of the man with the ink-horn,[2] to bring to sharpness the real point of the story. The group has all the edge of some such old steel engraving as *Rent Day*. It is the strenuousness of Christianity, shown as usual in a clear decision, that is here portrayed. We can see that *stout* [3] countenance. He goes ' as a man going to claim an inheritance.' Sam Jones, the Georgian preacher, says, ' God despises a coward . . . God entrusts all the noble causes on this earth to men who are game.' [4] Meredith makes his Victor say, ' I cannot consent to fail when my mind is set on a thing.' [5] Yet it must be remembered that more is needed than a stout countenance, and that many say, ' Set down my name,' who never go into the fight.

The strenuousness of Christianity is a congenial theme with Bunyan. He believes that it is always safest as well as most joyous to fight one's way through. He would rather sing in the bare old Puritan churches, ' Praise God from whom all blessings flow,' than, in the new luxurious ones, ' Art thou weary, art thou languid.' He certainly saw no necessity for being ' carried to the skies on flowery beds of ease, while

---

[1] *The Fourteenth Century*, p. 260.
[2] *Cf.* Ezekiel. ix.
[3] German *stolz*, proud—the right sort of pride.
[4] *Sermons and Sayings*, p. 266.
[5] *One of our Conquerors*, chap. xxvii.

others fought to win the prize.' For him, ' the kingdom of Heaven suffereth violence, and the violent take it by force.'[1] In his *On Greenhow Hill*, Kipling has a passage well worth the consideration of those who name themselves fighters of the good fight of faith. The whole passage has much in common with Robert Browning's typical view of life as expressed in such poems as *Prospice* and *The Epilogue to Asolando*.

The couplet at the end curiously haunts the memory. Compare Shakespeare's rhymed lines at the close of passages, such as [2]:—

> 'Come, side by side together live and die;
> And soul with soul from France to Heaven fly.'

VI. THE MAN OF DESPAIR

This is the darkest of all Bunyan's pictures. The very title of it, 'A Man of Despair,' ranks with such other titles as 'The Man with the Iron Mask,' etc., and lays hold upon the imagination. The picture is drawn largely from Bunyan's own experience, but it is as old as the religious life.[3] In Bunyan's case, however, this desperate condition was largely induced by his reading a book containing the deathbed confession of an Italian apostate, Francis Spira. It is a very dreadful book, now fortunately out of print. Morbid in the last degree, it tells how the friends of that poor wretch hovered round his deathbed, deriving what they took to be profit for their own souls from what were obviously the results of an unhinged reason.[4] The book produced a terrible effect upon Bunyan, as he tells us in *Grace Abounding*, and planted

---

[1] Dr Brown (*John Bunyan*, chap. xi.) recalls a parallel passage in *The Heavenly Footman*, 'They that will have Heaven must not stick at any difficulties they meet with, but press, crowd, and thrust through all that may stand between Heaven and their souls.'

[2] *I. Henry VI.*, Act. iv. sc. v.   [3] *Cf.* Ps. lxxxviii., etc.

[4] *Cf.* p. 35.

THE INTERPRETER'S HOUSE

in his soul, to rankle there like a poisoned arrow, those words, detached from the Epistle to the Hebrews concerning the repentance of Esau, which had already slain Spira. It is said that certain savages poison their arrows by dipping them in the decaying flesh of a corpse;[1] here certainly is a spiritual parallel. It is very striking that the dreadful phrase, 'O now I cannot,' in which the bitterness of the passage reaches its climax, is taken verbatim from Spira's book.

It is a morbid picture, such as is produced by an age of extremes whose intense black and white is relieved by no shading.[2] We can recognise in the picture elements of that hallucination which goes with religious melancholia in all ages, yet we have not dismissed the subject when we have said that. Mental pathology is as real a branch of science as any other, and these phenomena are facts which must be reckoned with as real possibilities in any life. They are the tragedy of Christianity; and however little one sympathises with the onlooking friends of Francis Spira, yet a talk with one in despair may be a lifetime's education. Remorse, alas! is a perpetual phenomenon, appearing as the latter end of the story of Passion.

One or two of the details of this narration are well worthy of notice.

'*I am what I was not once.*' This is the very essence of despair, touching even a lower depth than 'might have been.'[3]

'*I left off.*' This has been supposed to teach Arminian

---

[1] *Cf.* Henry Drummond, *Tropical Africa.*

[2] For an interesting historical account of the times in this light, see the first two pages of Cheever's first essay.

[3] *Cf.* Mrs Browning's *Loved Once*, and A. L. Gordon's *A Voice from the Bush* —

'They used to be glad to see me once,
They might have been to-day,
But we never know the worth of a thing
Until we have thrown it away.'

doctrine, but there does not appear to be any theological intention in it whatever. It is simply a piece of human experience terribly true to life. Behind the sense of God's departure and the devil's coming there stands the memory that one has chosen it to be so, and no stoicism can stand out against that. It is the ' burning worm ' of remorse—a phrase whose combination of the two elements of the New Testament Gehenna recalls Edgar Allan Poe's lurid poem, *Conqueror Worm*. In connexion with the phrase, ' I tempted the devil,' it is interesting to contrast the two *Fausts*—Goethe's and Marlowe's. Goethe's Mephistopheles enthusiastically tempts his victim; but the older Mephistopheles is a sad and almost reluctant figure, drawn into his work of temptation by Faust's passionate insistence. This leaving off is but one more form of that pet aversion of Bunyan's which he so constantly scourges. Here it is seen all the more vividly in contrast with the strenuousness and thoroughness of the Fighter of the Palace. Fatalistic despair is the natural doom of spiritual indolence.

The centre of all this passage is found in the fact that the whole matter turns upon the treatment of Christ. This was Bunyan's own experience, for the black heart of his despair was, ' this one consideration would always kill my heart, my sin was point blank against my Saviour; . . . I had in my heart said to him, Let Him go if He will.' It is striking that Christ should just here be called the Son of the Blessed. God is Himself happy, and is the fountain of all happiness for man. All our reserves of happiness and the sources from which it can be ultimately drawn, lie with Him who is to us the revelation of that God. Thus on our relation to Christ hangs our whole chance of joy. To count Him as our adversary who is the Eternal Friend of man is to court despair. It is a solemn thought that for each man there is only one Christ—*his* Christ—who stands for all that ideal

THE INTERPRETER'S HOUSE

of faith and truth and life and joy which shines before each man as his highest goal. When the Jews had crucified Jesus, their world was as empty of Him as Herod's world was of the murdered Mariamne. For him who crucifies his own Christ there is no other, and his world is empty.

It is certain that Bunyan did not believe that such a state of mind as this, represented the truth of the case as a necessary and final doom. His own experience had shown him escape from it, such as he portrays in Doubting Castle. Even the driest and most rigid of his commentators confess that it is difficult to draw the line, and that ' many have written the same bitter things as here, but to them they have in no wise belonged.' One thing may be taken as certain, that no one whose heart is in the least degree troubled about it has committed any unpardonable sin.

VII. THE VISION OF JUDGMENT

This vision, into which are woven parts of the gospel prophecies of Judgment, along with other elements, such as appear in the classic pictures of the Judgment Day, gives Bunyan an opportunity for a final assault upon conscience with the full force of his extraordinary spectacular imagination.[1]

It is characteristic of Bunyan that in this final vision he should revert to the form of a dream which was always peculiarly impressive to him.[2] No doubt much must be discounted from any such impression, especially in the case of imaginative natures like his, yet it is often true that dreams do reveal with appalling frankness the real bent of the soul. When we wake we check our frankness even with ourselves.

---

[1] For an interesting note regarding the central figure seated upon a cloud, see Lessing's *Laocoön*, chap. xii. Browning's *Easter Day* gives the finest modern parallel to the whole picture.

[2] *Cf.* p. 1.

There are two striking points in the vision. The first is the opening of the pit *just whereabout I stood*. That has the note of true conviction. The hell of many people gapes just whereabout some one else stands. Second, there is the haunting conception of him that *still kept his eye upon me*. This is the shattering of all privacy. He who has once realised it shall never be alone again. According to a man's relation with the great Onlooker, it is the greatest fear or the greatest hope of life.

Yet the picture as a whole is unsatisfactory, in spite of such magnificent sentences as, 'Then I saw the man that sat upon the cloud open the book, and bid the world draw near.' When the man is asked why he is afraid, he simply recounts again some of the details of the spectacle. Conviction has not gone deep enough yet, for there is no real thought here, and especially no real thought of sin. The time of the vision is the first moment of waking in the morning, when the imagination indeed may be excited, but the intellect is not collected. Then, when the lights of life are low, conscience stalks forth like a spectre, with imagination behind her; but the result is mere hysteria and not a rational view of life and sin at all. Very often such experiences pass away, leaving harm rather than good as their legacy, and on the whole the man in the iron cage is nearer salvation than this man.

CHAPTER IX

THE WAY OF THE CROSS

CHRISTIAN has already been impatient to leave the Interpreter's house for the journey. It is a common way with pilgrims, and we find Dante [1] hurrying his guide in similar manner,—'Sir! let us mend our speed.' One of the older annotators of the *Pilgrim's Progress* asks, 'Why in such haste, Christian? Poor, dear soul!'—and goes on to explain that the reason for this indecent hurry is his desire to get rid of his burden and to arrive at the Cross. Bunyan's idea is probably simpler. Action is always easier than thought for some natures, and it is necessary for this man to stay and learn, when going on were more congenial. It is a lesson which most pilgrims need to learn.

The prototype of THE FENCED WAY might be found in many a lane and cross-country road of Bedfordshire. Any day's journey of the author's would serve to remind him that the way of true life is always fenced. The Traditions of the Scribes were the old wall bordering that way, and the Rabbis actually called them by the name of 'the fence.' The new fence is Salvation. Nothing could be more significant than this change. Restraint by command and threat will indeed keep men in the straight way and be effective so far; but Salvation—with all that it involves of the sense of that *from* which and *to* which we are saved—that is a far surer fence. Alike by the sense of safety and the sense of honour it hedges in the narrow way. This wall is not well represented by those pictures of dull masonry which

[1] *Purg.* vi. 50.

suggest a lane to right or left of which nothing can be seen. It is true that at the first a man may pass through a stage when he can see nothing in all the world but just the one fact that he is saved. Yet that fact itself has very varied aspects, and this wall, like Dante's sculptured rock-face in Purgatory,[1] is both a prospect and a companionship in itself.

Up this way burdened Christian ran. At this stage there was little comfort, but there was much progress; and, indeed, at no stage is the one of these the measure of the other. It is when God has enlarged our hearts, rather than when He has lightened us of our burdens, that we go quickly on our way.[2]

The description of Christian at THE CROSS is one of the finest passages in the book, and is well worth learning by heart. It is interesting that so uncompromising a Protestant as Bunyan should have introduced a symbol generally associated with the Roman Catholic faith.[3] But John Bunyan was not the man to be kept back from anything which he found useful, on the ground that any one else, however different from himself, also found it useful. Really, the Cross is a Christian symbol, and it is an unnecessary and unfortunate thing to allow it to be appropriated by any one branch of the Christian Church. In Cynewulf's *Christ* it is used with terrific power, bloody and radiant, as the standard erected on Judgment Day. In Dante's

[1] *Purgatorio*, x.
[2] *Cf.* Ps. cxix. 32, and also Dante's *Purgatorio*, xv. 79.
[3] The explanation is really very simple. In Roman Catholic days, crosses were erected on many of the village greens of England, and through later times these remained, the customary places for public proclamations and the centres of village sport. There was such a cross on the green at Elstow, and the stump of it still remains. It was beside that cross (as Foster very strikingly points out) that Bunyan himself was playing tip-cat on the Sunday, when 'A voice did suddenly dart from heaven into my soul, which said, "Wilt thou leave thy sins and go to heaven, or have thy sins and go to hell."' *Cf.* Foster, *Bunyan's Country*, pp. 30, 67, 68.

THE CROSS,
ELSTOW

THE WAY OF THE CROSS

Paradiso, the Cross is the very emblem and centre of the glory. These and other uses are the property of Christendom, and this may well be ranked among them.

In this story, coming to the Cross is the last incident in the man's salvation. In many cases the Cross and the Gate stand close together, the experience of conversion being completed at one event, so to speak. The separation of the Gate from the Cross is here surprising, as it represents rather the modern than the Puritan type of experience. The Cross, which used to be the emblem of slavery, now becomes the means of liberty and lightening. The point to notice here is that *we are saved by what we see*.[1] The sinful man loses his burden upon realising a fact, and the essence of Christianity is a magnificent realisation. Sin had been too much for him, but now God has vanquished it. The joy that follows is inevitable. Bunyan tells us in his *Grace Abounding*, that when the joy of this release came to him, he could have spoken of it to the very crows that sat upon the ploughed land by the wayside.[2] The power and beauty of the simple sentence which tells of the burden tumbling into the mouth of the sepulchre make that passage one of the religious classics of the world. No commentary is necessary or possible, except the memory of that experience in the hearts of those in whose lives it has happened.

THE ANGELS are part of that 'machinery' of the supernatural which Bunyan introduces sparingly, but always with particularly striking effect. It does not seem to be necessary, on the one hand, to take them as theological symbols representing the three Persons of the Trinity, nor yet, on the other hand, to regard them merely as figures introduced for the merely artistic purpose of heightening the

---

[1] *Cf.* p. 9; also *John Bunyan*, by the author of *Mark Rutherford*, p. 98.
[2] Two hymns in Dr Bonar's *Hymns of Faith and Hope* recall this passage: 'Bear thou my burden' and 'Rest, weary Son of God.'

impressiveness. Rather are they simple symbols of actual experiences, and they may belong either to the inner or to the outer world. Browning's *Guardian Angel* very beautifully touches this subject, and the line in that poem—'My angel with me too,' reminds us that these messengers, dear and fair as 'birds of God,' may be human friends. It is interesting to note that it is only to the solitary man (Part I.) that angels come: the members of the company of Part II. have to be angels to one another.

The gifts of the Angels are four:—

I. *Peace.*—This is the friendliest gift that is ever given to man. It refers to the angelic message,[1] which Milton so wonderfully expands in his *Hymn on the Nativity*. But before that gift could be realised, much had to happen; and it is at the Cross of Christ that sinful men find the perfect peace.

II. *New Raiment.*—His garments stand for the outward seeming of a man as judged, not from the point of view of human onlookers, but of the eyes of God. One of the most curious and pathetic figures in our older literature is that of Langland's 'Haukyn, the active man,' who is so busy that he has not time to clean his coat. This, however, is deeper than those careless, casual sins of a busy life; for this is the view of himself as covered with sinfulness which the Puritan conscience so often gave to a man. It will be noted that the angel does not clean the coat of the active man, nor does he cover the former rags of the conscience-stricken with a new robe. At the Cross old things are passed away and all things are become new. The rags are stripped off and the robe is given.

III. *The Mark.*—This also has to do with the outward appearance, but it is more intimately connected with the individuality of the man than the raiment. It seems to

---

[1] Luke ii. 8-15.

stand for something distinguishable by others, which is in a stricter sense ourselves than even our character is—a subtle change wrought upon the very personality by the Cross of Christ, as the marks of the Cross were printed upon St Francis of Assisi in the familiar incident of the stigmata. In the Bible there are such references as the mark of Cain; the mark of Ezekiel's man with the slaughter-weapon; the mark of the beast and the mark in the foreheads of the chosen ones, recorded in Revelation. All these illustrate in various ways the subtle change in men, recognisable by others, produced by supreme experiences of good and evil.

IV. *The Sealed Roll.*—This is the inward memory and record of the experience at the Cross, which gives assurance to the Christian life. It is sealed, for it is incommunicable. Like the name written in the white stone, it is known to none but to him who bears it. It is worn within a man's breast as part of his own consciousness—the true *mens conscia recti*. It is just his own name, but to him that now means no longer a citizen of Destruction, but one of the redeemed.[1]

Bunyan's side-note is ' A Christian can sing though alone, when God doth give him the joy of his heart.' This is in strongest contrast to the House of Mourning which is immediately visited in Part III.; in which part, by the way, there is no word of Formalist, that being in truth the name of the author of the volume. Bunyan's side-note reminds us of Burns' test of a true poet, that he can wander all day beside a burn, ' an' no think lang.'

At this point we suddenly come upon the three sleepers, SIMPLE, SLOTH, AND PRESUMPTION, who stand, as Mr Stevenson with fine insight has said, for three types of Religious Indifference. The violence of the contrast between this scene and the last is evidently intentional. Just beside

[1] *Cf.* a very striking interpretation of ' The White Stone ' in Peabody's *Mornings in the College Chapel*, i. 96-98.

the emblem of safety and the inspiration of Christian's most intense vitality, we suddenly come upon three men in extreme danger and fast asleep. Next to the danger and sin of turning back, Bunyan would place that of standing still. There are, indeed, things which a man may stop for and take no harm. He stoops over these three hapless ones, not to gossip nor to thank God that he is not as they, but to help and save them if he can. Such an interruption to any Christian's journey will prove in the end to have hastened his arrival.

Bunyan's groups are carefully constructed, and these three have certain points in common. They are the only human trio in the book, though there are plenty of couples; and in the *Holy War* two of them have been elevated to the titles of Mr Simple and Mr Sloth. The things they have in common are but idleness and fetters; each of the three is asleep, and each is bound. That in itself is sufficient commentary upon the state of all who are unawakened to spiritual things; but in David Scott's very striking picture of the scene, the sense of danger is heightened by the protruding bones of a skeleton human foot above the surface of the marsh beside them. Christian is keenly awake, fresh from the Cross, with his heart full of the sense of their danger and tender for their sakes. To him, they are like those who sleep on a mast. The accurate translation of Prov. xxiii. 34 is ' poop, behind the rudder,' but Bunyan takes it in the other sense, and is thinking of the dizzy spectacle of wheeling stars and sky seen from the mizzentop of an old ocean trader. The threatening lion is a favourite image with Bunyan, as we shall see later on. It is peculiarly congenial to his own somewhat boisterous view of life. But perhaps it was the fetters more than the danger that appealed to his pity here.[1] He knew what spiritual chains were, and he knew the feel of deliverance. In *Grace Abounding* he says : ' Now did my

---

[1] *Cf.* Stevenson on Chains of Habit, *Text-Book*, pp. 63, 64.

chains fall off my legs indeed; I was loosed from my afflictions and irons.' To such a man it seems out of the question and impossible for any one to be indifferent to these supreme issues. He is baffled, and takes it ill. One of the saddest lessons that Christians have to learn is the limit of their responsibility for those who are bent on sealing their own doom.[1]

Simple[2] is one whose position is due not so much to ignorance as to want of power to put two and two together. But this want of power is not caused by natural defect so much as by the paralysis of systematic self-indulgence. It is significant that in the Book of Proverbs the Simpleton is so closely connected with lust. Simple sees no danger[3]—a kind of courage which is mere brutishness, for the brave man has the keenest eyes for danger. *Sloth* loves sleep for its own sake. Procrastination is his favourite art. Whymper traces the stagnation of the South American Portuguese to their constant word 'mañana' (to-morrow). It is an inseparable feature of genuine spiritual and moral truth that it demands earnestness, and presents a situation which is urgent and immediate. *Presumption* shows his quality by telling his would-be helper to mind his own business. It is a right answer to impertinence or curiosity. In the life of Robertson of Brighton an amusing incident is told of a busybody who interrupted his work with talk about the inconveniences of being a popular preacher, and was answered that the only such inconvenience 'is intrusion like the present.'[4] But where any earnest and kindly friend, seeing what he takes to be a danger, offers help, this man's answer is presumption.

---

[1] *Cf.* Ezek. xxxiii. 8, 9.
[2] *Cf.* Prov. xiv. 15.
[3] The bronze panel on the door of the Bunyan Meeting, Bedford, which represents this scene, cleverly introduces a lion approaching from behind while Simple says 'I see no danger.'
[4] *Life*, chap. x.

Even though the judgment be mistaken, if the help be given in friendship, a rebuff like this shows the mingled pitifulness and contemptibleness of the self-important Philistine.

These three are often supposed to be enemies only to themselves, but as a matter of fact every one who is an enemy to himself is an enemy also to others, and to the human race, in which ' no man liveth to himself.' It is significant that in Part II. even Mercy is uncompromisingly severe in regard to these, because of their danger to others. *Simple*, though he looks so inoffensive, may be a very subtle kind of evil influence. Of Robert Elsmere, in Madame de Netteville's drawing-room, Mrs Ward says : ' There is an amount of innocence and absent-mindedness in matters of daily human life which is not only *niaiserie*, but comes very near to moral wrong. In this crowded world, a man has no business to walk about with his eyes always on the stars. His stumbles may have too many consequences.'[1] *Sloth*, like all stagnant things, breeds malaria. It is impossible to live well beside an idler. Either by infection or by irritation, Sloth destroys his neighbours' souls. *Presumption* is like Browning's children, ' playing with a match over a mine of Greek fire.'[2] He is ready to hold himself responsible for all consequences, but that will be poor comfort for his neighbours after the explosion. There is much crude and ignorant scepticism, and much of the most dangerous sin, flaunted in the present day by foolish persons who have no idea either of its meaning or of its results ; but unfortunately for us all, it is not necessary to be intelligent in order to be dangerous.

[1] *Robert Elsmere*, p. 43.   [2] *Karshish*.

CHAPTER X

FORMALIST AND HYPOCRISY

THE next incident of the journey is the advent of FORMALIST AND HYPOCRISY, who came tumbling over the wall on the left hand of the narrow way. The figures have a connexion on the one hand with the Cross, and on the other hand with the Hill Difficulty. It is at these two points, more perhaps than at any other in the whole journey, that *reality* tells and is indispensable. It is interesting to note that it was at the Valley of the Hypocrites, in Dante's *Inferno*,[1] that the earthquake of Calvary had broken all the bridges.

Formalist, the man of precedents, the stickler for correctness, or the lover of ritual, has many representatives in every generation and in every church. There are many varieties of him, from the artistic lover of beauty for its own sake, apart from truth, down to him whom Creech calls ' the person who adopts the forms and externals of religion to quiet a stupid conscience.'[2] The point that all formalists have in common is this, that they prefer form to substance, the mere art of expression to that which is to be expressed, manner in general to matter. The modern types which are most in evidence are the religious people who practise this fashion in the extreme High Church on the one hand, and in the worship of dead orthodoxy on the other; in art it is represented by that extreme realism which exaggerates and abuses the excellent maxim, ' Art for art's sake.'

Hypocrisy is Formalism run into falsehood. When the form is there without any reality corresponding to it within,

---

[1] *Inferno*, canto xxiii.   [2] *Edinburgh Fugitive Pieces.*

you have the hypocrite. The easiness of profession and the interestingness of outward show are apt to beguile men into this vice, apart from baser motives. The profession has so many points fitted to engage one's own attention, and to catch the eyes of others, that it is quite possible to live for it, engaged with the outside appearances of things, while all the time the inner life and character are decaying. This may happen consciously or unconsciously, and it has happened so frequently that by some persons the name of hypocrite is applied to any one who makes a clear religious profession. Duncan Mathieson is said to have asked a child in a Northern town whether there were any Christians there. The child replied with a prompt denial. The evangelist, nonplussed for a moment, remembered how things stood, and asked whether there were any hypocrites there. He was at once directed to the house of one of the truest saints he had ever known. Hypocrisy does not consist in making a profession, but in making it when one has nothing to profess.

Even for this part of the allegory, Bunyan was able to draw from his own experience. It is very curious to think of him in the capacity of Formalist, yet here are his words. He is describing a time when he would 'go to church twice a day, and that, too, with the foremost.' 'I adored,' he says, ' and that with great devotion, even all things (both the high place, priests, clerk, vestment, service, and what else), belonging to the Church . . . had I but seen a priest (though never so sordid and debauched in his life), I should find my spirit fall under him, reverence him, and knit unto him; yea, . . . I could have laid down at their feet, and have been trampled upon by them; their name, their garb, and work did so intoxicate me.'

Bunyan as a hypocrite is still more difficult to conceive, yet in the same book he tells us, 'for though, as yet, I was nothing but a poor painted hypocrite, yet I loved to be talked

FORMALIST AND HYPOCRISY

of as one that was truly godly. I was proud of my godliness, and indeed I did all I did, either to be seen of, or to be well spoken of, by men; and thus I continued for about a twelvemonth or more.' This, however, we must take, like much else in the same strain, *cum grano salis*. The sin was peculiarly alien to his frank and truthful nature, and the following quotation seems better to express him. 'Even then' (*i.e.* at his worst time), 'if I had at any time seen wicked things, by those who professed goodness, it would make my spirit tremble. As once above all the rest, when I was at the height of vanity, yet hearing one to swear, that was reckoned for a religious man, it had so great a stroke upon my spirit, that it made my heart ache.' This natural abhorrence explains the singularly small attention given to Hypocrisy in the *Pilgrim's Progress*. Dickens puts this vice into the forefront in his Chadband, Pecksniff, etc.; Carlyle seems always to be aware of a multitude of hypocrites in the background of his audience. Bunyan's outlook upon life is healthier, and hypocrisy is not interesting to him.

The two figures are closely connected, for they have much in common. Each flippantly lives on the surface of things, lightsome and fashionable, but heartless. The hypocrite is of course a formalist, and becomes only more so as he goes on. He may be in the fullest sense conscious of his hypocrisy, knowing his life to be a lie but counting upon other people not knowing it. But more frequently he deceives himself as well as others. Busy here and there upon the surface respectabilities of life and religion, he does not know that the soul has died out of them. Again, the formalist tends to become a conscious hypocrite. His natural delight in form inevitably tempts him to exaggerate or at least to touch up his experience and to pose as more spiritual than he is.

'They made up apace,' for sham is always easier in one

sense than reality. They are quite willing to make friends—in which, by the way, Formalist is not by any means like all his kind; the one-fingered handshake of the supercilious ecclesiastic is a perpetual source of mingled pity and amusement to all human men. Their account of themselves is frank; they 'are going for praise to Mount Zion.' This is an old conventional phrase which means no more than 'doing a praiseworthy thing'; but even in Bunyan's use of it, some sarcasm is lurking. No doubt they hope to get praise as they go, as well as at the end of the journey. This is indeed the root of their offence. These are essentially theatrical religionists who play to the gallery, and can do nothing without having an audience in view. Christ, in His own second temptation, in some of His words to Peter, and in many sayings to the Pharisees, condemned all such theatrising. Indeed, common sense condemns it. These men expect praise for a life in which one fails to see anything specially praiseworthy. They wish to be saved; and yet, in the spirit of Little Jack Horner, they wish vast credit for what is, after all, an act of prudence rather than of virtue.

They came 'tumbling over the wall.' This is one of those short cuts to holiness and salvation which always prove in the end the longest way round. Dante, in the beginning of his journey, tried such a short cut up the steep mountain, but was driven back, by the blessed intervention of the wild beasts, to that long and dismal journey which ended in the heights of heaven. These men plead, in defence of their entrance, the plea of custom. Their short cut is a right-of-way, justified by use and wont; nay, is it not often a 'church road' to boot? In this there is, no doubt, a reference to the ritualistic habit of leaning back upon antiquity. There is a real and great value in authority, and he who despises the experience of the past proclaims, not his independence, but his ignorance of history. Yet it is often forgotten that all is not venerable which is old. In every generation there have been fools and knaves as well as worthy men ; and an error, after a thousand years, is an error still. The mere fact of authority and antiquity can set no man free from the responsibilities of individual judgment. But *custom* applies to the present as well as to the past. There are so many respectable people who have never entered in at any wicket gate, that to talk of ' one way ' of entrance is to seem presumptuous. Nothing takes the edge off warnings so much as the comfortable feeling that we are lost in the crowd. It is this ignoring of the individual and solitary character of all religious experience that beguiles perhaps the majority of those who go astray.

The answer to all this is the question whether it will stand a trial at law. The witness-box has nothing to do with custom, with vague feelings of hopefulness and a general sense of well-being. Law deals with evidence and facts, which are easily forgotten when a man is making out a case for himself, but come up with terrible awkwardness in cross-examination.

They meet this argument by hard fact, as they think,— ' if we are in, we are in.' They are walking this stretch at least of the Christian road. It is an old fallacy which asks the question, At any given moment, suppose you were not a Christian, how many things would be different from those which as a Christian you are now doing and saying ? Genuine Christianity is not a mere mass of detail. It is good works and profession springing from a relation with God. Christ is continually calling men's attention away from the questions of leaves and flowers to the essential matter of the root. The details may be imitated for other ends : they may even, as Dr Dods expresses it, be ' done to keep Christ at a distance.' So that the answer of Christian refers men back to the Rule and the Master—great commanding facts which put all other reasonings out of court. The whole passage reminds us of Mr Gifford's advice to John Bunyan: 'He would bid us take special heed that we took not up any truth upon trust; as from this or that, or any other man or men; but cry mightily to God, that He would convince us of the reality thereof, and set us down therein by His own Spirit in the holy word.'

The men proceed to taunt Christian about the coat on his back—a sneer in which there is yet the recognition of a difference between him and them. There is something about a true Christian which the world recognises. The worldling in his essential nakedness often sneers at the robe of righteousness, but in his heart he envies it, as the poor envy the well-clad rich. Sometimes, indeed, the worldling seems fashionably clad, but his is a stage dress at best, and not meant for rough weather. The Christian's coat may seem clumsy and ill-fitting, but it will wear and keep him warm.

So these men 'looked and laughed,' and went their separate way. It was the silliest thing to do, as silly as it was rude; but it served to take the edge off the rebuke, and soon 'they were released from the honest eyes of Christian.'[1]

[1] *Hudibras*, the contemporary of *The Pilgrim's Progress*, was professedly one long and bitter tirade against hypocrisy. *Cf.* especially the well-known passages in Part III., Cantos I. and II.

CHAPTER XI

THE HILL DIFFICULTY

THIS hill [1] is put in the allegory for one of those tests of reality which life is sure to supply to every pilgrim, and the test is here applied to Christian, Formalist, and Hypocrisy. The way of Christ, like the ancient Roman roads, runs straight on over everything, and there is no doubt how Christian will do, if he remains in the way. But there are other ways to go; there is almost always the chance of somehow avoiding Difficulty. In the interval since the *Pilgrim's Progress* was written, the advance of civilisation has been, in one aspect of it, one long scheme for making life in all departments easier. Every new machine which is invented supplants a more by a less strenuous day's work. Every new idea in education seems to have for its aim the removal of those difficulties which called forth and exercised the spirit of the past.[2] The same tendency is apparent in the field of religion also, and there is much meaning in Nathaniel Hawthorne's sending the train of the Celestial Railroad through a tunnel bored beneath this hill. To a certain extent, no doubt, this is rather to be welcomed than regretted, for life, religious and otherwise, has in the past suffered much from unnecessary obstruction and unreasonable difficulties. Yet there is a very real and serious danger of losing strenuousness when

---

[1] *Cf.* the Stoics' 'steep hill of virtue' and Dante's Mountain of Purgatory.

[2] 'Foreign languages were but as so many hedges surrounding gardens wherein grew desirable fruits and flowers of literature, to obtain which hedge after hedge was scrambled over.' Mrs MacCunn, of John Leyden in *Sir Walter Scott and his Friends*, p. 114.

difficulty vanishes, and of the degeneration of muscle by disuse of climbing.

Formalist and Hypocrisy are quite in character when they avoid this hill. Both of them represent devices for avoiding the spiritual and finding an easier way in religion. ' Formalist and Hypocrisy may be a ridiculing and persecuting religion—never a suffering one.' It is, however, striking that while formerly they took a short cut to avoid the Cross, here they have to take a way round about to avoid the hill; which things are also for an allegory—many of the longest wanderings in life have been begun to avoid a very little hill.[1]

Even before we knew the names of the two roads by which they went, we note that the hill has separated them. Difficulty is the common lot, and it unites those who face it bravely; while each man seeking to avoid it has to find out his own solitary, sinuous way.

Danger, presumably the way of Formalist, is a great wood reminding us of that in which Dante lost himself.[2] Here it stands for the hopeless tangle of Formalism, the endless maze of complicated ritual through which a man may wander in the ' dim religious light ' of the forest. *Destruction* is a wide field full of dark mountains, where a man stumbles and falls, and rises no more. The idea reminds us of the field in the closing stanzas of Browning's *Childe Roland*. The hypocrite inevitably produces for himself a place full of stumbling-blocks and hemmed in with barriers.

There is no propelling power like reality, and the great reality which has entered into Christian at the Cross gives him impetus enough to carry him far up the hill he is facing. There is no sense of grudging nor feeling of unreasonableness

---

[1] *Cf.* R. L. Stevenson's *Footnote to History*, where the splendid chapter on The Hurricane is the finest sermon in the language on the text ' Steer for the centre of the storm.'

[2] *Inferno*, canto i.

about this experience. In other things men expect difficulty —in business, in study, in athletics—and it is part of the secret of our British character that as a nation we have ' welcomed each rebuff that turns earth's smoothness rough.'[1] So it is in the Christian life, and often the difficulty seems to increase as it goes on. Nothing is more true to life than the sense of decreasing pace in Isa. xl. 31. The apparent anticlimax really gives a brilliant suggestion of climax in the increased steepness of the way.[2]

The Third Part here introduces an unusually fine addition to the allegory. In the double cave on the hill where the pilgrim rests and recovers breath, the outer cave is that of Good Resolution—a chamber of pure alabaster whose rooflights show sculptures, like the rock sculptures of Dante's *Purgatory*.[3] In the inner cave, Contemplation sits 'in a chair of pure diamond, musing and silent.' Drawing back a curtain, he reveals to the pilgrim a characteristic mediæval vision of the heavenly city ' full of lustre and magnificence.' Bunyan gives his allegory a very different turn, with the arbour, the sleep, and the loss of the roll. The sleep is all the more striking that it comes just after Christian's words to Simple, Sloth, and Presumption. And yet, after all, his sleep was unlike theirs in two essential points, for (1) he had done something to earn repose, and (2) he repented when he was awakened. The incident is an exaggeration of permissible rest, showing that it is easy to rest too long and too deeply. It is the danger of meditation where action is demanded, or of that relaxed, holiday mood in which all serious thought is abandoned. He who mistakes this arbour

---

[1] *Rabbi ben Ezra*.

[2] 'I perceived,' says Bunyan at this point, 'that Christian fell from running to going, and from going to clambering upon his hands and knees.' God perceived it also, and was well content. Stevenson, *Text-Book*, p. 72.

[3] *Cf.* p. 70.

in the open air for the chamber in the House Beautiful is liable to many dangers. There is the delay itself, which disarranges the future journey, the loss of the roll, which is apt to happen at the hasty start, and the chill which stiffens the limbs of the climber in too many cases. The arbour is not meant for sleeping in, it is but a breathing-place.

The reference to the ants reminds us of Watts' lines—

> ' The little ants, for one poor grain,
> Labour, and tug, and strive,
> But we who have heaven to obtain
> How negligent we live !'

The next incident in the journey is the flight of TIMOROUS and MISTRUST. It is by a fine touch of analysis that fear is made to follow so closely upon sloth. Just as sleep leaves the body open to cold, so slothfulness leaves the soul sensitive to fear. Dr Whyte has pointed out that in Bunyan's days many were terrified and ran back from civil and ecclesiastical tyranny. The lion then roaring was too often the Royal Lion of England. Bunyan had felt the fear of it, and he describes graphically his feelings when about to be imprisoned. Afterwards, he too found that the lion was chained.[1]

Timorous and Mistrust may be taken as types of character —Timorous representing physical fear, the natural dread of pain ; while Mistrust represents mental fear, the state of mind in which a man is incapable of trustfulness. In David Scott's picture, one of these two is drawn with a helmet on his head. The sarcasm reminds us of that ancient day when ' by the watercourses of Reuben there were great resolvings of heart.'[2] These are such as can brave difficulty but not danger ; there are others who can brave danger but not difficulty.

The two may be taken as an example of the abuse of the

---

[1] *Cf. Grace Abounding,* and Brown's *John Bunyan,* chap. xi., etc.
[2] Judges v. 16.

imagination. The tyranny of vague fears over those who are not courageous enough to face facts is very terrible. Rudyard Kipling's lines on panic are striking here—

> 'It was not in the open fight
> We threw away the sword,
> But in the lonely watching
> In the darkness by the ford.
> The waters lapped, the night-wind blew,
> Full armed the Fear was born and grew,
> And we were flying ere we knew
> From Panic in the night.' [1]

There is nothing that calls for more strenuous self-control than imagination, and to flee from danger without having faced it is in every way bad policy.

It was bad policy for their own sakes. There are some people who seem to get all the trouble and none of the reward of the Christian life, who go on almost to the end of the journey and then turn back when the real trouble of it is over. David Scott, whose picture of this scene is peculiarly happy, makes the chained lion look down after them with something very nearly approaching a smile. The reason for this kind of failure is very generally to be found in the weariness and strain which the climb has cost; and it needs a peculiar effort of determination to force tired nerves to face danger.

It was bad policy for the sake of others. In Part II., we hear of the grim punishment which Mistrust and Timrous suffered 'for endeavouring to hinder Christian on his journey.' As we have already seen in regard to the three sleepers, cowards are dangerous, and the weak brother may easily become a serious nuisance. All who exaggerate danger tend to discourage others, and all that is best in us rises in sympathy with Bunyan's anger against discouragers. Church work, social work, public work of every kind suffer from them, and the roaring of the lions themselves does not do so much harm as the roaring of those who are frightened at

[1] *Plain Tales from the Hills.*

them. Bunyan calls them tempters, for they would obviously have been pleased if Christian had retreated. This would have confirmed their own course of action, and vindicated their cowardice as proper caution. For this sort of caution there is no room in Christianity, because caution here means mistrust of Christ, and, indeed, mistrust of life itself. The cynic is generally a coward at heart, and cynicism is but a fashionable name for the fear of man, or at least for the fear of life. To all true men, experience worketh hope and not distrust. If we live and think honestly, what is there anywhere to be afraid of ?

A study of Bunyan's *The Sum of my Examination* and *Reflections upon my Imprisonment*, is well worth while at this part of the allegory. In one passage he actually speaks of himself as one that ' sticks between the teeth of lions in the wilderness.'[1] Christian here is not represented as one of those constitutionally fearless people, like Browning's Clive, or Kipling's Gunga Din, who ' never seemed to know the use of fear.' With Christian there are three stages of experience mentioned : (1) You make me afraid ; (2) I must venture ; (3) I will yet go forward. Thus we see that it is not fear that is fatal, but the yielding to fear. Our salvation generally has to be worked out with fear and trembling, and this is part of the trial in each new venture. There is a story of an old veteran riding into battle beside a young recruit. The boy noticed the older man pale, and said to him, ' Surely you are not frightened ? ' ' Man,' said the veteran, ' if you were as frightened as I am, you would run away.' Herrick's couplet is well worth remembering :—

> ' 'Tis still observed those men most valiant are
> That are most modest ere they come to war.'

The fact is that this pilgrim is between two fears, and he chooses to face the lesser. In the memorable words of Dr

[1] *Cf.* Brown, *John Bunyan*, i. 177.

THE HILL DIFFICULTY

Whyte, ' What is a whole forest full of lions to a heart and a life full of sin ? Lions are like lambs compared with sin.' So Christian wisely says, ' I will go forward '—the Christian fatalism of which *Grace Abounding* is so full ; Bunyan is prepared to die, so long as he may at least die at the feet of Christ.

In the accounts of the ARBOUR and the LOSS OF THE ROLL, the author's marginal annotations (whose compressed meaning, by the way, contrasts curiously with the thin commonplaces of many of his annotators) are well worth attention here. The arbour is a *ward of grace,* and *he that sleeps is a loser.* It is significant that it is at the moment when he is professing courage that Christian discovers his own lack of assurance. A fear of enemies is upon him, that vague fear so wonderfully described in Pater's *Marius the Epicurean.*[1] Something is wrong, for his manhood has become suddenly demoralised. He does not, as we would do, refer to the weather or to his own state of health. He traces it at once to sin. It was neither the lions, nor yet Timorous and Mistrust, who were to blame, but a well-remembered moment of carelessness upon the hillside. Readers of *Grace Abounding* will be reminded here of the reasons given for his own two years of terrible despondency. Before doing anything else, Christian asks God's forgiveness, and thereby shows his spiritual wisdom.

There follows the dreary walk back in search of the lost roll. Sometimes, indeed, we cannot find and recall the exact moment of our failure in this fashion. Sometimes, however, we can ; the places in life where we sat and slept are miserably clear to memory. Then there comes upon the journey a sense of waste. The backward steps are taken in vain, and the time spent in seeking to gain assurance is lost time. Hedley Vicars tells that upon one occasion, when he had

[1] *Marius the Epicurean,* chap. x.

neglected his private devotion, his soul was for three weeks the worse of it. This man finds his sun gone down too soon, and the evening is chill with regret. Doddridge, in a passage which might have been written by Bunyan, says: ' Yea, the anguish of broken bones is not to be compared with the wretchedness of a soul which has departed from God, when it comes to be filled with its own way.' *Filled with its own way* —Christian knew the meaning of that phrase before he had finished his journey over that toilsome bit of path.

And yet perhaps, after all, the time was not really lost. In God's great alchemy there are secrets whereby evil things may be changed to good. It would have been far worse if he had lost the witness of the Spirit without regret. If he had said of his former assurance that it was delusion and childishness, his danger would have been extreme. Thus the experience was not really in vain, for every step backward in self-examination is in reality a forward step. Indeed, the nimbleness of his third journey, and the sudden access of delight, were such as to make the whole episode almost worth while. In high contrast to this passage is Christina Rossetti's sad poem, *A Daughter of Eve*, where the last word which the remorseful soul can speak is—

> ' A fool I was to sleep at noon,
> And wake when night is chilly.'

The pilgrim now has to face THE LIONS at the gate. The imagination of lions as guardians of palaces is as old as Assyrian and Egyptian architecture, in each of which the expression of the lion is characteristic of the national sentiment. The lion, as a symbol of defence, is familiar on the gate-pillars of old English houses, and is one of the commonest features in mediæval romances. The figure was a very favourite one with Bunyan, and occurs in many passages of his books.

Here the lions guard the edifice of the Church, and stand for those things which keep would-be Christians from entering it.

THE HILL DIFFICULTY

1. It may be, as it is here, some fierce and unexpected danger or trial, which comes at the top of the long slope of the Hill Difficulty. Readers of *Childe Roland* will remember the sudden little river, petty and spiteful, which crossed the wanderer's path after long and difficult struggling.

2. It may be some mere trifle, exaggerated by the imagination of the timid or the unwilling, that keeps men back from entering the Church,—an ass in a lion's skin.

3. It may be the roar of the world that we mistake for a lion's roar, not knowing how little the world can do against any resolute spirit, nor realising how little its opinion matters to any wise one.[1]

4. The lion may be one's own past sin, that ' lion of our own rearing ' which Dr Whyte describes so graphically.

5. One's own mistakes and blunders may play this part,— apes rather than lions, jabbering at us and caricaturing us from out the past.

6. The lion may actually be the lion of the tribe of Judah. Dr Whyte's paragraph about man's fear of his own salvation is a very memorable one. There are times when we are more afraid of Christ, and the demands of Christ, than of all the dangers in the world.

What the particular significance of the lions was for Christian we are not told. No doubt, the long strain that had been upon him, the vexation of losing his roll, and the weariness of the search for it had shaken his nerves. But the rousing words of the porter are enough to recall him to himself. ' Is thy strength so small ? '—strength, that is, not to fight the lions, but to urge on his own trembling limbs. That question was enough to touch the honour of Christian. But there immediately followed the assurance which puts the whole episode in a ludicrous aspect. The lions were chained,

---

[1] *Cf.* 'The Roar of Piccadilly,' one of the most striking passages in that charming book, *London in the 'Forties*, by the late Professor Masson.

and from first to last the danger had been imaginary. This is a very exhilarating passage for us all. You may make up your mind when you are in the way of God that there is a safe passage through anything that may be met with. Napoleon's command to his troops at Austerlitz was, ' Charge through whatever is in front of you ! ' God has meant life to be difficult, and even formidable ; but from beginning to end of the journey He keeps its dangers upon leash. That is the reassuring fact which a wise faith may always lay hold upon ; but there is, on the other hand, a corresponding warning. The traveller must *keep the middle of the path.* We are evidently intended to remember that this necessity follows upon sin and repentance. No past sins or mistakes are fatal to a pilgrim, but they may narrow the way for him, and necessitate a caution which others do not require. The lion's claws may even catch the flowing garments of the light-hearted walker. What is safe for others is no longer safe for the penitent blunderer, who must observe a special self-control. When he was a little child, this man may have played at the children's game of walking delicately about a crowded room so as to touch nothing of its furniture. It is not a good game to be compelled to play in after-life. Those are wisest who do not, through sin or folly, render still narrower the narrow path of duty.

CHAPTER XII

THE HOUSE BEAUTIFUL

THIS is one of Bunyan's most charming conceptions. Its significance and its interest are as strong from the literary as from the religious point of view. The traveller, coming in the dusk of evening to the house from whose door and windows warm lights are streaming, with their offer of rest and hospitality, is one of the pleasantest figures in the poetry of every generation.[1] The old romances are full of such pleasant episodes, and they find echoes in every one of the long list of those who have written of life under the figure of a pilgrimage or journey.

There can be little doubt that so distinctive a piece of portraiture as the HOUSE BEAUTIFUL must have been suggested by some actual building, especially in a country so rich as Bedfordshire in 'stately homes of England.' The balustrade of the staircase in the Swan Inn (in whose chamber Elizabeth Bunyan pled in vain for her husband before Sir Matthew Hale and Judge Twisden), was brought thither from a house of a former Duke of Bedford, and may suggest the interior. Two houses dispute the honour of this identification. One of these is that beautiful ruin which stands on the site of the ancient Abbey of Elstow, close to the parish church.[2] This mansion, in the days of its glory, was very familiar to Bunyan. But the stronger claim appears to be that of Houghton House, on the Ampthill Heights, about six miles south of Bedford. It was built by the Countess Mary, sister of Sir Philip Sidney, in 1615, and

[1] *Cf.* the closing sentences of R. L. Stevenson's *An Inland Voyage.*
[2] *Cf.* p. 62.

the architect is supposed to have been Inigo Jones. In Bunyan's time it was the home of the Earl of Ailesbury, Lord Lieutenant of the County, a famous antiquary and book-lover, who, after Bunyan's death, appears on the side of the King against the non-conformists. Foster strongly advocates the identity of Houghton House with the House Beautiful, and finds near it the spring and the arbour of the Hill Difficulty, which is represented by the magnificent glade along which the north side of the house looks down to the plain of Bedford.[1] Apart from such details, a visit to the ruins with the *Pilgrim's Progress* in hand is certainly very convincing.[2]

Such a rest-house, with relief and good fellowship for the tired and solitary traveller, is a symbol that may be very variously interpreted. One of the most beautiful and familiar of modern instances is R. L. Stevenson's 'House Beautiful,' where the lonely cottage on the moor, dreary enough to outward appearance, and unromantic as the plainest life, is glorified for the open eyes of the appreciative spirit by the simple but marvellous work of nature through the seasons of the year. This, however, is analogous rather to Bunyan's Interpreter's House in one of its broader aspects of spiritual communion than to this, which, as we shall see, has a specialised meaning. Christina Rossetti, in her poem of *Uphill*, has a weird description of the road that winds uphill all the way, only to end in what Sir Walter Scott, in a similar metaphor, in the *Lord of the Isles*, calls ' that dark inn, the grave.'

Bunyan's House Beautiful stands, in contrast with the inner spiritual meaning of the Interpreter's House, for the external Church, the Church Visible and its membership; and it gives a peculiarly rich and attractive view of these.[3]

[1] *Cf.* Frontispiece.
[2] *Cf.* Brown's *John Bunyan*, i. 21; ii. 72, 74, 75. Foster's *Bunyan's Country*, chap. iii.
[3] *Cf.* Bunyan's *Discourse on the Building, Nature, Excellency, and Government of the House of God*, as described in Dr Brown's *John Bunyan*, chap. xvi.

HOUGHTON
HOUSE

THE HOUSE BEAUTIFUL

In Part III. it is represented as a convent, with much discourse on fasting instead of the feasting of this part. From the *Celestial Railroad* it is omitted altogether, and only referred to with a few scornful jests; the way is so easy that there is no need of rest in that journey, and the Church of Christ is far too old-fashioned for the new religion.

The Church is here seen in its social aspect. It is just by the wayside; not out of the world, a secluded place of dim religious light, shut off for the purposes of mere mystery. It is a home, with the fireside element strongly emphasised, in which we hail as our first view of the Church one which lays its stress on the social side of it, welcoming and genial. The incident stands for the beginning of Christian fellowship, that memorable fact in religious history—memorable not on earth only, but in heaven, for when ' they that loved the Lord spake often one to another,' we are told that a book of remembrance was written. The fellowship also is again that of encouragers. In times of depression, weakness, and regret, the friendly hand of the Church may do much for the saving of a man, and the whole passage is an excellent manual for those who are teaching a class of young communicants.

In the light of this interpretation of the House Beautiful, we see the more precise significance of the events which have immediately preceded. The lions and the loss of the roll represent the difficulties about entering the membership of the Christian Church which were and still are felt. Most serious is the loss of assurance, which in all generations delays the entrance of many. With Bunyan's arbour story, compare Question 172 of the Larger Catechism of the Westminster Divines.

The whole of this brilliant and charming passage makes one think of some of the old Morality Plays, whose spectacular influence was long and far-reaching on the English imagination. Each person represents a group or type of certain aspects of the religious life, and the whole picture taken together gives a very complete view of the manifold functions of the Church.

It has been noted that this is a household of women, and that may strike the reader as odd when he remembers Bunyan's words about his relations to women in his *Brief Account of his Call to the Work of the Ministry*.[1] Here again there may have been a local suggestion. The church at Elstow had risen upon the foundations of a Benedictine Nunnery and Abbey, founded by Judith, a niece of William the Conqueror, and destroyed by Henry VIII. in 1539. This nunnery seems to have been an aristocratic one, but lax in discipline. 'The Ladies of Elstow' must have been famous personages in local imagination; and, with the necessary changes in deportment, may well have suggested this house of religious women to the author, whose birth occurred within a century after the end of their varied career.[2] But the three women of the Palace have at once humbler and nobler originals in those other women of whom we are told in *Grace Abounding* : ' But upon a day the good providence of God called me to Bedford, to work at my calling; and in one of the streets of that town [said to have been St John Street], I came where were three or four poor women sitting at a door, in the sun, talking about the things of God. . . . And, methought, they spake with such pleasantness of scripture language, and with such appearance of grace in all they said, that they were to me as if they had found a new world; as if they were " people that dwelt alone, and were not to be reckoned among their neighbours." ' These, as the excellent caretaker of the Bunyan Meeting suggested to the writer, may have given Bunyan the idea

[1] *Cf.* p. 167.
[2] *Cf.* the very interesting account in Foster's *Bunyan's Country*, chap. ii.

not only of the women of the Palace, but also of the angels at the Cross.

The trust and fellowship of this house may, indeed, remind us of many a pleasant passage in such a book as Du Chaillu's *Land of the Midnight Sun*, and the kindliness to the wanderer of the Norwegian women in their guest-houses and sæter farms. But Bunyan knew well the difficulty of managing platonic friendships in real life, especially in regard to religious matters. Here he is simply following tradition, where the virtues of pagan thought are female, and the Christian Church is the Bride of Christ. Victor Hugo's opinion that women are the best Christians has found many supporters both before and since his day. Whether or not it is a correct one, is a question which will be differently answered by different individuals, and the answer will depend upon the women they have met. In this passage the tender womanly element, along with the strength and wisdom of noble women, are represented as among the finest products of religion. No doubt the conception is traceable, at least in part, to the commanding influence of the figure of the Virgin Mother upon so many centuries of Christian thought.

The religious conversation of the House Beautiful can hardly seem dull to any reader, though at first it may strike him somewhat as *Cranford* does, as typical of that old-fashioned propriety which is now so rare in conversation. On closer examination, however, the talk proves not only instructive, but thoroughly interesting and even entertaining. Most probably much of the talk is modelled upon that of the ' three or four poor women sitting at a door, in the sun, talking about the things of God,' to whom we have already referred. These, like the dwellers in Bacon's *New Atlantis*, had indeed ' found a new world.' It is a world with a language of its own, and there is no way either to speak or to understand this language but to live in the world where it is spoken. To those who have not travelled thither it is, like the New Atlantis, 'a land unknown': to its inhabitants it is 'here is God's bosom.'

Conversation is now more than ever a difficult art. Modern life has not leisure for the coffee-houses of Fleet Street, and modern men open with a kind of wistfulness the rich pages of Boswell and Eckermann, of Landor and Holmes; or they turn to the lavish brilliancy of Meredith's conversationalists with a kind of wonder. Religious conversation especially has felt the change. It is so difficult to keep it interesting and at the same time entirely real, that while some religious talkers still bore their neighbours with the dullest kind of speech, others exaggerate their experience and become romancers. It is little to be wondered at, and still less to be blamed, that many Christians are reticent, and some are silent about the deepest things. Yet there is such a thing as worthy and interesting religious talk, and this passage, allowing for the differences in the fashion of centuries wide apart, is a model of it. It is bright and sparkling, with clever play of wit in parts. There is no lecturing nor conventionality of 'improving conversation.' There is nothing morbid in it, as religious conversation is so apt to be—none of that sentimental anatomy and dreary self-analysis which is sometimes associated with intimate religious talk. It is the right kind of *gossip*—i.e. *god sib*, personal talk between intimate friends. It is an art well worth cultivating, for there is much helpfulness lost through undue reticence; and the old commentator knew what he said when he coined his fine phrase, 'the blessedness of experimental savoury conversation.'

The porter, the one man of the place, stands for the official aspect of Church life. A certain formality and carefulness is absolutely necessary for the right management of all public work; and when the work is religious the necessity is even

THE HOUSE BEAUTIFUL

greater. Those are not wise who resent any reasonable officialism and authority, and are continually demanding that everything in connexion with the Church shall be informal. What they mean by informality is very apt to become slovenliness; no Church work gains in spirituality by being done in an unbusinesslike manner.

The conspicuous feature in the figure of Watchful is a certain subordinate faithfulness. He is indeed broad-minded enough not to assert that the Church is altogether indispensable,[1] yet his whole demeanour is that of one who takes his office with the utmost seriousness. Thus the contrast is very striking between this gatekeeper and him of the wicket-gate. Goodwill speaks with authority, Watchful wholly as a subordinate. If he be supposed to represent the minister of the Church, then certainly it is his office and not his personal claim that he magnifies.[2]

The pilgrim's words as to his name are interesting. 'Graceless' carries us back to the title *Grace Abounding*. The words about the race of Japheth and the tents of Shem remind us of John Bunyan's young and surely very unnecessary heart-searchings as to whether he and the rest of the British people were descended from the Israelites.

These dialogues, both in regard to matter and arrangement, show minute carefulness and completeness on the part of the author, and the story of the House Beautiful is as noteworthy as a work of literary art as it is for its religious teaching.

Discretion comes first, for the place, though so hospitable, is well guarded. Sometimes, indeed, this Discretion has gone too far. The excessive strictness with which the entrance into the Church is guarded in exclusive religious communities is quite as great a danger to the Church as the laxity of which we hear in other quarters. In the one case carelessness,

---

[1] Compare the porter's words about Faithful to Christian as he is leaving the House Beautiful.   [2] *Cf.* p. 55.

in the other spiritual arrogance, betrays the high trust committed to mortal man. It is true, as Dr Kerr Bain says, that on the whole it is 'better to err on the side of letting in than of keeping out.' Still, questioning is necessary, and especially self-examination. Were it not for these, we might have Worldly Wiseman, Hypocrisy, and Sloth using the House Beautiful for their own ends, in which case it would soon require to change its name.

The order of Discretion's questions is significant. First come those about his experience, and last that about his name. There are many people whose first question is that of names. This is what they judge by and are interested in. A famous name telling of old family, or influence, or wealth is all that is needed for entrance to many a house of good society on earth. Here it is good to find in regard to all such matters the grand equality of the Church. Of lord and labourer alike it asks first—or ought to ask—not 'What is thy name?' but 'What has been thine experience?' and 'What is the direction in which thy life is moving?'

Before any further examination, Christian is hospitably welcomed. There is much more to be said both by him and by the damsels of the house, but he has already proved himself a genuine pilgrim, and that is enough for his admission.

To understand the precise grace which is referred to under the name of *Piety*, we may contrast it with the Piety of Part III., which gives the convent idea of Christianity, and has retreated far from the bright and busy world. Again, this Piety is distinct from that extreme type of Puritanism which has been well described as 'bitterly pious.' In modern times, partly through the influence of such sarcasms as Burns' *Holy Willie* and Dickens' richly deserved caricatures, the word *piety* is connected with the idea of a weak and hypocritical type. As a corrective, it is worth while to remember the original Latin meaning of *pietas*, with which Virgil has familiarised the world. Standing as it does for all that is tender and strong in family loyalties, this may serve to give us back a fine but lost word.

Piety in this narrative is not a striking character, but simple and true. She exhibits no cleverness nor attempts any cross-examination, leaving that to the more competent Prudence A gentle, loving, and ingenuous person, she is quite as anxious to get good as to give it. And yet she is no weakling, for the truest spirituality is founded not upon conventional phrases, but upon real experience. Of course, much more is needed for complete character than this, but it is always well to judge people by what they have rather than by what they lack. There is room in the Church for such lesser lights of grace as hers, and after all there is much to admire and be very thankful for in them.

The conversation begins with a very naïve reminder of their kindness in admitting him. This is the egoism of the little child, which is so familiar in many of the Psalms. The following discourse is entirely retrospective. It avoids all discussion of religious questions in the abstract, and confines itself to details of personal experience. An interesting view of the pilgrim's mind may be had by noting the things he has felt to be most impressive in his past. The thought of the Fighter of the Palace, which we shall find to be a forecast of what is coming immediately upon Christian himself, is added only as an afterthought. It is a curious and surely intentional touch of humour by which Bunyan makes the pilgrim say that he 'would have stayed at that good man's house a twelvemonth.' Either his conscience is still uneasy about his impatience to get away from the Interpreter's House, or else he has forgotten that impatience. The past, with its halo, makes things seem very precious which we did not fully value at the time. Of course, the most noticeable thing in the memory of the journey is the Cross and what befell him there. It is interesting to note that here he speaks of one who hung bleeding upon that tree, whereas before, so far as we are told, it was the empty Cross which he saw. Looking back upon that supreme experience, we recognise that it is not the mere fact of the Cross, or any doctrinal interpretation of it, which holds the sinner's eye through a lifetime.[1] It is the person of the Crucified, in which is seen the Incarnation of the Eternal Love. The pilgrim says he had never seen such a thing before, and that is both false and true. The Cross has been familiar from childhood to many a man who has never before seen it like this.

There is only a word or two about the bad people he had met. No mention is made of Mr Worldly Wiseman, and the notice of the rest is very brief and gentle. Jeremy Taylor, in his *Holy Living*, has a fine passage of which this reminds us : ' Upbraid no man's weakness to discomfort him, neither report it to disparage him, neither delight to remember it to lessen him, or to set thyself above him. Be sure never to praise thyself or to dispraise any man else, unless God's glory or some holy end do hallow it. And it was noted to the praise of Cyrus, that, among his equals in age, he would never play at any sport, or use any exercise, in which he knew himself more excellent than they; but in such in which he was unskilful he would make his challenges, lest he should shame them by his victory, and that himself might learn something of their skill, and do them civility.' Along with this passage it is interesting to place the following from the life of Bunyan himself : ' It is well known that this person . . . made it his study above all other things not to give occasion of offence, but rather to suffer many inconveniences to avoid it, being never heard to reproach or revile any, what injury soever he received, but rather to rebuke those that did.'

[1] *Cf*. p. 70.

CHAPTER XIII

THE HOUSE BEAUTIFUL (CONTINUED)

In *Prudence*[1] we meet with a very different questioner indeed. Clever, knowing the world and the heart of man, she searches into Christian's character in a fashion that gives us the assurance that he is dealing now with a practised cross-examiner. He is not facing here mere outward questions of conduct or speech. The inquisition is running its search deep into the secret motives of the life, its imaginations, and desires.

This examination is significant, for, on the one hand, the Church of Christ ought to have a place for Prudence, and a large place. Any public association so influential as the Church still is, can only be a menace to society if it allows itself to become, through a mistaken charity, the cloak and guarantee for dangerous men. On the other hand, the function of Prudence is not solely exclusive. It is a huge mistake to imagine that moral perfection is expected in Church members, or is the guarantee of their worthiness to be such. Bunyan knew far too well the evil of his own heart to tolerate any such doctrine. Once, we are told, when in the disguise of a waggoner he was overtaken by a constable, the latter asked him if he knew ' that devil of a fellow, Bunyan.' ' Know him! ' Bunyan said. ' You might call him a devil if you knew him as well as I once did.' The true worthiness lies in the heart, far below the surface of the outward life. It would be difficult to find a more perfect definition of it than that which is contained in these sentences of John Knox's

[1] Contrast Chaucer's Prudence, in the *Tale of Melibœus*.

Communion Service : ' For the ende of our comming thither is not to make Protestation, that we are upright or just in our lyves ; but contrarywise, we come to seeke our Lyfe and Perfection in Jesus Christ.' ' Let us consider, then, that this Sacrament is a singular *Medicine* for all poore sicke creatures ; a comfortable *Helpe* to weake soules ; and that our Lord reqyreth none other worthinesse on our part, but that we unfeignedly acknowledge our naughtinesse and imperfection.'

It is a curious fact and a touching one, that Protestantism cannot escape the need which created the confessional in the Church of Rome. Something deep as human nature itself— the loneliness of sin, or the desire to face the worst—drives men to confession in all Churches and outside of them. Only it is well to remember that while confession to a friend gives a relief which is legitimate and has warrant in Scripture, yet the practice is a delicate one and beset with dangers. There are only very few among even our most trusted friends whose natures are wise and fine enough for the office of confessor. Again, the act of confession must never be allowed in itself to satisfy the sinful conscience ; indeed, when it ceases to humiliate a man and to give him real pain and shame, it has become dangerous, and should at once be stopped. The luxury of confession may develop easily into the disease of confession, than which there is no more unwholesome and morbid condition of the human spirit.

The list of questions addressed to Christian is extraordinarily well chosen :—(1) His longing after the past evil life. She asks him simply whether he thinks of it, and he is able to answer that he does so only with shame and detestation— a declaration which, made honestly, shows a very considerable and, indeed, unusual reach of attainment in the spiritual life.

(2) Carnal cogitations, however, still linger in memory and imagination. They are, indeed, his grief, and if he had his

choice he would never think of them again. Bunyan knew by experience this strange battle with his own imagination which both haunted and disgusted him. In more than one paragraph of the most violent language he describes the battle between fascination and repulsion in *Grace Abounding*. It is the same battle which St Paul describes as that between the living body and the corpse to which it is chained. It is pathetic to think of men now so long at rest who were troubled with this constant and discouraging human warfare, and it is interesting in the present instance to note how sore and evil such memories appear when the eyes of a pure woman are looking into the pilgrim's eyes. This is for many of the young their sorest battle, and if Bunyan shall in this conversation give us any hint as to how it may be won, he will indeed be a benefactor to the generations. Meanwhile it may be noted that we may learn to hate even an attractive sin, if we have learned sufficiently to fear it. One commentator quotes from an anonymous writer a curious passage which is relevant here. He gives the test by which you may know a sheep from a swine when both have fallen into a slough and are indistinguishably bemired. 'How, then, distinguish them? Nothing more easy. The unclean animal, in circumstances agreeable to its nature, wallows in the mire; but the sheep fills the air with its bleating, nor ceases its struggle to get out.'

(3) Unaccountable changes of experience give him sometimes a lucid interval. It is a terrible confession for a Christian man that such intervals are but seldom, and are to him golden hours; yet there is great comfort in this for those whom Abbott has described as 'often falling into sin yet always struggling against sin.' Evidently life is meant to be a battlefield. Human nature will keep the battle at the gates, and God will have it so.

(4) But how to conquer? The man who can tell us this

will be the greatest of all God's gifts to us. Most men find that the more they fight the hotter the battle becomes. The drift of objectionable imagination is often trifling, unpleasant, and altogether unworthy of regard, yet sometimes the more one tries to forget, the more surely he remembers. Bunyan's plan is simple and in every way wise. It is contained in the one sentence that one set of thoughts must be fought by another set of thoughts. There is no possibility of fighting this battle *in vacuo*, for idleness and vacancy of mind are the opportunities for every unworthy thing. Only when mind and body are kept actively engaged is there any chance of victory.

It is important to note that the thoughts which drive out the evil ones are in a totally different line. They are the Cross, the robe, the roll, and that heaven which is the end of the journey. These are all subjects into which nothing that defileth can enter. They are God's blessed distractions by whose means the feet that have been in miry ways may find clean paths. The one thing essential to this means of victory or escape is that these subjects shall be so presented to the mind as to be vitally interesting. The roll, the question of one's assurance, has the interest which attaches to all study of one's self. The robe has the interest of a spiritual *amour propre*, reminding us of the dignity and self-respect due to the Christian life. The Cross has its own eternal interest. On a rustic crucifix above Zermatt there is the following inscription in badly spelt German :—' Look up to Me, child of humanity, before thou goest further, for I have suffered and died for thy sins which thou so lightly committest. Ah! repent and bewail thy sins and say, O Jesus have compassion! God so loved the world that he gave his only begotten Son for our sins.'

(5) The mention of heaven as a distraction from unworthy thoughts suggests her last question to this shrewd examiner.

THE HOUSE BEAUTIFUL

Why does he wish for heaven so much? It is an interesting question, for one of Bunyan's characteristics is the surprising delight in the spectacular which often throws up a heaven of almost barbaric splendour against his grey earth. This passage, however, is singularly free from all that side of things. It is ethical from first to last, and is prompted, point by point, by the confessions he has just made. It is one of the most exquisite passages in the book, and the sigh of weariness and longing that breathes in it is the most authentic proof of the genuine thirst of his soul for purity.

Christian is approaching the table of the sacrament, and in order to complete his preparation for that, one more element is necessary. The Lord's table is a place for human affection, where family love and remembrance should share the thoughts with self-examination. The conversation with *Charity* is an afterthought of Bunyan's, appearing only in a later edition. Charity is the pure heart of affection, which does not concern itself with any other interest than that of friendship. Charity begins at home; how about his wife and children? As we have already noted, some have accused Bunyan of the selfishness of his conception, sending his pilgrim forth to find his own salvation, and leaving his family behind him.[1] This passage is Bunyan's vindication. No one knew better than he that Christianity demands not only earnestness and pity for those who are outside a man's own circle, but ' affection for those that are within.' If proof of this be needed, it may be found very abundantly in his account of the *Discourse between my Wife and the Judges* and *Reflections upon my Imprisonment*. In the latter he speaks most sadly of the parting from his wife and children and their hardships in his absence, ' especially my poor blind child, who lay nearer my heart than all besides. Oh! the thoughts of the hardship I thought my poor blind one might go under would

[1] *Cf.* p. 27.

break my heart to pieces. . . . Thou must be beaten, must beg, suffer hunger, cold, nakedness, and a thousand calamities, though I cannot now endure the wind should blow upon thee. But yet recalling myself, thought I, I must venture you all with God, though it goeth to the quick to leave you.' The bitterness of Christian's separation reminds us of some of the saddest words in English poetry, where the Blessed Damozel realises that her lover will not come to her home in heaven—

> And then she cast her arms along
> The golden barriers,
> And laid her face between her hands,
> And wept. (I heard her tears.) [1]

The *Parsifal* of Wolfram mourns, through long wanderings in search of the Holy Grail, his severance from wife and children; but the heathen knight in the same romance helps the solution of the problem by the announcement, ' I believe in the God of my love '—

> . . . 'If thou speakest, Lady, the thing that indeed shall be,
> If God as His knight doth claim me, and they are elect with me,
> My wife and my child, then I wot well, tho' a sinful man am I,
> God looketh with favour on me, and hath dealt with me wondrously!' [2]

Charity, in the capacity of advocate for the man's wife and children, examines him as to what he had done to induce them to follow him. Three things are especially inquired into: (1) how far he had talked with them (*N.B.* not talked *at* them); (2) how far his relation with them had been the subject of his prayers; (3) how far his conversation with them had been confidential and personal, relating his own experience instead of discoursing on generalities. Bunyan's ideas on the subject are strangely mingled. In one passage he says, ' My judgment is that men go the wrong way to learn their children to pray. It seems to me a better way for

---

[1] D. G. Rossetti, *The Blessed Damozel.*
[2] Wolfram's *Parsifal,* (Jessie Weston, vol. ii. p. 160).

people to tell their children betimes what cursed creatures they are, how they are under the wrath of God by reason of original and actual sin,' etc. In another passage, however, he asserts, ' I tell you that if parents carry it lovingly towards their children, mixing their mercies with loving rebukes, and their loving rebukes with fatherly and motherly compassions, they are more likely to save their children than by being churlish and severe to them.' With so strange a combination of sentiments as this in our mind—the inevitable result of the blend in Bunyan of Puritan professor and human man—we cannot help feeling that perhaps the wife and children may have had something to say for themselves. The *Book of Sports* had called forth a Puritan reaction, and we can see in John Bunyan's soul-searchings about bell-ringing the inflamed state of the religious conscience of the time. Perhaps it is just to suggest that if this man had been as wary to gain their friendship and confidence as he was to check their amusements, he might have had more influence with his family. If a man be found with four sons, and all of them mocking his religion, the chances are that there is something wrong with the way in which that man had dealt with his four sons. Dr Whyte's commentary on this passage is peculiarly rich in insight and genius. One of the driest of the old commentators at this point breaks into unwonted vivacity : ' Though, like an angel, you talk of Christ, of the gospel, or of the doctrines of grace and of heaven, yet, if you indulge devilish tempers and live under the power of any sinful lusts and passions, you will hereby harden others against the things of God, and prevent their setting out in the ways of God.'

Yet even Charity is convinced that in this case it was not the man's fault. Four cruel children had behind them a woman whose heart was set upon the world, and her worldliness had eaten out whatever love she may have ever had for her husband. Charity is not easily provoked, yet she can be provoked. Indeed, without the power of anger, Charity is but one of those thin sentimentalities on which Meredith pours out his scorn in *Sandra Belloni*. Charity is not easily provoked, but her indignation, when it appears, is that dreadfullest of things—' the wrath of the Lamb.'[1]

The description of *the Supper Table* ranks with that of Christian at the Cross as one of the most perfect of Bunyan's writings. It is a model for all who celebrate the sacrament of the Lord's Supper, and its literary and devotional qualities give it a very high place in the literature of England. For delicacy of touch, for unconscious art and exquisite simplicity, for fulness of religious meaning and wealth of spiritual imagination, it would be difficult to find its equal.

The most noticeable feature of the passage is the sense that Christ is with us as we read it, supplying the Real Presence in the sacrament. No part of the Allegory recalls so vividly the words of Cheever's preface—' In all things we are brought to Christ, and thrown upon Him; and this is the sweet voice of the *Pilgrim's Progress*, as of the Gospel, Come unto Me, all ye that labour and are heavy laden, and I will give you rest.'

Four points may be noted in the description of the Supper Table, all of which give the aspects under which the writer presents Christ here.

1. *A Warrior.*—It is a masculine view of Christ's death, which is regarded not as a doom nor in any pitiful light, but as a thing of blood deliberately shed at an hour which the warrior himself had fixed. The stern facts of life may be brought to this place, and the most anxious conscience finds

[1] Much in these conversations reminds one of passages from Bunyan's *Christian Behaviour*, and from the *Plain Man's Pathway* and the *Practice of Piety*, all of which are well worth consulting at this point.

peace in the assurance that they will be sternly dealt with here.

2. *Love.*—This is the key to the meaning of the three moments mentioned, before, at, and after the Cross. None of these can be understood until we realise that every one of them was done out of a ' pure love to his country.' It is not the mere ' loss of much blood,' but the pure love that was in it which gives that ' glory of grace ' for which Bunyan has so happily found the phrase, to all the events commemorated at this table.

3. *Resurrection.*—The element of love in the Resurrection, as here presented, is of the deepest significance. The witnesses to the Risen Christ are summoned—Mary, Peter, Thomas, the men of Emmaus, and the rest. But it is that we may realise that we are near them not merely in our common faith, but also in a great and unceasing love. They bore witness not to the mere fact that Christ was risen, but also that He was a ' lover of poor pilgrims.' That was why He rose from the dead, and Bunyan's interpretation of the Resurrection as an act of love is one of the most illuminative and far-reaching of all his gifts to religious thought.

4. *He would not dwell alone.*—' Father, I will that they . . . . be with Me.' It is a simple touch, but it presents a whole aspect of the soul and character of God. Many readers have been struck by the daring presentation of God's loneliness, which Coulson Kernahan has given us in *A Book of Strange Sins*. Many of us have felt in the negations familiar to all students of dogmatic Unitarianism an irresistible feeling of dreariness. The demand for a social aspect in our conception of God lies at the back of all wise doctrines of the Trinity, Creation, and Redemption. These things we believe, because our souls have discovered that ' He would not dwell alone.'

The sleeping chamber closes, in a few simple and choice

words, the delightful story of this day. In the second part Bunyan adds a sidenote, 'Christ's bosom is for all pilgrims.' It would be impossible to promise peace to all pilgrims after the first sacrament. Sometimes disappointments and anxieties mar that memory. Yet it is the normal experience, and no communicant should be content until he has gained it.

So the night falls and memory is lost in sleep. Many, like the poet, have written of the awfulness of 'that sad, obscure sequestered state,' and we may well wonder how we or any dare lie down in peace, unless it be in the full assurance that in it 'God unmakes but to remake the soul.'[1] It is to be noted that this sweet sleep comes to Christian on the eve of his most terrible battle, and we are reminded of the great words of St Paul, 'The peace of God shall guard your heart and mind.'

The chamber window opened towards the sun-rising, giving us for the last word of the night a promise of hope that reaches beyond the morrow's battlefield. Cheever quotes two very remarkable poems written by Bunyan upon the sunrise.[2] These are so brilliant in their way, and so full of the naïve genius of the dreamer as to excuse and almost justify Cheever's comparison of them with lines in *Comus* and *Romeo and Juliet*.

[1] Robert Browning, *The Ring and the Book*.
[2] *Lectures on Bunyan*, 120, 121.

CHAPTER XIV

THE STUDY AND THE ARMOURY

On the second and third days the Pilgrim receives from the Church three different kinds of preparation for the journey of the Christian life that lies before him. These, like so many of Bunyan's symbols, are admirably chosen, and together they present a very complete view of 'the preparation of the Gospel of Peace' with which the apostles would have the feet of all pilgrims shod. The three are—(1) Intellectual study ; (2) Spiritual realisation ; (3) Armour.

(1) INTELLECTUAL STUDY.—The Protestant Church has always laid great stress on study. However earnest and wholehearted in his devotion a man may be, however rich in spiritual experience, however quick with those instincts which go to make what is called religious genius, yet this further preparation is required. Religion is and ought to be a thing of knowledge, and the more thorough the intellectual labour of faith is, the more effective will the believer be in the world. Consequently the Church must ever put in the forefront of her responsibilities the question of religious instruction both for her ministers and for laymen.

Naturally, the great subject of such study is the Bible—those 'records of the greatest antiquity,' which are the first things shown to Christian.[1] In *Grace Abounding* we read in one place : 'The Bible was precious to me in those days. And now methought I began to look into the Bible with new

---

[1] With the words of this passage the late Dean Stanley began his course of lectures on Ecclesiastical History in Oxford, in fulfilment of an early resolution. *Cf.* Brown's *John Bunyan*, chap. xix.

eyes, and read as I never read before; ... and, indeed, then I was never out of the Bible.' Every reader of that book will remember the recurring phrase, 'to be set down in the Scriptures by the Spirit of God.' Bunyan's was a simple way of Bible study. At times, indeed, we find the suggestion of modern questions which have perplexed the student, but these are generally brushed aside as temptations of Satan, and the spirit of the study is that of childlike simplicity and faith.

The order in which the various subjects are taken is not without significance. First comes the Person of Christ; second, the saints and heroes of the faith; third, the message of the Gospel, confirmed by prophecy. It is not until the next day, and then not until after he has seen the weapons of defence and attack with which a man must be endued, that he looks into those curiosities which too often have a more important place assigned to them.

Christ is first, and in that we have John Bunyan's great secret. There is a Royalist ring in the first words of this passage, as of one appealing from the cruel and perverse government of the English kings of his day, not to a republic, but to the King of kings. It used to be maintained that Bunyan's fighting was done on the Royalist side of the English struggles, and certainly there is in all his thoughts of Christ the feeling of hereditary and exultant allegiance.[1] It may be that this partly explains the view which he shares with all contemporary theologians, that the study of the doctrine of the Person of Christ should precede that of His 'recorded acts.' No change is more significant than this, that while the older theology came down upon the record of Christ's

---

[1] Dr Brown has proved that Bunyan served in the Parliamentary army, as Macaulay stated. Mr Froude considered it probable that he fought on the King's side. The evidence adduced by Dr Brown is complete and conclusive. (*Cf.* Froude's *Bunyan*, chap. i.; Dr Brown's *John Bunyan*, chap. iii.; Carlyle, *Cromwell's Letters*, Letter xxx.; Firth, *English Association Leaflets*, No. 19.)

words and deeds from a doctrine of His Person found in the region bordering upon Metaphysics, the modern order is from the human Christ to the divine.

The Saints and Heroes come next for consideration. The order of the Roman Missal, closing the Church year with the singularly beautiful services of Commemoration of All Saints and All Souls, brings this into equally close connexion with Advent, which immediately follows. It is a subject which, with the decay of reverence and the greater independence and self-assertion of these later times, is apt to receive scant justice. Those who have thrown off the yoke of authority because it has become tyrannous, should beware of ignoring the value of history, and losing the immense gains won by the experience of holy and brave men. Similarly for the individual, while there is a slavish use of biography, there is also a wise and necessary use. It is foolish to imitate the experience of even the noblest, by forcing one's own life into the grooves which fitted another; but it is equally foolish to repeat experiments already made, and to blunder exactly as others have blundered, or miss the right paths which they have found and pointed out.

Having seen the goal of life in Christ, and heard the call of the mighty dead who urge the living to follow in their footsteps, it is natural that the Gospel message, the willingness of the Lord to receive sinners, should next impress itself upon the pilgrim. This is but the personal application to himself of all that he has heard and seen. It will be observed, too, that it is only now that there is any mention of fulfilment of prophecy. As a set of curious and puzzling problems in history, the prophecies are of little use, and the study of them, diverting the minds of the earnest from more practical and intelligible thoughts, has done great harm. As the guarantees and buttresses of faith, encouraging the wavering spirit and assuring it of God's power and love enlisted on the side of all who believe, they are among the highest of the means of grace.

Last comes the list of curiosities, which the museum instinct of Bunyan finds so congenial. These are not, however, speculative curiosities such as distract the mind with idle attention to side issues. Rather are they a continuation of the remembrance of saints and heroes—relics of stories drawn mostly from those rough and heroic ancient days of Israel which the Puritan times in many ways resembled. In his *House of Lebanon,* Bunyan writes in a similar vein: ' There ' (in the porch of the church) ' are hung up the shields that the old warriors used, and on the walls are painted the brave achievements they have done. There also are such encouragements that one would think that none who came thither would ever attempt to go back. Yet some forsake the place.' The whole trend of both passages shows the characteristic horror of backsliding, and the urgency of the pilgrim and warrior spirit. Everything is leading up to the coming fight with Apollyon.

(2) SPIRITUAL VISION.—Yet there is another kind of preparation for the dangerous way. It is to be a battle between earth and heaven, between the spiritual life and its great enemy. Consequently nothing is more necessary than a quickening vision of some sort, which will confirm upon the pilgrim his sense of the reality of spiritual things. As yet it can be only a glimpse, for high and steady spiritual vision belongs generally to a riper age than his. Each period of the religious life has its own appropriate phase of spiritual experience, and much has to be learned and unlearned before this will be the characteristic phase for Christian. In *Rabbi ben Ezra,* Browning's great verses well describe the contrast between the normal moods of youth and age.

Yet sometimes we are permitted to feel what an experience will be like which is far beyond our present attainment.

THE STUDY AND THE ARMOURY

The Church (and especially some of its choicest and most experienced spirits) has the power and the duty of making such disclosures. In this way, through his very wistfulness, many a man is led to live worthy not merely of his present condition, but of that platform of the ideal which is still far ahead of him. When, even in a glimpse, 'it *doth* now appear what we shall be,' and we know that we shall be like Him, life inevitably throws off its baser things, and attains in some measure to that which it has seen beyond the present.

Also, such foresights 'make the journey manageable to a man's mind, and conquer in him the sense of remoteness' that clings about all spiritual things. 'From the Palace Beautiful the Delectable Mountains may be seen in the distance; and by and by, from those Delectable Mountains will the Pilgrim see the gates of the Celestial City.' Thus is the way to heaven divided into stages, which give new meaning to the words, 'A day's march nearer home.'

It is interesting to compare this passage with Wordsworth's lines from his *Ode on Immortality* :—

> Hence in a season of calm weather
> Though inland far we be,
> Our Souls have sight of that immortal sea
> Which brought us hither,
> Can in a moment travel thither,
> And see the Children sport upon the shore,
> And hear the mighty waters rolling evermore.'

But Wordsworth looks *back* for that vision; his Golden Age, like Virgil's, lies behind. Christianity alone looks forward for the best. Both visions, however, have this in common, that they are only occasional. Wordsworth's is 'in a season of calm weather,' Bunyan's is 'if the day be clear.' Such experiences cannot, in most lives, be protracted until they are continuous. Those are wise who make the most of them when they come; and, when they have faded, brace themselves for the journey by dimmer light, but without forgetting the vision they have seen.

The phrase 'Immanuel's Land' is borrowed from Isa. viii. 8. It is a curious fact that here, as in many other instances, words first spoken in threatening have been sweetened by the Christian thought which took them over. Samuel Rutherford's use of this phrase is familiar to every one, embodied and reiterated in the extremely realistic verses of one of our hymns.

(3) ARMOUR.—Bunyan's interest in all that concerns battle reminds us of his own fighting days at the siege of Leicester and elsewhere. For him the Church Militant was no mere form of words, but a very plain reality. The effect of the Church on Christian was to transform him from a civilian into a soldier, and we have to change entirely our imagination of the pilgrim from this time forth. He becomes, as Dr Kerr Bain says, 'at once more serious and more competent'; but, besides that, there is about him something of the 'first-class fighting-man' which cannot be mistaken. It is that difference which Shakespeare describes in *Henry V.* between the 'modest stillness and humility' which are becoming in peace, to the 'terrible aspect' which comes upon the face of the warrior. 'Armour is Heavy, yet it is a Proud Burden, and a man standeth straight in it.'[1]

It is worn openly and without concealment. Readers of *Romola* will remember the tragic results of wearing concealed armour there recorded; and every Christian who is ashamed of being on his guard is liable to bring upon himself like troubles. In *Israel's Hope*, Bunyan puts this very plainly: 'Should you see a man that did not go from door to door, but he must be clad in a coat of mail, and have a helmet of brass upon his head, and for his life-guard not so few as a thousand men to wait on him, would you not say, "Surely

[1] Mark Twain, *A Yankee at the Court of King Arthur*, chap. xxviii.

THE STUDY AND THE ARMOURY

this man hath store of enemies at hand " ? If Solomon used to have about his bed no less than threescore of the valiantest of Israel holding swords, and being expert in war, what guard and safeguard doth God's people need, who are night and day roared on by the unmerciful fallen angels ? Why, they lie in wait for poor Israel in every hole, and he is for ever in danger of being either stabbed or destroyed.' However far we may have travelled from the point of view which these words indicate, we have certainly not yet reached a place where any man need be ashamed of armour.

But this is not the only armour which a man may put on, nor is the House Beautiful the only armoury. There is the brazen armour of cynicism and effrontery that is forged in hell. There is the armour of cowardice which the world forges—compromise and casuistry and conformity. But by far the commonest kind is that which we and our friends make for ourselves. Every Australian boy has heard of Ned Kelly's home-made armour, and some have seen those curious iron cylinders from which so many revolver bullets glanced off harmless. There are many men and women who know too well this secret. They encase themselves in mail of reserve, self-centredness, and the keeping up of appearances, and so go through the world. Mary Wilkins, in *A Far Away Melody*, speaks of a girl who, after she had put on her wedding-dress, found herself forsaken : ' She girded on that pearl-coloured silk as if it were chain armour, and went to merry-makings.' Such armour is apt to fail its wearers at the critical hour, proving like those ' leaden ' bayonets which stain the records of certain great wars. And even if it does not fail, such self-made armour is dangerous, and may be deadly. Some one has described a ceremony which used to take place at the funerals of the Czars of Russia. Two soldiers rode in the cortege as Black Knight and White Knight, representing Death and Life. The Black Knight's armour was an ancient, heavy suit, and the strongest guardsman was selected to wear it. At the funeral of one Czar the man dropped dead on the way, and at that of another he died after reaching his destination. So it is with many hearts that have encased themselves against the 'slings and arrows of outrageous fortune' in armour of hardness, coldness, or indifference. Their armour kills them while it seems to protect.

The detail of the arming of Christian is all taken from the Bible.[1] Bunyan might have found, in any of the Romances of Chivalry, abundant material for this part of his writing: yet the list already given of weapons exhibited in the armoury shows clearly that it is St Paul's inventory to which he refers. The list is familiar :—

The Sword is 'the Word of God'—the only offensive weapon included. Men of high spirit and temper like John Bunyan must have been glad of this restriction. Such men, fighting with any weapon which passionate earnestness might suddenly suggest, may have to repent of many of their strokes. It is true that there are portions of the Old Testament Scripture which, regarded as they were in those days, certainly offer great licence for vigorous fighting. Yet it is wonderful how restrained and how skilful Bunyan himself was in his controversial use of Scripture. In his answers to his enemies, whether human judges or evil spirits from the pit, he stays closely, and with infinite readiness and address, by the words of the sacred writings.

'*The Shield of Faith*' is one of the happiest figures in literature. The doubter stands naked to the darts of all enemies. He whose faith is lost finds the battle ever doubly sore upon him. No one who has not tried both ways, can have the least idea of the safety and protection given by a faith at once strong and not too heavy for his hand.

[1] *Cf.* Eph. vi.

THE STUDY AND THE ARMOURY

The Helmet protects the vital and most assailable part which gives direction and guidance to the limbs. Salvation is the Christian's helmet. He who is assured absolutely of his salvation can bear any suffering and undergo any length of conflict. That grand assurance gives coolness and skill in rush of battle, and wins on many a hard-pressed field.

The Breastplate is Righteousness. 'Thrice is he armed that hath his quarrel just.'[1] To question the rightness of the cause is to have the heart exposed, and many a man has lost the keenest conflicts of his life through a sudden touch of conscience making him a coward.

The Shoes are 'the Preparation of the Gospel of Peace.' The gospel is always and essentially a thing that moves. It urges forward those whom it saves, to all their spiritual adventures. The missionary spirit is in it, if it be true gospel at all. But yet it is the Gospel of *Peace*. Peace goes, in the long run, further than aggression. Its journeys and its victories are those fraught with the most permanent results. Those who would be successful pilgrims in the great pilgrimage should look well to the quality of their Gospel Peace, for upon that will depend much of their success as pilgrims. One of Zola's heroes, describing the lame and footsore army of the French in 1871, says : ' A soldier who can't depend on his feet may just as well be thrown upon a rubbish-heap. My captain was always saying out in Italy that battles are won with men's legs.'[2]

All-prayer is a word coined from Eph. vi. 18. In the Romances it was usual for heroes to have one weapon to which magic power was attributed. Just as the Arabian stories revel in magic lamps, rings, and carpets, so those of Teutonic and Celtic nations often introduce a magic sword, like the ' Blood-drinker ' of Frithjof's Saga, or Arthur's

[1] *II. Henry VI.*, Act iii. Sc. ii.
[2] *The Débâcle*, p. 67.

Excalibur. Here, however, the mystic weapon is not a sword, but something whereby a man lays hold on heaven. Scott's picture suggestively introduces gauntlets, by which All-prayer may be intended. It is significant, too, that the 'girdle of truth' mentioned in Ephesians is here omitted. Bunyan may have intended All-prayer for the girdle, and, if so, he certainly chose a figure very true to fact. Nothing girds the day's life together, and braces the man to face it without entanglement, so much as prayer. Yet the change is evidently intentional, and it reminds us of Dante's girdle thrown down into the abyss in the Inferno.[1] That was the emblem of the Franciscan vow, of which he felt he had no further need. Possibly Bunyan felt his struggle for truth over, and truth become so intimate a part of himself that it no longer required to be girded on.

The whole armour is simply equivalent to the command, 'Put ye on the Lord Jesus Christ.' Elsewhere Bunyan writes : ' Christ Himself is the Christian's armoury. When he puts on Christ he is then completely armed from head to foot. Are his loins girt about with truth ? Christ is the Truth. Has he on the breastplate of Righteousness ? Christ is our Righteousness. [Similarly, Christ is Shield and Salvation and Word of God—the shield, helmet, and sword of the Christian.] Thus he puts on the Lord Jesus Christ, by His Spirit fights the fight of faith ; and in spite of men, of devils, and his own evil heart, lays hold of Eternal Life. Thus Christ is all in all.' [2]

Grateful for the somewhat austere but helpful kindness of the Porter, the Pilgrim blesses him as he passes out of the gate. The Porter will be better for that blessing. His is a lonely post, watching pilgrim after pilgrim depart for the excitements of battle and the adventures of the road. Every blessing of this sort genuinely uttered keeps the heart alive

[1] Canto xvi.   [2] Quoted by Offor, *sub loco*.

THE STUDY AND THE ARMOURY

in the minister of the church, and preserves him from losing his human attachments in the routine of office.

So the guest departs. The very meaning of pilgrimage is that he shall feel continually the need for going on. One remembers Chaucer's great lines—

> Her nis non hoom, her nis but wildernesse:
> Forth, pilgrim, forth! Forth, beste, out of thy stal?
> Know thy contree, look up, thank God of al;
> Hold the hye wey, and lat thy gost thee lede:
> And trouthe shal delivere, hit is no drede.'[1]

For a certain distance friends may accompany us, and the sisters who convoy Christian do so not as symbolic virtues, but as human friends. Yet all the chief crises of the journey must be faced alone. These friends warn him of coming danger, and yet show him clearly that they believe in him and in his future success. Such trust is the best of parting gifts.

Descent is always dangerous. High spiritual experience entails this subsequent danger unknown to commonplace travel along the level plain. Spiritual pride, temper on edge, and other 'slips' of character worse than these, are the dangers of descent. There are few pilgrims who do not 'catch a slip or two' at such times.

So closes the story of the House Beautiful. Mr Froude reminds us of a passage which seems to indicate that Bunyan had read the Romance of Sir Bevis of Southampton, and states that recollections of that Romance 'furnished him with his framework' for this part of the allegory. 'Lions guard the court. Fair ladies entertain him as if he had been a knight-errant in quest of the Holy Grail,' etc. It is an interesting statement. How far it is an accurate one we shall see in our next chapter.

[1] *Truth.*

CHAPTER XV

THE BATTLE WITH APOLLYON

REFERENCE was made at the end of last chapter to the Romance of Sir Bevis of Southampton. Republished by the Maitland Club in 1838, it has again been reprinted by the Early English Text Society. The original of the English Romance was a French *chanson*, but it is said that the two have little in common but the name. The hero was referred to by Chaucer's Sir Thopas, by Browne in his *Religio Medici*, and in many other English books. The tale must have been a favourite one, for we find that scenes from it were depicted on Henry V.'s tapestries, and painted on the walls of some of Henry VIII.'s rooms. It was printed at Bologna in 1497, about the end of the times of court poetry. It is interesting as a link between the past and future ideals, for in it the figure of Arthur, which dominated the older Romances, was lost sight of in the greatness of England, although here and there a touch reminds one of the Arthur of Geoffrey of Monmouth. In its 4440 lines of swinging rhyme there is a continuous vitality and rush of action which must have fascinated John Bunyan. Whether he possessed the book, or whether he came to know it in fragments heard at some tavern or merrymaking of his early days, we do not know. Mr Froude speaks of it, without stating his authority, as the only book he possessed in his young days. Curiously enough, it is mentioned in *The Plain Man's Pathway to Heaven*, (one of the two volumes which his wife had inherited from her father and brought her husband as her dowry), in a list given by *Antilegon* as 'excellent and singular books against heart-

THE BATTLE WITH APOLLYON

qualms,' but rejected by *Asunetus* as 'vain and frivolous books of tales jests, and lies.'

The most interesting allusion to it which we find in Bunyan's writings is in the *Sighs from Hell*, a treatise on the parable of Dives and Lazarus : ' " They have Moses and the Prophets, let them hear them." This is the thing (to be short), My brethren are unbelievers, and do not regard the Word of God. I know it by myself, for when I was in the world it was so with me. The Scriptures, thought I then, what are they ? A dead letter, a little ink and paper, of three or four shillings price. Alack! what is Scripture ? Give me a ballad, a newsbook, George on Horseback, or Bevis of Southampton. Give me some book that teaches curious Arts, that tells old Fables.'

Mr Froude's statement that it furnished Bunyan with the framework of the story of the Palace Beautiful appears to be guesswork, possible only to one who had not read the Romance. There is absolutely no trace of Sir Bevis in any detail of the passage.[1] There are, however, other traces of Sir Bevis in the *Pilgrim's Progress*, as we shall see from time to time. The most interesting of them all are those passages which appear to have been in Bunyan's mind when he was writing this account of the fight with Apollyon. First of all, the name Apollyon occurs in the Romance. In Armenia, when Bevis falls in love with Josian, the fair daughter of the king, the condition on which alone he may have her is that he will forsake his God and take *Apolyn* for his lord, Apollyon being the dim figure seen behind the ' *Mahoun* ' of Saracen worship. Bevis refuses, and the Saracens are greatly offended:

' " Herkenyth felowes," said a Sarzin,
"How he dispiseth Apolyn." '

But the passage which relates to the battle is one in which a fight of Bevis with a giant is described. There is the usual

[1] The lines describing an encounter with " lions two, Rampyng and grennyng with their teeth," may be a possible exception to this statement.

vaunting speech which prefaces the combat, though that is shorter than Bunyan's war of words. Then comes the account of the battle, in which the incidents of the shield flying from Bevis' hand, the unexpected blow upon the breast, and the throwing of the dart, offer parallels to the allegory too close to be merely coincidences :—

> 'Beues is swerde anon up swapte,
> He and the geaunt togedre rapte,
> And delde strokes mani and fale,
> The nombre can nought telle in tale.
> The geaunt up is clobbe haf.
> And smot so Beues with is staf,
> That his scheld flegh fram him thore,
> Thre akres brede and sumdel more,
> Tho was Beues in strong erur
> And karf ato the grete levour,
> And on the geauntes brest a-wonde
> That negh a-felde him to the grounde.
> The geaunt thoughte this bataile hard,
> Anon he drough to him a dart,
> Thourgh Beues scholder he hit schet,
> The blold ran doun to Beues fet,
> The Beues segh is owene blod
> Out of is wit he wex negh wod,
> Unto the geaunt ful swithe he ran,
> And kedde that he was doughti man,
> And smot ato his nekke bon ;
> The geaunt fel to grounde anon.'

The general meaning of the descent into the Valley of Humiliation appears to be the first re-entering of the world after a time of special religious experience in the Church. Etymologically, it means simply coming to *earth* again. But there are two English words in which the Latin *humus* appears, Humiliation and Humility; and a Christian's ' coming to earth ' from spiritual experience may be in either of these two fashions. Thus Bunyan wisely refrains from giving this next passage in his Pilgrim's career the character of a universal or necessary experience. The valley is there for all, but there are some who find it altogether lovely. Faithful, after a few encounters with undesirable persons, ' had sun-

THE BATTLE WITH APOLLYON

shine all the rest of the way through that and also through the Valley of the Shadow of Death.' The story of the pilgrims of the Second Part, and especially of Mr Fearing, tells of this as a Happy Valley—green and beautiful with lilies, and, indeed, ' the best and most fruitful piece of ground in all these parts.' The character of the pilgrim determines his experience in this Valley. Gentle and humble souls that go softly— souls like that of Cowper or of St Francis, have no trouble here. But this Christian is a proud man throughout, with a large claim on life and a strong sense of personal identity. To such aggressive natures Humility has to be learned by way of Humiliation. The devil they meet is the devil of their own pride, a Satan proud as Milton's, and it needs many buffets to humble him. We may take it that in the present passage the bitter conflict is connected with those slips which the pilgrim caught while striding down the hill in his new and impressive armour. That descent corresponds with By-path Meadow that leads to Doubting Castle. In Part II. we are informed that the Valley of Humiliation is a spacious valley, but that part of it where Christian's battle was fought was *Forgetful Green*.

The name Apollyon is borrowed from Rev. ix. 11, where it is given to the king of those fearsome locusts, by which the writer probably meant to symbolise the hosts of Parthian horsemen threatening the Western world from beyond the river Euphrates. The name means Destroyer. At this stage of his writing, Bunyan appears to have had no clear or consistent system of demonology such as was commonly framed by serious men of his time. Even in the passage itself there is confusion, for while throughout the dialogue Apollyon speaks as the Archfiend himself, yet in the verses at the end we read of ' Great Beelzebub the captain of this fiend.' The *Holy War* has, for the purposes of its story, a systematic demonology, in which Apollyon occupies a subordinate place, and Diabolus is the general and king of the forces of Hell, like Milton's Satan. It has been suggested as a possibility that this change may have been due to the influence of Milton's great epic, published during the same period as Bunyan's allegories.[1] Further investigation of this point might throw a peculiarly interesting sidelight on the disputed question of Bunyan's acquaintance with literature and his use of books.[2]

In one of the most fascinating of modern English essays, Professor Masson's *Three Devils*, the contrast is drawn between Milton's *Satan* and Goethe's *Mephistopheles*: 'Milton's Satan, then, is the ruined Archangel deciding his future function, and forswearing all interest in other regions of the universe, in order that he may more thoroughly possess and impregnate this. Goethe's Mephistopheles is this same being after the toils and vicissitudes of six thousand years in his new vocation: smaller, meaner, ignobler, but a million times sharper and cleverer.' In the lapse we see a gigantic parable of the degeneration of mere activity when it is without any element of reverent contemplation. In contrast with these classical and superb literary creations, we have Luther's devil, who 'was a being recognised by him as actually existing—as existing, one might say, with a vengeance.'

Bunyan's Apollyon is a blend of the poetic with the actual. No reader of *Grace Abounding* is left in any doubt as to Bunyan's literal and haunting belief in the devil as an actual personality. Many passages strongly remind us of Luther. Luther went so far, under extreme pressure of conflict, as to tauntingly suggest to the devil that if (as he said) Christ's blood was not enough, then the fiend himself might pray for him; Bunyan, upon occasion, could go so far as to wish 'either that there had been no hell, or that I had been a devil; supposing they were only tormentors; that if it must needs

---

[1] *Cf. John Bunyan*, by the author of *Mark Rutherford*, p. 219.
[2] *Cf.* Kerr Bain's *People of the Pilgrimage*, ii. 437.

THE BATTLE WITH APOLLYON

be that I went thither, I might rather be a tormentor than be tormented myself.'[1] Yet there is nothing prosaic about this undisguisedly literal belief in Satanic agency and personality. The fiends of Bunyan are symbols as well as personages, and are kept lifelike by much reference to the knowledge of his own heart.

The question of personal diabolic agency is one to which too much importance is sometimes attached. The terrible destroying power of evil in the world, however explained, is unhappily far beyond dispute. Those who explain it as the work of a personal enemy need to beware of shifting upon him the responsibility for their own evil choices. Those who explain it otherwise will do well to see to it that their conception of evil is capable of producing anything approaching that sturdy and militant type of manhood which has so often been developed in men who have viewed their own lives as a prolonged wrestling match with a ghostly foe. As a matter of fact, every earnest man has encountered many devils, both without and within. He would be a bold dogmatist who, in the present stage of thought upon such subjects, should deny the possibility that these experiences are indeed the work of sinister agencies and malicious personal will in the unseen world. He would be equally hardy who should insist upon this as an essential element in saving faith, as if belief in God were not enough without it. He will be wisest who, upon either theory or none, shall remember the certainty of the coming conflict with evil, and the fact that his spiritual armour is not given him to make a show of or to talk about; and who shall act upon the sage's cry, ' In God's name fight the devil ! '

The description of Apollyon, ' striding large and leisurely across the low green ground,'[2] is in strong contrast to the

[1] *Cf.* also *The Heavenly Footman*, quoted by Dr Brown, *John Bunyan*, chap. xi.
[2] Kerr Bain, *The People of the Pilgrimage*, ii. 419. With Bunyan's description of Apollyon *cf. The Visage of a Devyl* in the vale perilous, Sir John Maundevile, *Voiage and Travaile*, chap. xxviii.

magnificent fiend of *Paradise Lost*, or the aged man in the wilderness of *Paradise Regained*. Bunyan's devil never appears as an angel of light. Strange, uncouth, and repulsive imaginations are lavished upon the picture. To find the origins of these we would need to go back to such monsters as the goblin of Frithjof's Saga, or the scaly sea-monster of Beowulf, with all that lies behind such conceptions drawn from the battles of primitive man with Nature, in the hot slime of the Persian sea-shore, or in the forests and morasses of the West. In every respect he is the extreme opposite of all that is human. Fish-scales, bear-feet, dragon-wings, lion-mouth—these suggest the reptilian mixture of cunning and cruelty, the swiftness and the silence of temptation. The flame and smoke may well stand for that blaze of passions in the heart which sets life on fire and plunges it in thick darkness.

Both the fascinating and the hideous representations of the devil are true to actual experience. The sin that tempts a man and fights with him for his soul is not always alluring of aspect. The case is but too common in which a sin known to be not only sinful, but deadly dangerous, tempts a would-be victim. The lust of drunkenness, and other lusts of the flesh, are often followed when there is neither magnificence nor any real hope of pleasure in them, but only a fierce and hideous strength before which the will of the tempted one goes down. Nothing in life is more tragic than this victory of evil over those who have no illusions, but who yield to what they see clearly in all its naked ugliness.

Christian's courage is well revealed, but never narrated. It is a witty touch in which we are reminded that no armour had been provided for his back, so that to turn and run away would be the most dangerous of all courses. Here Bunyan is at his favourite doctrine, but this time it is discretion, as at other times it is usually honour, which condemns the recreant.

THE BATTLE WITH APOLLYON

As usual, he is true to life. The assaults of temptation are always more dangerous to those who avoid than to those who face the battle. Christian is all for open combat and no quarter. This part of the allegory will be read with head-shaking by some who would fain be on good terms with evil for the sake of peace. Meredith has thrust hard at them in his *Farina*, where the merchant of Cologne is so angry against the man who has insisted upon fighting Sathanas: 'He hurt us not. We were free of him. Cologne, I say, is cursed! The enemy of mankind is brought by you to be the deadly foe of Cologne.' It is a word to the wise and to the foolish!

The conventional combat of the old Romances of Chivalry was prefaced with a high-sounding argument between the combatants. A typical example of this is furnished by that story of Sir Bevis to which we have already referred. Nothing could be more apt for an allegory of temptation, with its two stages of suggestion and passion. In the *Holy War*, where the military system is complete and elaborate, we have Apollyon as the devil, not of force, but of craft. Here he stands for both. In the first part of the conflict, the war of words, we discover the cleverness of the devil. This is a familiar idea which has become proverbial in Goethe's Mephistopheles. Milton's Satan, too, is intellectually a great figure, worth a great many of the commonplace Adam. But it may be taken as a rule that the cleverer a man is, the more subtle will be the devil that tempts him. It is part of the price that must be paid for genius.

I. THE WAR OF WORDS [1]

The conversation which follows is a rare study of temptation as an exercise of mind. Its arguments may be detailed as follows:—

1. *A Claim.* The king of hell is in search of his runaway

[1] *Cf.* a similar dialogue between Satan and a soul, in the first book written in prison by John Bunyan, a poem entitled *Profitable Meditations* (Brown, *John Bunyan*, chap. viii.).

and wayward liege. 'When Christian forgot himself as a pilgrim, the devil remembered him as a deserter,' every man being valuable to the devil as well as to Christ. We all know those times in which we are acutely conscious of the twofoldness of our moral nature—the Dr Jekyll and Mr Hyde within. And there are times, when the spiritual lights of life are low, in which we feel as if the lower nature had the stronger claim. In the light of modern evolutionary theories, this claim has come by some to be regarded as the obvious scientific one, and a man's spiritual nature is burdened with a terrible handicap when he feels that he is essentially of the earth, looking back for the truth of himself instead of forward.

Christian's first answer is that though he was born in the City of Destruction, he is going to Mount Zion. Whatever the past of the individual or the race may have been, it is open to each man to repudiate it in favour of the present and the future. He who has once seen the spiritual and moral possibilities of life may claim them as his inheritance, and go forward to realise them in spite of all claims that the flesh may urge.

The second answer is that Christian had tried the apparently natural service of Apollyon, and found it did not pay. The wage was not a living wage. It was not enough to keep a man's soul alive. In Rudyard Kipling's *Life's Handicap* the tale is told of a man who had paid for his sin his best possessions of faith in man and woman. ' " What return ? " says he, catching up my last words—" why, strength to live as long as God or the devil pleases, and so long as you live my young master, my gift." With that he puts something into my hand, though it was still too dark to see what it was, and when next I lookt up he was gone. When the light came I made shift to behold his gift, and saw that it was a little piece of dry bread.'[1] There is a twinkle in the pilgrim's eye

[1] *The Dream of Duncan Parrenness.*

as he repudiates the claim of the devil in the name of common sense. It would have been a stupid thing to serve for such poor wages, and he had done but as other considerate persons do.

2. *A Promise.* Here Apollyon speaks like a prince, and for a moment we are reminded of Milton's lordly fiend. The promise is the same as that of Christ's third temptation, and the answer is the same—a reference to God's claim. It is not wise to linger over the promises of temptation and argue with them one by one. It is safer always to cut the matter short. 'I have let myself to another'; and, that being so, even to discuss such promises were treachery.

3. *A Plea for Reconsideration.* To our weak flesh and wavering spirit it seems at times that all nobler choices are the exchange of a bad for a worse. To have made the venture of faith and found it vain is to be indeed in sorry case; and there are moods when that seems to be the truth of our experience. Just then, backing the temptation, comes the remembrance that it is ordinary to go back. We shall not be alone if we take the line of retreat; it is the most crowded of all life's highways. No words are more absolutely devilish than those which Mephistopheles spoke to Faust regarding Marguerite, 'She is not the first.' Few men have courage to brave the conspicuousness of originality in sin. The remembrance of the crowd in which they may lose themselves is an appeal to all that is basest in tempted souls.

The answer cannot be a denial, for 'Here the father of lies utters a most awful truth.' The point of honour is the only answer. 'I have given Him my faith' is the talisman which closes doors irrevocably behind, and blocks the open lines of retreat.

4. *A Reminder of Inconstancy.* When the devil says, 'Thou didst the same by me,' he seems to be opposing his own point of honour to that which had been quoted against him.

THE ROAD

It is strange, too, how generally he has managed to get his point of honour valued most. A gambling debt comes before the payment of tradesmen; a promise to boon companions cancels a promise to wife and children. In a thousand ways men feel it more incumbent upon them to keep faith with the devil than with God. It were well if we could all remember that there is only one absolute criterion of honour, and that treachery to the devil is the only ultimate good faith.

There is another point in this temptation, however. It is a reminder of the man's previous inconstancy, and so an appeal to shame.

The answer is one of the finest passages in the book, and needs no comment. With its repudiation of young folly, its trust in Christ's forgiveness, and its frank avowal of his heart's choice of his Saviour, it is worthy of a place in all books of devotion. The directness of its personal speech, and the evident heart that is in it, remind us of Christian's speech to Prudence, 'And to tell you the truth, I love him.' There is a peculiar winsomeness about such personal turns in Bunyan's writing which it would be difficult to match elsewhere.

5. *The Silence of God.* Evil can boast of more practical resources for the help of men in straits than good can show. We no longer expect miracles to happen, but every fraudulent business man knows tricks that can work deliverance of a sort. And behind all this is a deadly sense of the silence of God. The devil says in the hearts of many, that Christ 'never came from His place' to help them. The doubt is well expressed in Browning's *Fears and Scruples.* Through the long voyage of this storm-tossed life Christ seems to some to be ever asleep on the pillow.

Against all such thoughts faith sets its one assurance of a Love that is certain as life itself. He who wholly believes in and trusts that Love, may leave the mysterious silence and the apparent indifference to wait their explanation when Love shall find language in God's good time.

6. *Accusation.* No one has been more fully nor painfully aware of this backsliding and treachery since he pledged himself to Christ than John Bunyan. *Grace Abounding* is full of such revelations, and the history of Mansoul in the *Holy War*, after its capitulation to Emmanuel, is sad reading. It was with a pen dipped in his own heart's blood that Bunyan wrote Apollyon's detailed accusations of Christian's unfaithfulness.

But no one knew better than he the true and wise answer. Christian pleads guilty to everything, and even enlarges the accusations under which his conscience smarts. But all these things only serve to increase his hatred of Apollyon, who has wrought such shame in his Christian life, and to magnify and endear the Saviour, who has forgiven so much. Thus sin becomes a means of grace in him, and conscience by its very wounds brings healing.

II. The Combat

In its second stage, temptation changes from a discussion to an onslaught of blind passion. The activity and energy of Apollyon are here as great as his cunning was seen to be in the earlier part. Altogether, Mr Froude is right in calling him ' a more effective devil than Diabolus of the *Holy War*.' As for Christian, he has not rushed out to meet this battle before it naturally comes. All the initiative is left to Apollyon. In the argument we have observed in him a certain great and settled quality of character, which reassures us. For, to a worthy and intelligent man, the chief danger lies in the stage of thinking things out. We are less afraid of Christian yielding to blind passion than to sophistry.

Apollyon is represented as giving himself away by getting into this rage. It is a hopeful moment for a combatant in any fight when his enemy loses self-control and gives way to violence. The prize-fighter who begins to strike out wildly has come near to the end of his game. In Mansoul, afterwards, Apollyon advocates cunning, but Beelzebub decides for open rage, and loses by it.

Christian claims the protection of 'the King's Highway'—a claim which, in the condition of early English roads, was very intelligible, and even suggested the romantic. The worst of temptation is, that the position in which it finds a man often makes it seem legitimate. So long as we are in the King's Highway of honest duty-doing, temptation has no such rights. Yet there are paroxysms now and then when Apollyon straddles 'quite over the whole breadth of the road.' With rights or without them, the fact remains that for the moment the temptation is the only thing that the man can see, and the very Highway is blotted out by its menacing form. It is very close to experience, yet at this point Bunyan ventures to the edge of the ludicrous, when Apollyon assures his victim that 'I am void of fear.' Obviously, when the fiend finds it necessary to say that, the man is in good case, and the probability is that the fiend is lying. The closing thrust, 'Here will I spill thy soul,' is worthy of the villain in melodrama, and reminds one of the bombastic Pistol, with his—

> 'The grave doth gape, and doting death is near.
> Therefore exhale.' [1]

The actual onset of Apollyon recalls Tasso :—

> 'The grand foe of man
> Against the Christians turned his livid eyes,
> Bit both his lips for fury, and in sighs
> And bellowings, like a wounded bull enraged,
> Roared forth his inward grief and envy unassuaged.' [2]

---

[1] *Henry V.*, Act ii. sc. 1.
[2] *Gerusalemme Liberata*, iv. 1, quoted Kerr Bain, *The People of the Pilgrimage*, ii. 421.

THE BATTLE WITH APOLLYON

The flaming dart, another figure of the sharpest moments of temptation, is caught on the shield of faith. He remembers what Christ has done for him, and how He trusts him; or he recalls the eternal things and sets them against the momentary perilous thoughts and seductions. Thus it is in God's name that he fights the devil. Long afterwards, his friends, passing that way, will see the ground strewn with fragments of these shivered darts.[1] There is nothing more inspiring to see, or more likely to bring victory to new generations, than just the fact that the faith of a good man has in the past been effective against very keen temptation. He who assures posterity of the practical effectiveness of faith is a true benefactor.

As the battle grows closer, Christian is wounded in the head, the hand, and the foot. Temptation has got at his thoughts, his deeds, and his walk. In all of these he is aware of evil. He no longer fights as a pure man, a white warrior. The bloom of his innocence is gone. When this has happened, some men reckon that all is lost, their fight terminating with the first wounds; but in such an event as that there is more of self-conceit and pride than of necessity. Why should any of us make the condition with life that we shall have either a victory complete in every detail, or none at all? R. L. Stevenson sent on a true and wise thought in the ringing words: 'Honour can survive a wound: it can live and thrive without a member. The man rebounds from his disgrace; he begins fresh foundations on the ruins of the old; and when his sword is broken, he will do valiantly with his dagger. To cling to what is left of any damaged quality is virtue in the man.'[2]

The final phase of the combat is that sore wrestling, body to body with Apollyon, in which is portrayed the utmost intensity and nearness of tempting evil, which now seems

[1] Part ii.   [2] *Memories and Portraits*, p. 242.

to be close to his own very breast. At last he receives a dreadful fall, and his sword flies out of his hand. The incident is common in the Romances, and an interesting and revelant passage may be found in Weyman's *Gentleman of France*.[1] Not even for 'a dreadful fall' will this dogged fighter and tempted man give up the conflict. To the end of life he will be not only a wounded soldier, but a fallen Christian, who has no record of unbroken purity any longer to live up to. To fall thus in battle is to lose one of the main incentives to success—that of maintaining honour untarnished. Yet, once again, honour can survive a fall as as well as a wound, and it is just as noble a thing to fight in order to retrieve it, as it is to fight for its preservation. Sometimes it is even nobler, inasmuch as it is more difficult, and has to be done under a cloud of shame.

So, just then, a strange thing happened. When all seemed lost, the man caught his sword again and succeeded in wounding his enemy.[2] The devil then, it seems, is vulnerable; and it is a great thing to realise that fact. Milton's invulnerable spirits, who are put out of action without injury, are a clumsy part of his creation.[3] Bunyan's are truer to experience as well as to art. It is an actual fact that not only the tempted but the tempter is steadily losing strength. However difficult it may be to realise, it is nevertheless true that every hour a man can hold on is lessening the temptation he resists, even when that temptation seems to be steadily increasing. Temptation fattens upon compliances, and dies out at last by refusals.

So at last it comes to pass that the tempter flies away. After long resistance, when it seemed as if he were stationed for ever behind our shoulder, he one day suddenly is not there, and life without temptation is almost incredible in its

---

[1] P. 359.   [2] *Cf. Gentleman of France*, pp. 213, 359.
[3] *Paradise Lost*, bk. vi.

THE BATTLE WITH APOLLYON

peacefulness. 'A Greek poet,' says Lytton, 'implies that the height of bliss is the sudden relief from pain: there is a nobler bliss still, the rapture of the conscience at the sudden release from a guilty thought.'[1] Yet though the devil leaves him, it is only 'for a season,' as it was even in the Prince's tempting.[2] And the tempter seldom flees far away. In Part II. we find that he had gone from Christian only into the next valley.

There is a shudder in the words with which Bunyan dismisses the scene and its events. He still hears the appalling sound of the tempter's yelling, and the 'sighs and groans' which burst from Christian's heart. The phrase is one redolent of the religion of the seventeenth century, and forms the title of famous verses of George Herbert's which may have been known to Bunyan. The battle had lasted half a day—but into that half-day John Bunyan had seen compressed the experience of years of conflict. He must have envied his own Pilgrim!

> 'They said the war was brief and easy:
> A word, a look, would crush the throng.
> To some it may have been a moment's conflict:
> To me it has been fierce and long.'[3]

A man's temptations are often a good measure of his moral and spiritual manhood. Many men escape temptation such as this because there is not enough of them to be so tempted. So regarded, temptation is seen to be an honour and a high mark of God's confidence.

There follow some verses, in which Jesus is referred to as 'blessed Michael,' appropriately introduced as dragon-slayer in this place. Then the passage closes with the beautiful figure of the hand that brings healing leaves from the Tree of Life. The hand is ever the tenderest or the terriblest

[1] *My Novel*, xii. 31.   [2] *Cf.* Luke iv. 13.
[3] Quoted in Maguire's edition of the *Pilgrim's Progress, sub loco.*

of symbols, and the tenderest of all its works is healing. Wounds gained in the battle with temptation are not usually difficult to heal. From them comes no permanent pain, nor even any scar, except in desperate cases. The wounds that ache and throb through a lifetime, the chronic open sores of the soul, are those that are got in the service of the devil, whose servants are all sooner or later ' wounded in the house of their friend.'

The results of the battle appear in the later career of Christian. That is his last fight as an armed man, and after we have watched him go forward with drawn sword in his hand, watchful for new assaults, we shall not again hear anything of the armour or the weapons. Yet how precious that sword of his had now become to him, only those can realise who have seen the reverence with which an old campaigner handles a sword on which the blood drawn in mortal combat has rusted. Perhaps that watchfulness, with the drawn sword in hand, was the very reason why we hear no more of his armour. In this sense Bismarck's words are true indeed, ' Nothing but the sword can keep the sword in its scabbard.' For this part of the hero's adventures the present writer always sees Christian in the bodily likeness of a young farm servant of his acquaintance, who had suffered much tormenting for his religion from his fellow-servants, and who (without any suspicion of priggishness) said that he had found he ' needed persecution.' Another result of the combat was that it had made a man of Christian, fixing a gulf between his old life and his new as no other experience could. Many a man has *found himself* through temptation overcome. Again, this had turned Humiliation into Triumph, and shown him for all time to come, how sins and dangers may become means of grace. Yet there was no vainglory in his exultation. Bunyan did not find the conflict with Apollyon dangerous in that

THE BATTLE WITH APOLLYON

particular way. On one occasion he tells us how he was filled with a desire to preach; yet 'not for desire of vainglory,' he adds, 'for at that time I was most sorely afflicted with the fiery darts of the devil.' Lastly, it made him able to understand and sympathise and help others in their times of temptation. At one time Bunyan was himself oppressed with the fear lest he had committed the sin against the Holy Ghost. He opened his mind to 'an ancient Christian,' who told him he thought so too. 'Here, therefore, I had but cold comfort; but talking a little more with him I found him, though a good man, a stranger to much combat with the devil.'

CHAPTER XVI

THE VALLEY OF THE SHADOW OF DEATH

THIS part of the Allegory is one of the most famous, because the condition which it describes is but too familiar. One of the most graphic of Borrow's casual touches in *The Bible in Spain* is his description of the imprisoned murderer who dwelt in this valley.[1] The name,[2] seems to be a reminiscence of one of those narrow and malarial gorges which run like fissures across the eastern side of the Judean tableland. It is not Death itself that is meant, but the Shadow of Death, falling dark and deadly across some part of life. It is, in another form and a subtler, the continuation of the fight with Apollyon, who has, indeed, retreated no further than this valley from the place of his defeat. Christian need not seek repose as yet. He is kept from self-congratulation by new peril. One is reminded of the story of that young officer who in a long-continued battle came radiant to his superior, saying, 'Sire, I have taken a standard!' Receiving no reply he repeated his boast, only to be told, 'Then take another!'

The chief notes of this valley are *darkness*, *indefiniteness*, and *solitariness*. It is a time when the inner vitality seems dried up and dead, and there comes on the poisonous morbid mood of *Accidia*, which mediæval Christians found so tormenting. In modern language it would be called Reaction. It is the nerves that have to pay the price of victory. After all excitement of conflict there comes upon the overstrung victor a natural depression and melancholy. 'With me all is

---

[1] Quoted there in chap. xl.
[2] Used in Ps. xxiii. and again in Jer. ii. 6.

THE VALLEY OF THE SHADOW OF DEATH

blackness,' says Carlyle on one occasion, 'lit by flashes of lightning.' In such a time of desertion of soul, will, and heart, hope and faith seem dead. Only imagination appears to remain alive, and that is feverish and morbid.

In the anatomy of melancholy Bunyan was a past master, as every reader of *Grace Abounding* knows. Especially true is that reference to ' discouraging clouds of confusion.' At such a time, overstrung and then relaxed, it is not so much any definite horrors that assail the soul. The condition is one of nervousness about things in general, indefinite difficulties and impossibilities, moving states of mind whose uncertain moods cannot be expressed in words. The invisible has a ' power of darkness,' a fascination of horror, for all imaginative minds. All writers of the gruesome and uncanny know well and act upon the maxim that it is the unknown which holds the end of our chain.

Not only is such a mood possible to a Christian, it is peculiar to a Christian. There is a depth of darkness which, as Bunyan here cleverly changes his text from Jeremiah to tell us, ' no man (*but a Christian*) passes through.' [1] Only those who have lived in the glory of God's face can imagine the full bitterness of the times when that face is hidden. The question has often been asked, whether such an experience as this is necessary or inevitable ? The disciples of the Gospel of Healthymindedness—that greatest Word of God spoken in these latter days—will be apt to answer promptly and absolutely in the negative. Except in a few cases, where the mind is positively and chronically diseased, their answer is true. There are, indeed, some who are more naturally prone to such a state than others, but that only means that a greater or less effort is required according to the individual constitution. It is certain that by far the

---

[1] *Cf.* Ian Maclaren's story of ' A Highland Mystic ' in *Beside the Bonny Briar Bush*.

greater part of the suffering endured in this valley is avoidable, and that the majority of such sufferers accept as a doom those mental idiosyncrasies which ought to be taken only as a challenge. It may be further added that such experiences are not now nearly so excusable as they were in John Bunyan's time. Every reader of the *Pilgrim's Progress* must be touched by the constant recurrence of melancholy in one form or another. The Slough of Despond, the Castle of Giant Despair, and between them this valley, give a doleful itinerary of the Christian life. The times were evil then, and the thoughts of men had felt their gloom. Superstitious views of nature, unscientific theories of psychological phenomena, and a positive obsession of theological beliefs by conceptions both of God and of devils which are no longer held by educated men, contributed to this state of affairs. It is true that the *Weltschmerz*, in other forms, is with us still. But it may be confidently asserted that it is now neither so hopeless nor so general as it was in former days. All the more definitely should we regard as criminal those decadents of our new literature who would bring back as a fashionable modern disease that *Accidia* which attacked so many of the earlier generations. There are surely enough new diseases of mind and heart without reintroducing this old infection.

THE TWO MEN RUNNING.—The exceedingly clever passage about these two fugitives is one more variant upon Bunyan's favourite theme of the evils of retreat. These men have been interpreted by some as a mere literary trick, a revival of Timorous and Mistrust, introduced for the sake of heightening the sense of fearfulness and horror. Yet they are real men, and the dialogue is a consummate piece of portraiture of a quite distinct type of human nature. There are many who could face the lions from which the former pair of cowards fled, and who yet dare not enter such a valley as this. Lions, or human enemies, or the cannon's mouth, are definite dangers : this state of haunted depression, of melancholy suggestion and sinister hints of evil, unmans a different kind of mind by its indefiniteness. This is indicated by the vague answers which they give to Christian's questioning. They are in mortal terror, but they cannot tell what they are afraid of.

Christian, accordingly, meets them with a demand for particulars. Most of our troubles and all our fears owe much to the indefinite sense of something ominous. To analyse them is to end them. Set down in black and white, they will lose much of their terror and all of their impossibility. There never yet was a situation in which, when it was faced frankly and without flinching or reserve, there was not something immediately to be done.

When at last Christian has forced the new cowards to state as well as they can the causes of their terror, his reply is, ' I perceive not yet, by what you have said, but that this is my way to the desired haven.' It is a very great answer. and he would have said it whatever they had reported. The dangers ahead are not the point of the situation. They are irrelevant side issues, and have nothing to do with a pilgrim's course of action. The point—the only point—is, Which is the way of God ? To go in that way is indeed the only safe course : but even if it were not, it is the only right course, and therefore the only course. When Fear says to our soul, ' A man must live,' Conscience had better repeat the old rejoinder, ' I fail to see the necessity.' There is only one necessity in the world, and that is to be faithful to God.

From this point onwards, Bunyan puts forth the whole strength of his imagination, yet he never for a moment allows himself to be carried out of sight of the actual facts of experience. The path is narrow, requiring great carefulness. There is no need for the officiousness of Part III., which diminishes this narrow path to a plank slushing up and down in the mire. The narrowness, with its danger of stepping aside to right or left, is all that is intended. The fact which this represents is the extreme danger presented by abnormal conditions such as these, of sudden extravagances both intellectual and moral. The ditch, into which the blind have led the blind, appears to refer to theoretical error of belief and principle; while the quag [1] would stand for error in practice, of the nature of outward sin and scandal. These are the perils of such darkness as this. Anything, even what one would shrink from in normal times, may become a temptation and a danger if it only offer some definite and strongly marked sensation, in exchange for the vague and intangible gloom of the valley. Readers of *Jane Eyre* [2] will recall some striking instances of such temptation.

Hawthorne, in *The Celestial Railroad*, cleverly lights up this valley with gas drawn from the coals of the infernal pit. Such gaslight is only too common as a remedy for gloom. For the darkness which quenches the sight of actual facts as they are, actually kindles the imagination and so increases the terror. At every step the man is afraid, like Childe Roland, of what he is to put his foot on next:—

> 'Which, while I forded,—good saints, how I feared
> To set my foot upon a dead man's cheek
> Each step, or feel the spear I thrust to seek
> For hollows, tangled in his hair or beard!'

Through all this, the man steps on steadily. He who does this will find the darkness quicken his sight and so allay the very fear it induced.[3] Meanwhile there is—

---

[1] *Cf. quake*, and *quick*, in the old sense of *living*, moving.

[2] Ch. xviii., etc.

[3] Compare Sir Walter Scott's *Journal*, 22nd January 1826, which tells one of the noblest of our country's stories: 'I will not yield without a fight for it. It is odd, when I set myself to work *doggedly*, as Dr Johnson would say, I am exactly the same man that I ever was, neither low-spirited nor *distrait*. . . . Well—exertion—exertion.'

THE VALLEY OF THE SHADOW OF DEATH

> 'Nothing before, nothing behind;
> The steps of Faith
> Fall on the seeming void, and find
> The rock beneath.'[1]

But now new horrors multiply with a swiftness which shows the terrible fertility of Bunyan's brain in this sort of imagination. Once again the pilgrim sees that dreadful thing, the Mouth of Hell. Formerly it was just where he stood; here it is 'hard by the wayside,' for this is no theoretical vision of hell, but a matter of personal danger and fear. The mouth of hell, in the form of a whale's wide open jaws, was a familiar part of the property of the mediæval Morality Plays. Dante's conception of it is a cave in the wild wood. Bunyan supplied it with abundance of flame and sparks and smoke and hideous noises, suggesting a hillside vent from some volcano which intermittently rose and subsided. What exactly he meant by it, it would be difficult to say. It may have been simply the fear of damnation, or it may have been suicide, or the plunge into sin that he might end suspense. All these Bunyan could remember as temptations of his own, and there had been times when,

> 'He yearned to the flare of Hell-gate there, as the
> light of his own hearth-stone.'[2]

Whatever it was, the flames and the sounds of it chased him with the sense of 'rushings to and fro.' In this we have a fuller horror than could be supplied by any more definite portraiture. It is the omission and suggestion which by their indefiniteness give the most terrible quality to the picture. These also were things that cared not for his sword[3]—another very horrible touch. The enemy which you can see but cannot strike, the weapon passing through the spectre, supplies the point on which many weird stories have depended

---

[1] Whittier, *My Soul and I*.   [2] Rudyard Kipling, *Tomlinson*.
[3] *Cf. John Bunyan*, by the author of *Mark Rutherford*, p. 130.

for their horror. Shakespeare, indeed, boldly speaks of 'taking arms against a sea of troubles,' but Bunyan knew well that melancholy of this sort cannot be fought even by the armed power of will. This kind goeth not out but by prayer, and he betakes himself to the mystic weapon. It will be noted, however, that his will sends him steadily forward with undelayed and active march through all. It is one thing to pray in idleness, and a very different and more useful thing when prayer goes with the swift foot.

The rushings to and fro, and the imagined 'company of fiends,' have a very skilful reticence about them. Interesting parallels will be found in Dante,[1] but it is characteristic of the two writers that while Dante goes into a mediæval fulness of detail, which for us tempers the horror by its grotesqueness, Bunyan, with a finer touch, says just enough to stir the imagination, and leaves the effect to the reader's own mind. Nathaniel Hawthorne makes these fiends bear the faces of individual sins of his own which stretch out their hands to claim him.[2] It is true that the worst fiend for any man to meet is that which bears the likeness of his sin, and the conscience-stricken may grow mad by looking into the reflection of their own eyes. Yet the possibilities of this valley include many other kinds of horror. Whittier, expressing in his own way what Bunyan intends by his weapon All-prayer, gives us a great song of the valley in *My Soul and I*—

> 'Why fear the night ? Why shrink from Death,
>   That phantom wan ?
> There is nothing in heaven or earth beneath
>   Save God and man.
> Peopling the shadows we turn from Him,
>   And from one another ;
> All is spectral and vague and dim
>   Save God and our brother.'

---

[1] *Inferno*, cantos iii. and xxi.
[2] *The Celestial Railroad, sub loco.*

THE VALLEY OF THE SHADOW OF DEATH

Christian, however, has not reached so healthy a point of view as this. First of all, he hesitates, and is kept back from retreat mainly by the thought that the danger of going back might be greater than that of going forward. It may seem a poor defence, but a breastwork may be thrown up in an emergency out of any rubbish that lies in the neighbourhood. So Christian resolves to go on. During the Civil War in America, at one of the sieges the work of storming the walls fell to the black contingent. For a little time they advanced, but the fire of the guns was deadly, and they halted and were about to retreat. The only man who kept on his way was the old standard-bearer, who advanced alone with the colours. The colonel shouted to him, 'Come back here, old Sam!' The answer was, 'These here colours never go back, Colonel!—Come you up here, Colonel!' The advance continued, and the town was taken. As we see Christian advancing through the darkness, we hear the name of God uttered in a vehement cry like the stormy clang of consecrated bells bidding back the fiends. All-prayer again prevails. We may remember that scene in Faust where the soldiers, reversing their swords, present to Mephistopheles the sign of the Cross, so that he cannot advance. It is a happy fancy that the sword-hilt may become the mystic Cross, prayer thus being but another side of action.

Yet the confusion of the place has entered into him, and this element of disorderliness greatly intensifies the horror, introducing the classic dread of *Chaos*, of which Carlyle speaks continually. Perhaps it is the greatest victory of all when a man's courage does not fail him even then, but overcomes perplexity. The specific form which the confusion here takes is noteworthy. A fiend whispers to him from behind, and he mistakes the language for his own utterance. This experience is continually recurring in *Grace Abounding*, where all manner of blasphemies and foul thoughts persecute

Bunyan until he compares himself to a kicking and screaming child carried off by a gipsy. It is a curious psychological fact, this persecution by alien imaginations; and unfortunately it is a very common one in highly strung natures. It is safe to say that such haunting thoughts and words in no case become sinful until they are welcomed and deliberately harboured. Sinful things, disowned and repudiated, may seem to haunt a man only the more insistently for that; but until he chooses them for his own they are no sin of his.[1]

After this long misery of haunted loneliness there comes the infinite relief of the human voice, as he hears great words spoken by a man going before him. One remembers in Carlyle's *Everlasting Yea* the similar emergence of Teufelsdröckh from the darkness, when he breaks forth into the great passage beginning 'With other eyes, too, could I now look upon my fellow-men; with an infinite Love, an infinite Pity.' That is the highest meaning of this sudden companionship. Each of the two men had imagined he was alone, and each makes that most amazing and revolutionary discovery that there are other people in the world besides himself. The fountains of compassion and sympathy and the desire to help are opened, and the soul is refreshed by them. But the very sense of company, apart from its fuller meanings, is a blessed thing at such times. One of the most striking things that Nansen tells of his adventures is his account of the feelings with which he first heard a dog bark in Franz Josef Land, after his long wandering. Bunyan could not have invented anything which would have given the sense of relief more perfectly than this voice. We may perhaps be justified in remembering that, as yet, Christian has made no friends among other pilgrims. From this point onwards we shall never see him alone again. Had he from

---

[1] For a very wise and able treatment of this subject *cf.* the late Dr Bruce's *Parabolic Teaching of Christ*, p. 139.

THE VALLEY OF THE SHADOW OF DEATH

the first cultivated the love of men and clung to their companionship, it might have gone better with him in the valley. But then, in these first stages of difficult and anxious pilgrimage, a man has little heart for company. It is a part of the journey on which God sends most pilgrims alone.

The verse which the unseen man is repeating is from the 23rd Psalm, where there is as yet no word of ending, and the comfort comes simply from the fact that God is with the man. By and by the day breaks, and Bunyan, who was intensely sensitive to the changes of light and darkness, finds a deep satisfaction in the new light. His poems of sunrise are well worth consulting. There is in them that authentic note of true poetry which reminds us sometimes of Chaucer and sometimes of Spenser. They contain the finest touches in his printed poems. The verse that Christian utters is " He hath turned the shadow of death into the morning ":[1] it is the same that is engraved upon the tombstone of Dr Guthrie. Christian had need of light, for the second part of the valley which he had yet to travel was more dangerous than that through which he had found his way in the dark. All manner of traps and pitfalls seem to exhaust the cunning of the evil one. These may represent special circumstances of difficulty and temptation which beset a man whose nerves have long been on the strain, and who now comes out from mental wrestling into the practical difficulties of the world. Nothing could render him more unfit for sudden and petty irritations than the experience he has just passed through. Scott's note is valuable here, ' Believers are not in most danger when under the deepest distress.' The mood of the man is represented cleverly, by the fact that the daylight has not driven away the hobgoblins, but only kept them visible at a distance. Neither has it ended the dangerous narrowness of the path between quag and ditch, but only

[1] Amos v. 8.

revealed it. It is with the full consciousness of the horrors which had tortured him in the dark that he is now called upon to gather his wits together, and pick his way with the most painful carefulness among the new dangers of the active life. Part III. cleverly invents a kind of trap which is like a noose hanging in the air, so that at this point the only safety is in lowly stooping.

CHAPTER XVII

POPE AND PAGAN

THIS passage leads us to the subject of persecution. Bunyan had studied history mainly in the pages of Foxe's *Book of Martyrs*. In his own day Protestants were persecuting one another, taking up the rôle which the Papacy had so recently laid down. The Act of Uniformity, with its threats of the gallows, hung like a dark cloud over the imagination of John Bunyan. In Elizabeth's time the poet Southwell had been executed for avowing that he had come into England to preach the Roman Catholic religion, and, as Dr Brown says, Bunyan 'was too much of an Englishman, and too near the days of Mary and the Spanish Armada not to have a fling at the Pope.'[1] It was long after this before any adequate realisation of the real meaning of toleration could be found either on the one side or the other of the papal controversy. Naturally, however, both on account of the far greater extent of its persecutions and on account of his own attitude to it, it is the Roman Church which stands with Bunyan as the modern type of persecutor. The Bloodmen in the *Holy War* have Captain Pope for their chief, whose escutcheon is 'the stake, the flame, and good men in it.' Here and there in provincial hospitals an operating-table may be seen, round which there are iron rings fixed in the floor, by which the patients were tied down before the use of anæsthetics. The thrill of horror which such a sight produces upon those in whose

[1] *John Bunyan*, chap. xiii.; *cf.* also *John Bunyan*, by the author of *Mark Rutherford*, p. 161.

THE ROAD

youth this was the manner of operating, may give us some imagination of Bunyan's feelings towards the recent stake and axe.

There is a passage in *Sir Bevis of Southampton* which may have suggested the gruesome picture of the end of the valley at the mouth of the cave. There two lions inhabit such a cave, and

> 'Whan Bevys cam from hyntynge
> In the cave, at the begynnynge
> As he went inwarde for the nonys,
> He sawe a man gnawen al to the bones.'

Pope and Pagan inhabit the same cave. The reading of any Church History, of Lecky's *History of Rationalism* or of Hatch's *Hibbert Lecture,* supplies innumerable instances in which it is seen that the policy of the Church of Rome has been to incorporate and baptise the ancient Paganism; and the same thing may be witnessed in the policy of Roman missionaries in many mission fields to-day. As a matter of expediency, there is, no doubt, much that may be said on both sides of this question. Many of the pagan beliefs and customs which have led men in some fashion towards God, may offer the best means in certain circumstances for sending on the new life. On the other hand, there are obvious dangers connected with such a policy, and no law can be laid down which will cover all the individual sets of circumstances.

There is, however, a deeper sense in which Pope and Pagan have often been allied. It has been said that 'Romanism is the paganism of Christianity . . . her strength is a pagan strength.'[1] This means that the same outwardness, materialism, and worldly power have characterised the two systems; and it is true that not in persecution only, but in her whole point of view, the Church of Rome has elements that make this her danger. At the

---
[1] Kerr Bain, *The People of the Pilgrimage,* ii. 465.

same time, it would be unjust and untrue to imagine that that is a complete statement of the case. It cannot be forgotten that there is a spiritual side to the ritual and the doctrines of Rome which has produced some of the finest types of devotional Christianity. The danger in all such discussions is that, through the circumstances of the individual thinker's case, only one aspect of that which he is opposing will present itself to him. Nathaniel Hawthorne puts Transcendentalism into this cave instead of Pope and Pagan; and a well-known divine has asserted that not the Pope but Hegelianism is the 'man of sin.' The cave is wide, and there is room in it for the *bêtes noires* of many generations of earnest men.

It is very curious to remember that, with a few alterations, the *Pilgrim's Progress* has been adapted for the use of Roman Catholics.[1] It is interesting to remember that at one period Bunyan seems to have been in a state of mind, according to his own confession, far more congruous with the Roman Catholic than the Protestant way of thinking. Cheever says of him, 'his mind seems to have been in that state of bondage which we call *priest-ridden*; heartily as he afterwards hated the Pope, it would not have taken much at this time to have carried him completely over to Rome.'[2]

However this may be, it is certain that in later times his antipathy to Roman Catholicism was intense, as may be seen from his uncompromising discourse on *Antichrist and his Ruin*.[3] The view he here takes of the Roman Church is that its day is done, and the picture of the Pope is that of one outworn. Through the days of Charles II. and James II., when the Papacy threatened the English throne, he kept in the main

[1] For an account of Roman Catholic editions, *cf.* Brown, *John Bunyan*, chap. xix.
[2] Cheever, *Lectures on Bunyan*, p. 19.
[3] Published posthumously in 1692.

aloof from politics,[1] and trusted the march of progress to render the Roman power obsolete. Like Christian, he held his peace and passed on.

The wisdom of this point of view has been called in question. It is said that the genius of Roman Catholicism 'has the old will if he had the old way.' Now and then some priest or cardinal is quoted as advocating the revival of the Inquisition; and there are some who absolutely disbelieve in progress within the Roman Church, and distrust the power of society to defend itself from the barbaric methods of the Middle Ages. Of such an attitude Dr Kerr Bain happily says that ' Chronic alarm does more to foster and flatter the giant than to quell him.' It is to be hoped that all sensible people in every Church will eventually agree with Praed's vicar,

> 'That if a man's belief is bad,
> It will not be improved by burning.'

As to the undoubted recent advances of the Roman Church in this country, these bear witness to the fact that there is a perpetual section of society for whom authority and high ritual is the natural way of worship. Protestantism appeals to those who are willing and able to undertake the intellectual and spiritual responsibility of religious thought and life, and who are prepared in a time of questioning such as the present to do without the comfort of a more luxurious trustfulness.

The passage in Part III. which corresponds to this is peculiarly interesting and happy. Over against the cave of these two giants it invents another cave where there sits 'a middle-aged man of a mild, grave and venerable countenance.' The name of this man is *Reformation*, and his function is to guard and keep clear the inscription on a pillar which is erected there—the pillar of History. Nothing could be better than that, as a view of the situation

[1] *Cf. John Bunyan*, by the author of *Mark Rutherford*, pp. 62, 235.

between Protestant and Catholic faith. It is history that is against the Papacy, and its form of faith is an anachronism. Its house is in the valley of the shadow, and humanity moves towards the light and the sunshine. Of course, there will always be people who prefer to live and to worship in that mediæval gloom, and they will and ought to be allowed to do so. It is progress and not propagandism to which Protestants have to trust. There will always be pre-Raphaelites in the Kingdom of God as well as Moderns, but there is no danger of Roman Catholicism becoming again the general faith in Protestant countries. There may be a real danger of its being allowed to speak in the name of Christianity; in which case the bulk of the nation would cross over into scepticism. The moral of the situation appears to be that the Protestant appeal to conscience and to reason must be insisted on with all urgency and human sympathy, so that the Christian faith shall always present to the thinking world the aspect of a living force of thought, and not the mere beauty of ancient tradition.

Pagan is, in the allegory, said to be dead, and the reference is to the persecutions of the past centuries. It must be remembered that in the times of the Crusades and the Romances the word pagan was applied to Mohammedans, and their God or idol was spoken of as a Mawmet.[1] In such outward senses as these, it is quite true that Pagan is dead, and yet no one knew better than Bunyan how terribly alive in the heart of man is the subtle spirit of paganism. In every generation of men there is the inward conflict of Pagan against Puritan. Given certain conditions, social and otherwise, great masses of the population lapse into a state which justifies the title 'Heathen England'; and even in those who have not lapsed there is an element which responds but too readily to the Pagan ideals. Readers of Fiona Macleod's

[1] *Cf. Sir Bevis of Hampton.*

Annir Choille will remember the Christian youth's rush back to Nature; and though the popularity of Omar Kayyám is a literary rather than a moral phenomenon, yet there can be little doubt that its frank paganism has made a wide appeal. The victory of Jesus Christ over the pagan world has to be fought out and achieved in the heart of every Christian.

CHAPTER XVIII

FAITHFUL

AT this point in the allegory we come to a very important change. Christian goes up a little ascent, which may be taken for a moment of encouragement and good spirits in which a man rises above the past, and is able to see before him some distance into the future. The great discovery which he makes there, is that he is not alone. He has already, indeed, heard the voice of a man in front of him, but now he sees him. Montgomery has pointed out the artistic skill of this introduction. Hitherto the story has sustained its interest upon the solitary adventures of Christian. Just when these have reached a climax, and it might have been difficult to sustain the vitality of the tale with other similar incidents, Bunyan resorts to the device of introducing a companion.

Nothing could be more natural than the manner of this introduction, and nothing more true to experience. In times of depression and difficulty we are all apt to imagine that we are alone in this trial, and it is half the deliverance to know that there are others with us, and ours is but the common lot. Elijah, after his valley of darkness, emerges into the assurance that instead of his being the only faithful man surviving, there are yet left seven thousand who have not bowed the knee to Baal.[1]

The conversation which follows is in lighter vein than we have yet listened to in the story, and there is a touch of humour in Christian's next adventure. When Christian calls

[1] 1 Kings xix. 18.

to the man in front of him to stay until he comes, there is no deliberate thought of detaining him, and yet a man like our pilgrim does not like the second place in any situation. The answer is that of one who, like Bunyan himself, had learned not to trust new friends easily. Whatever the future relations may be between these two, the foremost of them has made it clear at the outset that neither friendship nor love shall be allowed to hinder religion. It is better to postpone companionship, or even to go alone upon the journey, than to lose ground or time when a man is ' upon his life.'

The answer, however, stirs up the emulation to which it was sure to appeal in a character like that of the Pilgrim. If the other will not wait for him, then he will pass the other. So far so good; but emulation easily runs into vain-glory, and the smile is soon followed by a stumbling fall. A suit of armour is a heavy thing to run in; and when ironclad men fell to the ground they often found it impossible to rise. A terrible instance of this is recorded in the great battle between Saladin and the Crusaders at Hattin, when the grass and herbage were on fire, and fallen horsemen lay and perished in the flames. So this forward Christian has to be helped to rise by the man he was smiling to have surpassed. There is in Bunyan's Christian an encouraging persistency of the natural man—encouraging, because conscience rebukes us all for that smile, and there are few of us who cannot remember some fellow-pilgrim whom we had not taken very seriously, yet standing where we had fallen, and helping us to rise. It is worth while to compare this supercilious smile of Christian's with that 'one smile' which he himself had received from Evangelist after his rebuke in the matter of Mr Worldly Wiseman.

What does Faithful stand for in the allegory? One theory is that he represents another part of Christian's own life, so that Faithful, Hopeful, and Christian stand for Faith, Hope, and Charity. This might have been possible in the earlier allegories of French and English literature, but Bunyan's was a simpler genius than theirs, and this is not in his style. Two things seem plain. (1) That a second type is here presented. The writer feels the insufficiency of any one human life as an all-round portraiture of manhood. To crowd into one personality all the virtues were to create a figure at once unnatural and unhelpful. In all Christian men there is one Spirit, but there are diversities of operations corresponding to the complexity of human nature. (2) It is also clear that Faithful and Hopeful are friends of this man Christian whose life-story we are reading, and that the value of friendship is here insisted on. Bunyan himself had known this, and readers of *Grace Abounding* will remember the extreme warmth of affection with which he speaks of Martin Luther and his book on the Galatians. Luther was Bunyan's Faithful in more than one dark valley.

Emerson says that 'the condition which high friendship demands is ability to do without it.' That, in a sense, is true; for it ensures that independence which retains one's own personality, and without which self-respecting friendship is impossible. Manifestly Faithful would have stood this test. He was sufficient unto himself, and could have gone on alone safely to the end. Yet the friendship was good for both. The increasing multitude of Israelites travelling to the feast at Jerusalem was well described by the Psalmist as 'going from strength to strength,'[1] and in this story it is remarkable that no mishap befalls either of the pilgrims while they are together. It is equally remarkable, as Dr Kerr Bain has admirably pointed out, that these two men supplement each other's characters. They are of entirely different nature in some respects, and when first they meet

[1] Ps. lxxxiv. 7.

the contrast is noticeable; but as the journey proceeds we can see both characters being moulded, Faithful melting into richer human sympathy, and Christian gaining robustness. Faithful's first address to Christian is indeed cordial—'Dear Friend'—but later it becomes 'My Brother.'

From first to last the character-drawing in the sketch of Faithful is marvellous. The man is distinct, living and vivid. As with Shakespeare's characters, we feel as if we had met and known him in the flesh. In him the two senses of *faith* are combined, the passive sense of belief and the active one of trust and fidelity. On the whole, the active aspect is predominant, and the impression he leaves upon the mind is that of an intensely vital and purposeful man. It is a stalwart figure, rather than an intellectual or emotional one; strong of nerve, notable for momentum, braced in will. His characteristic word is 'I firmly believe it,' and he has been well described as a type of 'Strong-willed urgency,' and 'a man whom Christian will need a good deal of his sagacious charity rightly to understand.' He reminds one of the glorious Early English figure of Beowulf, who wins his battle by the sheer grip of the hand; and if he is somewhat thick-skinned, that serves the better to throw up the sensitive delicacy which appears from time to time in Christian.

The conversation which here opens between Christian and Faithful is breezy, natural, and human. Cheever has well said that 'Few men could have gone through Bunyan's experience and not come out fanatics.' The common sense and sprightliness of this conversation on the further edge of the Valley of the Shadow of Death shew how entirely he had escaped that danger.

Their talk first turns to the City of Destruction. It appears that after Christian's setting out there was much excitement and interest in those parts, but the notable point in this description is the combination in the citizens of the fear of judgment, and the derision of Christian. It is a very common combination, quite irrational indeed, but no less popular on that account. There was no firm belief, and yet the threatening aspects of religion had laid hold upon the imagination. There is probably no condition more corrupting to the moral nature than this. In Browning's *Easter Day* we are reminded how easy the Christian life in its extremest demand of devotion and sacrifice would be, granted an unhesitating intellectual conviction.[1] The attitude here described is that of those who do not take the practical step of committing themselves to their convictions, their belief not being firm enough ; and who, on the other hand, are not able to throw off that belief, and escape from its ring of terrors. The result on character is that they seem to be perpetually braving danger and violating conscience, upon the chance that what they think they believe may turn out eventually not to be true.

The conversation turns to Pliable, and it appears that that ill-fated person had little thanks for his returning. Bunyan is always glad of a chance of saying what he thinks about pilgrims who turn back, and here he further tells us what the world thinks of them. When Pliable returned to the City he found that his change of mind, although it had brought him back among them, had shaken their trust in him. They very naturally argued that he who had been faithless in one line of action was not likely to be very trustworthy in another, and no one would give him work to do. Marbot tells how a spy was caught and pardoned in one of Napoleon's campaigns, but when he offered to turn traitor, and supply

---

[1] 'Could I believe once thoroughly,
    The rest were simple.
    . . . give my body to be sawn
    Asunder, hacked in pieces, tied
    To horses, stoned, burned, crucified
    Like any martyr of the list ? '—ii.

information regarding the movements of his own army, Napoleon had him shot.[1] In the *Holy War* we read this interesting and parallel passage: 'Mr Anything became a brisk man in the broil; but both sides were against him, because he had been true to none. He had, for his malapertness, one of his legs broken, and he who did it wished it had been his neck.' Unfortunately for all concerned, apostasy is not always so thankless a business.

At the close of the talk about Pliable, Faithful utters one of those sentences in which we can hear the undertone of fatalism, 'But who can hinder that which will be?' For a character like Faithful's, that note is inevitable. It is Bunyan's own attitude towards the doctrine of election, and is abundantly illustrated throughout his writings, and especially in *Grace Abounding*. At times he is able to discuss details in it with singular ingenuity; but he, like all other really great spirits, knows that at the depths it must remain a mystery. Man's will and responsibility are obvious facts in the case, but the deepest fact in the universe is the will of God. And in the present connexion it has been beautifully said that 'it is not in the days of man's free will, but in the days of Christ's power, that any soul becomes a stranger and a pilgrim.' Nothing could be a more striking testimony to that fact of the ultimate mystery than a sentence like this of Faithful's, which leaves Pliable out among the great unexplained forces of the universe.

It is easy to fall into ill-natured gossip about others, and these wise pilgrims avoid that danger by turning the talk upon themselves. It is the instinct which has created the class-meetings of Methodism, and the pre-communion gatherings of 'the men' in the Highlands of Scotland. No doubt this, too, has its dangers. Introspection, besides an inherent tendency towards morbidness, is apt on the one

[1] *Memoirs of Baron de Marbot*, p. 370.

FAITHFUL

hand to foster vanity and self-importance, and on the other hand to exaggerate experience and lead to fiction. Worse than any other danger is its tendency to violate the sanctities of the individual life. All our deeper spiritual experience is essentially solitary, and by talking of it we are apt to cheapen it, and so to vulgarise our souls. Yet now and again, when it is done in the confidence of an intimate friendship, with simplicity and without parade, it may be a precious and valuable exercise.

The conversation proceeds to the discussion of Faithful's past journey. Of this we have already had two glimpses. One was when the porter at the House Beautiful told of his passing by with the simple answer to his question regarding his name. Thus Faithful has passed by the Church, as such independent spirits sometimes do. In many cases, no doubt, such men have had reasons for this course, such as the defects of Church organisations and the faults of Church members. But in this case the reason for his passing by seems to be that he did not feel the appeal of the Church as a wider intelligence and a more richly sympathetic nature would have done. A man of narrower interests, whose one thought is his own salvation, misses much which goes to enrich the life of so interested a spirit as that of Christian. Yet, though Faithful does not appreciate the Church, the Church appreciates him; and he is probably mentioned by the porter as a hint that the Church is arranging for a companion who may accompany Christian. The second glimpse we catch of him is in the Valley of the Shadow, where, as we have seen, the man of one idea and of narrow interests fares better than the more many-sided and imaginative Christian.

For the rest, even in the City of Destruction, he had still been Faithful—applying then, however, the faithfulness of his character only to worldly affairs. He had been saved by the fear of Hell, which with such natures as his sometimes does

THE ROAD

excellent work. By his natural dutifulness he had been kept from falling into the Slough of Despond. We hear nothing of a burden for him, nor of any adventure with Mr Worldly Wiseman. On the other hand, he has apparently missed the revelations of the Interpreter's house, as well as those of the House Beautiful. While Christian had lingered and learned, Faithful had done nothing but press doggedly on, and the result is a stronger manhood, though one which is neither so full nor so ripe.

CHAPTER XIX

FAITHFUL'S TEMPTATIONS

FROM what we learn by his own speech, Faithful has been a very sorely tempted man. His temptations fall into two classes, both characteristic :—

(1) Wanton and Adam, which appeal to the sensual side of his nature.

(2) Discontent and Shame, which appeal to its social side.

Thus he is tempted first by his lower nature, and then by his higher; first by the flesh, and then by the world. The devil will come by and by, as one writer has sententiously remarked. It is interesting to contrast these with Christian's temptations in the Valley. Each man has to bear his own burden of temptation, fixed for him by the peculiarities of his disposition. Christian is tempted through his imagination; Faithful, having little imagination, is tempted through his flesh and his pride.

WANTON

The reticence and chaste delicacy of this passage is remarkable in the age of Bunyan, and is in strong contrast to the treatment of the same subject in Part III. In a curious passage in the account of his *Call to the Ministry*, Bunyan writes : 'And in this I admire the wisdom of God that He made me shy of women from my first conversion until now. . . . It is a rare thing to see me carry it pleasantly towards a woman : the common salutation of women I abhor; it is odious to me in whomsoever I see it. Their company alone I cannot away with; I seldom so much as touch a woman's hand.'

Faithful, however, is a man of a quite different stamp. His flesh is hard on him, and its appetites are strong. While Christian wrestles with spiritual enemies for the most part, Faithful's first two temptations are of an opposite sort. It is in keeping with this that even after his escape he is still troubled. 'I know not,' he says, 'whether I did wholly escape her or no.' He is not, in spiritual matters, an imaginative person. But the unimaginative are perhaps all the more subject to this kind of imagination, which needs not any great amount of finesse and subtlety, but assaults them with crude and gross thoughts. On the coarsening effect of such imaginations there is a remarkable and weighty passage in the first of Matthew Arnold's *Discourses in America*.

The character of this forceful man, blunt almost to roughness, is the result of such conflicts. He hates lust because he fears it, and because he knows that he has good reason to fear it. It is that hatred, with fear behind it, which keeps him braced and ever on the strain. The easy good nature which might be safe for some is not safe for him, and he makes no attempt to risk it. He is austere, and graver than untempted men see any reason for. Such men as he are apt to be harshly judged. Their asceticism appears bitter, and their strictness and straitlaced severity appear inhuman. Yet if we knew their inner life we would often find that they are but choosing the only way in which it is possible for them to keep themselves pure. Their 'choice between faith and sense must be decisive and exclusive.' If lust has to be fought, there is no use of striking gently. Pleasures, genialities, even friendships otherwise helpful, must be sacrificed, and the sacrifice is well worth while.

The refuge which Faithful found is the best and indeed the only way of escape. The texts which he remembered [1] are uncompromising and ungentle ones. Yet, where argument

---

[1] Prov. v. 5; xxii. 14; Job xxxi. 1.

and dalliance of any kind are so dangerous, this is the only kind of answer that is wise or safe. The rough blow that clubs down an evil imagination with the word 'hell,' shows a finer skill than any moral discussion would do. And the following words are still wiser: 'I shut my eyes . . . and I went my way.'

The sudden change in Wanton from sweetness to railing was only to be expected. It is characteristic of that cruelty and coarseness which falsely calls itself love. The railing does not matter. The important thing is to shut the eyes and go away. Get, perforce, into another region of interests, and out of this. It is the old story of Ulysses stopping his sailors' ears with wax as they passed the Islands of the Sirens. There is no combating such suggestions. They must be gone away from; and the keener and more manifold a man's general and innocent interests in life are, the easier will be his chance of escape.

It is curious that the six remedies against this kind of sin, given in Bunyan's favourite *Plain Man's Pathway*, are 'Labour, abstinence, temperance, prayer, restraint of senses, shunning of women's company.' As to the last, its wisdom may be questioned. It may well be, that if Faithful had dwelt in the Palace Beautiful for a time, he would have had less trouble from the attacks of such temptation.

Adam the First

Mr Froude has, in the second chapter of his *Bunyan* an interesting and able *résumé* of the course of Christian thought regarding the Platonic theory of the inherent evil of material susbtance and the body. John Bunyan approaches the subject from the point of view not of philosophy but of experience; and while his Adam is the Adam of Paul rather than of Genesis, he is nevertheless a very human figure. His bluff entrance almost suggests the old man on the comic stage. He is the most distinctly drawn of all Bunyan's pictures of tempters, and he is loathsome as the elderly sensualist always is—a man like him of Tennyson's *Vision of Sin*, in whom all ideals are dead. He is an extension of the idea of Wanton, representing an appeal not to any one appetite, but to the entire sensuous side of a man—to all that is of the earth, earthy. Easy-going, luxurious, conscienceless, he stands for the natural man that is in us all, with his clamant senses and his indifference to questions of sin and goodness. His daughters are the Lust of the flesh, the Lust of the eyes, and the Pride of life.

To a full-blooded man like Faithful the appeal of this old Adam must ever be strong. And the time at which that appeal comes is significant. After the first impulses of pilgrimage begin to flag and to give place to the discouraging sense of difficulty, a reaction is inevitable. This episode corresponds to Christian's sleep in the arbour on that same Hill Difficulty, and the difference of experience is determined simply by the different natures of the two men. It was natural for Faithful to take his relaxation in a broader and more voluptuous form than Christian. Yet the temptation is the same.

This temptation, in one form or another, ' comes to every Christian, and always from Deceit.' There is only one way of successfully meeting it. Faithful for a time combats it with questioning, but all the time a soul spends in arguing with him, the old Adam is winning. He can be monstrously specious, and the strictest of men know only too well that there is much that can be said for him. But at last Faithful looks him straight in the face and sees the truth. The flesh ever wins by side glances and suggestions. Looked at directly, with an unclouded eye, it only disgusts; for the spiritual eye is sensitive to broad effects, though it can easily be bewitched by things seen only sidelong.

This temptation has found beautiful and daring language

in every generation. In our own time Swinburne and Rossetti have sometimes pled its cause. Kipling has made us feel its power in his *Mandalay*, Fiona Macleod in *Annir Choille*, Fitzgerald in his revival of *Omar Kayyám*. As records of phases of human life, these have their unquestioned place in Art. But if any of them aspires to be prophetic, and to claim a serious place among the spiritual counsellors of our time, that is a different matter. If we have to make a choice, it must be wiser to be merciless to the flesh in order to save the spirit, than to be merciless to the spirit in order to gratify the flesh.

The very characteristic passage about Moses has for its sidenote in the first edition 'the temper of Moses,' which yields in later editions to 'the thunder of Moses.' Really they mean the same thing, Moses' temper being always (when he is allegorical at least) more or less thundery in this wicked world. This episode corresponds with Christian's experiences at Mount Sinai, only that here we see more clearly the thoroughness of that Law, which reaches to the heart's desires and buffets a man even for inclining to the flesh. No more illuminative commentary has ever been written on Rom. vii. 7-11. It was when the Law said to Paul's conscience, 'Thou shalt not *covet*,' that sin revived and slew him. And John Bunyan was the very man to write this commentary. Here are two of his own experiences of the Law : 'There is no middle way in the Law. It hath not ears to hear, nor heart to pity its penitent ones.'[1] 'Also the law, that can shoot a great way, have a care thou keep out of the reach of those great guns, the Ten Commandments.'[2] The biographer of the wretched Spira, in words which well represented the sufferings of that poor soul whose tortures had so deeply impressed Bunyan, spoke of 'the continual butchery of his conscience.'

[1] *Defence of the Doctrine of Justification by Faith.*
[2] *The Heavenly Footman.*

THE ROAD

Luther advises sinners to 'Hit conscience on the snout,' by faith in Christ. But how much finer is the account of deliverance which this ardent disciple of Luther gives. 'One came by and bid him forbear,' and that one had holes in His hands and in His side. Thomas à Kempis, too, is with Bunyan here : ' Oh, if Jesus crucified would come into our hearts, how quickly and fully should we be instructed in all truth.' 'If thou canst not contemplate high and heavenly things, rest thyself in the passion of Christ, and dwell willingly within His sacred wounds.'[1]

There can be no doubt that here the wounds of Christ are set over against the old Adam as well as over against Moses. True, the realisation of the crucified is primarily introduced as the man's salvation from an accusing conscience. Bunyan himself often found that it is ' the object of the threatenings to make the promise shine.' The most brilliant visions and illuminations of *Grace Abounding* usually break through passages of the blackest despair. Yet in this place there is an unusually subtle touch of spiritual art in setting Christ's wounds over against the fleshly appetites—the bleeding body of the Lord in controversy with the lusting flesh of His poor pilgrim. This contrast is exactly expressed in Christina Rossetti's poem of *The Three Enemies*, in which the first part relates to the Flesh—

> ' " Sweet, thou art pale." "More pale to see
> Christ hung upon the cruel tree,
> And bore His Father's wrath for me."
>
> " Sweet, thou art sad." " Beneath a rod
> More heavy, Christ for my sake trod
> The winepress of the wrath of God."
>
> . . . . .
>
> " Sweet, thou art footsore." " If I bleed,
> His feet have bled ; yea, in my need
> His heart once bled for mine indeed." '

---

[1] *Imitation of Christ*, Bk. I. ch. xxv. par. 6 ; Bk. II. ch. i. par. 4.

FAITHFUL'S TEMPTATIONS

DISCONTENT

At this point we come to the second group of Faithful's temptations. He had been preserved from yielding to the lower ones of the first group, and now those very qualities of pride and self-respect which help a man to resist the flesh become the means of a new order of temptation. The man of high spirit is attacked by Discontent and Shame. There is a further parallelism between the groups. Just as Wanton is a herald and foreshadow of Adam, so Discontent is of Shame. Indeed, a sufficiently drastic and final dealing with Wanton and Discontent may obviate any encounter with the larger sins.

Discontent is not always and wholly an evil thing. There is indeed not only a right discontent, but it is from a divine discontent that all Christian life springs. Nothing is more un-Christian than that silly kind of optimism which is satisfied with anything that comes, good, bad, or indifferent —like some courageous but futile weathercock, fixedly pointing south through a north-westerly gale. Lasalle, in the early days of Socialism, bitterly accused the Alsatian peasants of a 'damned want of needs.' One of Matthew Arnold's most telling passages is directed against the fallacy that 'excellence is common and abundant.' [1]

This, however, is a different sort of Discontent. The difficult path of Christ, when it leads through the valley of Humility, is apt to present the double aspect of lost chances and lost friends. There is no honour in it which the world can recognise, and it is very lonely. These are rather wafts of sentiment that play for a moment upon the pilgrim's heart than definite and clearly stated arguments. He brushes them aside by the answer that the loneliness is there

[1] *Essays in Criticism*, i. 58.

already, and there is no use in lingering over any pathetic aspect it may present; as to the honour, that is a matter of standards, and he has chosen another code of honour than the world's.

Yet upon many a pilgrim, Discontent makes the heavier assault of a grumbling spirit about things in general.[1] That ancient sin of Accidia [2] which mediæval saints found so sore upon them, is ever with us. It is an exhilarating reflexion that its evil has wrought out so much good as it has done in literature, setting Chaucer and Dante, and so many others of the greatest, to sound the bugle note of the Duty of Joy. In our own time Browning has enriched that literature by much of his noblest poetry, and R. L. Stevenson will be remembered for this more than for all his other gifts to posterity.

Shame

This Section has a peculiar importance in view of the fact that, as Cheever says, ' the delineation of this character by Bunyan is a masterly grouping together of the arguments used by men of this world against religion, in ridicule and contempt of it, and of their feelings and habits of opinion in regard to it.'[3] It is peculiarly significant in view of the conditions of Bunyan's time, when Shame entered very largely into the controversy between Cavalier and Roundhead. Of course, there were many whose whole pride was enlisted on the side of plain living and high thinking; but there must have been many also who felt the glamour of that brilliant world from which they excluded themselves by espousing the cause of the people and their form of faith.

---

[1] The late Professor James MacGregor, in his Commentary on Exodus has the following caustic note on Ex. xv. 24:—*Murmured:* N.B. the *first* separate action of this people now set free!—grumbling (cp. John Bull).

[2] *Cf.* p. 142.

[3] *Lectures on Bunyan*, 231.

FAITHFUL'S TEMPTATIONS

Even in dress this temptation was widely felt. In the *Plain Man's Pathway to Heaven* there are ten pages in regard to the pride of dress, which show the height to which feeling ran at the time. We hear much of starching and steeling, busks and whalebones, supporters and robatoes, full moons and hobby-horses, etc., and are told that 'to be proud of apparel is, as if a thief should be proud of his halter, a beggar of his clouts, a child of his gay toys, or a fool of his bauble.'

It is 'proof of our having lost the image of God that we are ashamed of the things of God.' So says the old commentator Scott, and in this chapter we see the curious reversal of a great and valuable natural instinct. Shame has its uses. Dr Whyte (whose chapter of 'Shame' is one of the most suggestive in his book) points out that it is 'an original instinct planted by God to act as a check on dishonourable action.' It is meant to be a social conscience, adding, as it were, a more popular appeal, to the great language of the moral sense herein. Unfortunately that very fact of its lower moral elevation has attached more shame to the discovery than to the commission of sin, and in this code of judgment the great commandment is not to be found out.

The arguments of Shame (to borrow Dr Kerr Bain's division of them) are as follow :—

1. *The Spiritlessness of Religion.* This is the old Greek and Roman stumbling-block against Christianity—the offence of the Cross. Faithful is a gentleman and an aristocrat who cannot help having a keen regard for the world's opinion. His experience reminds one of passages from the biographies of great soldiers, who have often had to endure a severe conflict of this kind. In Bunyan's time Puritans had much to bear, but the most trying part of it all to sensitive natures must have been the shame and contempt which was cast upon

them.¹ Offor tells us that it was then safer to commit a felony than to become a Dissenter, and Bunyan himself, in one of his clever swinging verses, writes :

> 'Though you dare crack a coward's crown,
> Or quarrel for a pin,
> You dare not on the wicked frown,
> Nor speak against their sin.' ²

When ridicule is added to the sense of shame the situation becomes still more difficult, for it takes a very big man to bear being laughed at, and a very commanding faith to enable him to bear it. To be treated as one who has no claim to respect, who is unmanly and undignified, and whose place in society is that of the butt for caricature, must put a strain upon all that is sensitive in feeling and fine in character. As one reads *Hudibras* and feels, even after all the years, how gibe after gibe must have cut home, alike by their cleverness and injustice, one realises how vital a character this Shame was then. To a considerable extent he has retreated now within the four walls of homes where dear friends ply the rack and thumbscrew as only dear friends can ; and although in many an office, shop, and factory the battle is open enough, yet there is something to thank God for in the change of times.

2. *The Worldly Worth of the Irreligious.* This is an argument as old as the days of the Psalmist, who was puzzled and grieved at the prosperity of the wicked, in their great power spreading themselves like a green bay tree.³ Like the Psalmist, many a man has been led into the House of God, where he has considered their end ; and, judging them by their death instead of by their life, has escaped the snares of

---

¹ Even Churchmen were by no means exempt, as may be seen from Pepys' curious account of a conversation with Mr Holliard : 'Much discourse about the bad state of the Church, and how the Clergy are come to be men of no worth in the world.' *Diary*, Feb. 16, 1667.

² *Prison Meditations*, 56.

³ Ps. xxxvii. 35.

THE
OLD PULPIT,
ELSTOW CHURCH

Shame. But the sting of this argument is in the tail of it. The Christian has cut himself off from the strong and prosperous life of the irreligious, venturing the loss of all 'for nobody else knows what.' Once again we are brought back to Faith, the absolute essential in our conflict with Shame. Whether anybody else knows or not, we *must* know what we are venturing everything for. There is no hope against Shame but clear Faith that can withstand the whole brilliance of the world by the simple assertion, 'I know whom I have believed.'

3. *The Worthlessness of the Religious.* Judged from the world's point of view this has always been a stumbling-block to all who were tempted by the pride of life. From the early days of Christianity, when so many of the converts were slaves, the sincerest piety has often been found among those who counted for nothing in the great world. Two pulpits are to be seen, with which the name of John Bunyan is associated. One, under which he was converted, is still on exhibition in the beautiful and charmingly situated Parish Church of Elstow. The other, that in which he preached at Bedford, is now in a bare and small chapel in a back alley at Goldington, surrounded by poor and squalid brick houses. Which things also are for an allegory.

4. *The Shamefulness of Religious Ways.* In this part of his argument Shame has more to say for himself than in any other part of it. When religion presents for its chief outward appearance a spectacle of 'whining,' 'mourning,' 'sighing,' and 'groaning,' it is not only false shame, but true shame, that may rebel. No doubt there were elements in the Puritan worship which justified this assertion, and as these elements have been caricatured in many accounts of Puritanism,[1] we may thankfully admit that a religion which lays emphasis upon the healthier side of things may also

---

[1] *Cf. Hudibras*, etc.

be, and has actually been, a great gift of God; and yet after all, though the best repenting is generally done in secret, it is permanently true that the really shameful thing is *not repenting*; and however exaggerated the expression of repentance may be, it is the most honourable act of which a man is capable. The same sort of thing may be said in regard to asking forgiveness. Nothing is more unworthy than to be always making apologies, and there are no more irritating people than those over-sensitive souls who go about with an air of apologising for their very existence, and are oppressed with a chronic sense of having offended somebody. Yet, the real shamefulness of such an attitude is due to the very sacredness and honour of the difficult task of asking forgiveness. The blessed moment of frank confession is far too sacred to be thus vulgarised. To many natures it is indeed a bitter thing to have to ask forgiveness, and the apology is not always generously received; yet there is something sacramental and cleansing in the humiliation, and he who takes it so may find it a great means of grace.

5. *Social Degradation.* This is practically the same as the third argument of Shame, the new point being that subtle blending of moral and social estimates by which the vices of the great assume finer names, and the virtues of the base seem to share in their lowliness.

Such was and still is shame—that 'final effort of unspirituality' which makes its appeal to an attractive infirmity of noble minds. So far as this is concerned, it is easier for a dull and humble spirit to be a Christian than for one tempted by the brightness and welcome of the open doors of the world. It clings persistently through a lifetime, if it be not very resolutely and deliberately fought. It can be overcome, and Faithful shows us the way.

Being a sin of the imagination, it, like Faithful's other temptations, depends upon the adroit and immediate

FAITHFUL'S TEMPTATIONS

guidance of that faculty towards other and more commanding realities than those which have been engaging it.[1] The fact of God, the Word of God, the day of doom, the love of Christ, the soul's salvation, the coming of the King—these are the facts with which Faithful confronts the men of his time and the hectoring spirits of the world. Shame speaks only of men and their opinion, but there is God and His judgment to reckon with. The shrinking mind must be forced up to that, and in the strength of that vision of great certainties Shame can be thrown off. It is a case of the rivalry and conflict of the seen with the unseen, the present with the future, the human with the divine. Every day we are accustomed between man and man to find it a great privilege and delight to bear reproach out of loyal affection to those we love. Let but love find in the eternal region images equally clear and sweet, and the same loyalty will gain an easy victory over Shame. It is but another instance of the victory of Faith.

So Faithful sings his first song, as well he may. He is a considerably worse poet than Christian is, but he is a *man*, conspicuous through the centuries. Dr Kerr Bain sees his ' broad shoulders, well-set head, and military walk,' and we see them. His is no smart virtue ready with words, cocksure and lighted-hearted. He has hesitated twice, but he has overcome.

[1] *Cf.* pp. 167, 168.

CHAPTER XX

TALKATIVE

We come now to the longest and not the best managed of the dialogues. The first part of it is in Bunyan's best vein, but the second is somewhat dull and long drawn out. He has devoted much time and space to the exhibition of this type of character, and doubtless there must have been a reason for it.

Talkative is ' a fellow of infinite discourse.' The redundant style of his first sentences proves this, with their lack of the abruptness familiar in these conversations. Bunyan's own plain style is part both of his attraction and his greatness. His own words about it are : ' I could have stepped into a style much higher than this in which I have discoursed, and could have adorned all things more than I have seemed to do ; but I dare not. God did not play in tempting of me ; neither did I play when the pangs of Hell caught hold upon me, therefore I may not play in relating of them ; but be plain and simple, and lay down the thing as it was. He that liketh it, let him receive it ; and he that doth not, let him produce a better.' As we read the rolling periods of Talkative, this tall and somewhat comely man ' walking at a distance besides them,' we cannot but be thankful that Bunyan's style bears the marks of God's earnest in it. When we read Part III. we are still more thankful for Parts I. and II. There is something about Talkative that reminds us at times of Shakespeare's loquacious folk, and suggests a man whose conversation is always that of one addressing a public meeting, and receiving frequent applause from his imaginary auditors.

This lengthy and scathing satire gains a special interest

TALKATIVE

from the fact that Talkative was the very type of Puritan singled out by the enemies of Puritanism for their scorn. What poor wretch was it, we wonder, who sat for this portrait? For certainly Talkative is drawn from life, and some long-haired and leather-jerkined man talks again in him after the silence of two hundred years in an unknown grave.[1] It is characteristic of the fidelity of Bunyan that he has drawn this portrait. He is no partisan who is afraid of a truth, even against his own side, any more than the frank writers of the Bible are, who have told the stories of Jacob and of Peter. Here is a Puritan writing of what he knows. He has seen the evil excesses of some of the prophets, lunatic preachers, and loquacious hypocrites of his day, and he exposes it ruthlessly. The whole picture is a protest that this is not the true type of Puritan, and he has sent it down for the benefit of those who in every age are tempted to a religion of speech instead of deed. It has been well remarked that this type has become an almost traditional figure with light and thoughtless writers. There is a limit beyond which such caricatures cease to be amusing, and to-day they are perhaps less necessary than they may have been in the past. There have been in our country generations of great talkers, and these were sure to have their followers who talked without having their great things to say. Our age appears to have lost the art of conversation,[2] and Talkative nowadays would be voted a dull fellow. Indeed, the abruptness of our modern telegraphese has cost literature and life a heavy price, and we are tempted at times to feel that we would take the risk of being bored a little for the wealth and finish of the style of former days. All the more honour should be given to Bunyan for attacking and satirising a fashionable excess of his own time.

[1] Compare the conversations in *Hudibras* between the Knight and his servant.   [2] *Cf.* p. 97.

Of course, fluency in the gift of speech is still to be found, though it takes more courage to exercise it nowadays. It is largely a matter of temperament, and one is apt to judge wrongly in regard to it. On the one hand, Offor's note is wise, ' Reader, be careful not to judge harshly, or despise a real believer, who is blest with fluency of utterance on divine subjects.' On the other hand, one must be equally careful not to characterise all silent Christianity as the work of a ' dumb devil,' or to attempt to force either in ourselves or others the fluent expression of private experience. Silence is better than unreality or exaggeration. There is in fact a golden mean in this as in other matters, and those who can talk upon religion naturally and without verbiage, are its most valuable advocates.

The permanent warning of this passage is that fluency is always a dangerous gift. Faithful has already told us how in the City of Destruction there was great talk that came to nothing, and any reader of the Epistle of St James may see by the frequent and striking metaphors for the tongue, how great a danger this was in the early days. Dr Whyte has told a story of a Carthusian, which Browning tells in another form in his *Pambo*. It is the tale of a young man going to a teacher, whose first word to him was, ' I said I will take heed to my ways, that I sin not with my tongue.' [1] The student broke off the lesson, and found that enough for a lifetime. It is not so much particular sins such as profanity, or foulness, or backbiting that are here rebuked, but simple excess of language. He who talks too much is sure to exaggerate his experience, and to use words without meanings. In this way the blight of unreality comes across the whole field of conversation. Speech ceases to be expressive or persuasive ; and, worst of all, it becomes a substitute for the very things about which it discourses.

[1] Ps. xxxix. 1.

TALKATIVE

1. *His Talk.* ' Well, then,' said Faithful, ' what is the one thing that we shall at this time found our discourse upon ? ' ' What you will : I will talk of things heavenly or things earthly ; things moral or things evangelical ; things sacred or things profane ; things past or things to come ; things foreign or things at home ; things more essential or things circumstantial—provided that all be done to our profit.'

This drench of talk, in which Talkative replies to Faithful, gives characteristic promise of the surfeit which we are to have. Bunyan's sidenote, twice repeated, is ' Oh, brave Talkative.' Concentration is not this man's forte, as it is Faithful's. There is no one thing on which he will found his discourse. He will talk about anything and everything. This programme is too rich for any man except one of encyclopædic powers, and in most cases such men do not talk like this. ' The greatest talkers,' says Montaigne, ' for the most part, do nothing to purpose.' Tolstoi, in his *Invaders*, says of one of his heroes : ' If a great saying in regard to any subject came into my hero's mind, I believe he would not have uttered it : in the first place, because he would have feared that in saying something great he might spoil a great deed ; and secondly, because when a man is conscious within himself of the power to do a great deed, there is no need of saying anything at all.'

2. *Talk about Sacred Things.* Those subjects interested him most, but simply as a department of human study and activity, just as another man is most interested in archæology and a third in coleoptera. The marked defect of all the talk is that lack of accuracy and of the tendency towards practical and personal experience which is never absent in religious talk that rings true. A man to whom religion has meant much, who has been saved by it, and has realised the meaning of salvation, will never to able to discuss it dispassionately as an outsider. Consequently, in such talk as this we shall find that the words are almost the correct ones, but not quite. The accuracy which only experience can give is absent. The statement of religion seems right enough, yet with a difference. Luther, in that commentary on the Galatians which was so dear to Bunyan's heart, commenting on i. 6, writes : ' For the devil will not be ugly and black in his ministers, but fair and white. And to the end he may appear to be such a one, he setteth forth and decketh all his words and works with the colour of truth, and with the name of God. Hereof is sprung that common proverb among the Germans, *In God's name beginneth all mischief.*'

The application of this to the case of ministers of religion is too obvious for any commentator to omit. ' Nothing so belittles a man,' says Dr Jowett of New York, ' as undue familiarity with great things.' But ministers have to deal with things not only great but sacred, until perforce these things become familiar. Stewart of Aberdeen, a notable preacher of the earlier nineteenth century, in a great sermon upon the text, ' Thou art unto them as a very lovely song of one that hath a pleasant voice, and can play well on an instrument,' exposes this danger in a memorable fashion. The terrible thing for ministers is that they have to talk so much about these things, whether they have anything to say or not. And the lesson is that of Isaiah,[1] where the sin of the lips is burned away from the minister after his great vision of the Lord. Only by a life in which that supreme vision repeats itself in the changing lights of varied experiences and circumstances, can a man retain the wonder which alone makes it safe for him to carry on so spiritually dangerous a profession. When that wonder has died away, every word uttered about sacred things may bring the doom of those who lay light hands upon the ark of God. Many a

[1] Isa. vi. 7.

man has shared the fate of Uzzah, and been slain by this—slain in heart, in conscience, and in spiritual imagination and insight. Poor Francis Spira had said terrible things to John Bunyan's conscience on this subject: 'A man had need be exceeding strongly grounded in the truth, before he can be able to affirm such a matter as ye now do; it is not the performance of a few formal duties, but a mighty constant labour, with all intention of heart and affection, with full desire and endeavour continually, to set forth God's glory. ... It is no light or easy matter to be a Christian; it is not baptism, or reading of the Scriptures, or boasting of faith in Christ (though even these are good), that can prove one to be an absolute Christian.'

3. *Quotation of Scripture.* Mr Froude tells us that 'The language of the poor women has lost its old meaning. They themselves, if they were alive, would not use it any longer. The conventional phrases of evangelical Christianity ring untrue in a modern ear like a cracked bell.'[1] This judgment cannot be accepted without qualification. The whole worth of speech of this kind is determined by whether the speaker is using language with real thought or without it. Every reader of Matthew Arnold must have been struck, however widely his point of view may have differed, by the startling suggestiveness of the Scripture texts that are introduced. It is an indisputable fact that men to whom every text stands for something experienced and thought out, still use that language both in prayer and in preaching with the most pointed and convincing effect, both literary and spiritual.

Yet all depends on the sincerity and vitality of the thought that lies behind the quotation. No quotations of Scripture are more apt than those which are introduced in New Testament speeches of the devil, but their lack of sincerity

---

[1] Froude, *Bunyan*, p. 29: *cf. antea*, p. 64.

is at once apparent. On the other hand, quotation without vitality of thought is equally distasteful. The familiarity of the words makes them a line of least resistance, into which the laziest and most sapless discourse may naturally run. But the sham is easily detected, and the quotation of Scripture is perhaps the most unfailing test for sincerity of utterance that could be named.

4. *The Slightness of Talkative.* In her bitter essay on *Worldliness and Other-worldliness*, George Eliot points out how slight a fund of real knowledge is necessary for the equipment of a popular preacher. The lust of speech is a very subtle kind of egotism, for Talkative always greatly prefers to hear himself talking than to listen with attention to anybody else. Tolstoi, in his sententious way, asserts that, 'as everybody knows, in a business conversation it is absolutely unnecessary for you to understand what is said, but it is necessary only to bear in mind what you yourself wish to say.'[1] In the present age, when so large a multitude of people who do not read books have extracts and scraps, reviews and criticisms of books served out to them, nothing is easier than to acquire just such a superficial acquaintance with a vast mass of information as will enable them to talk freely about what they do not know. Here is the mirror for such talkers. Talkative has no system of thought. He has no capacity for it in that slight and restless mind of his. Consequently he is easily made to contradict himself, though he cannot be made to see that he has done so.

But his slightness is a more serious matter than that of superficial intelligence and discursive information. When he speaks of 'learning by talk to suffer,' we begin to know him for what he is. A man might as well speak of the art of prayer, or the preparation by talk for death. What this man wants is experience, by which, and not by talk, all that is

[1] *Polikushka.*

TALKATIVE

best worth learning must be learned. This is a man, not of practice but of theory; and the religion of Christ is a religion of actual repentance and forgiveness, of actual dealing with life and with God. Talkative's religion is a hopelessly cheap religion, and the Christianity of Christ is always costly, though it is also in another sense without money and without price. Every one of those who in Bunyan's day would have been called ' exercised Christian men ' will say that ' with a great price obtained I this freedom.' We shall presently see that Talkative was a hypocrite, and that the words of Burke are true of him : ' Those who quit their proper character to assume what does not belong to them, are for the greater part ignorant both of the character they have and of the character they assume.'

5. *Talkative's Idea of himself*. From what we have already seen, we should expect the vanity of the talker that goes with his slightness. This was a favourite butt for the scorn of John Bunyan. 'The Pharisee goes on boldly,' he writes in his *Pharisee and Publican*, ' fears nothing, but trusteth in himself that his state is good ; he hath his mouth full of many fine things, whereby he strokes himself over the head, and calls himself one of God's white boys, that, like the Prodigal's brother, never transgressed.' In *Grace Abounding* he writes : ' Shall I be proud because I am sounding brass ? Is it so much to be a fiddle ? Hath not the least creature that hath life more of God in it than these ? '

What strikes one most in Talkative is the utter want of escape from self. His life has no exit, either in helpfulness, love, or real faith. He speaks of edification, but that means for him being built up on self, not on God or truth. He is hiding from God, and from all realities, behind words. He takes it for granted that he is a Christian, and seeks the company of the good as a matter of course. But he who is ' of course ' a Christian falls at once into the dangerous vice of patronising both men and God. He is the professional critic and sermon-taster so familiar in lands like our own, where preaching is in a nation's blood. In such lands there is always a large company of interfering persons whose function it is to keep the workers right. Looking down upon the backs of the actors from their exalted but inglorious post behind the stage, they neither see nor feel the power of the play. The fact is, that they are thinking not of it, but of themselves. One note of this attitude is Talkative's accusation that Faithful is 'lying at the catch.' The self-conscious man is more interested in the bearing of the conversation upon himself and his dignity than upon any of the great matters with which it deals. It is but one of many ways in which the personal element hinders true knowledge.

6. *Talkative as Hypocrite.* The false presupposition regarding himself imparts an element of unreality to everything about such a man as this. But he is too much engrossed with himself to be aware of the unreality: he is a hypocritical talker before he becomes a talking hypocrite. From the first he is hopelessly unnatural, a theatrising person whose word-built world is wholly artificial. The actor, playing his part in such a world, may for a time imagine it to be the real world, and honestly mistake words for realities. But there comes a time when he knows himself to be posing, and then hypocrisy becomes conscious and daring. In general, however, the hypocrite first deceives himself before he sinks to the conscious deceiving of others.

It is a word to the wise, especially if they be also constitutionally eloquent. When talk runs ahead of thought, you have a fool; when it runs ahead of feeling, you have a flatterer; when it runs ahead of will, you have a liar. This is the natural history of hypocrisy. No one at the beginning says, 'Go to, I will be a hypocrite.' But when expression outruns experience, the hypocrite is the inevitable result.

TALKATIVE

It has been well said that ' No angel with drawn sword disputes Talkative's entrance to the way of pilgrimage.' That is the pity of it and the horror of it. The angel at the gate of Paradise is an angel of mercy. Any barrenness of the outside wilderness were better than to be wandering, an alien and unwelcome intruder, among the trees of the garden. Yet that is the heavy doom of all hypocrites who have by their talk entered the unguarded gate of a professed religion.

7. *The Life of Talkative*.[1] Near neighbourhood betrays the hypocrisy of the man. He is one of those who will not stand knowing. He must always be among strangers. He can make friends easily, but cannot keep them long. The test is the home life of the man. He is hard and selfish there. His servants feel the full weight of his hypocrisy. The state of matters is elsewhere described by Bunyan in a passage eloquent of one phase of the domestic life of his time : ' Servants that are truly godly care not how cheap they serve their masters, provided they may get into godly families, or where they may be convenient for the Word. But if a master or mistress takes this opportunity to make a prey of their servants, it is abominable. I have heard poor servants say that in some carnal families they have had more liberty to God's things and more fairness of dealing than among many professors. Such masters make religion to stink before the inhabitants of the land.'[2] It is indeed quite true that below-stairs opinions of specific actions, being formed upon imperfect information, are often wrong ; yet servants are rarely mistaken in their general estimate of a master's or a mistress's character. It matters little to any one what those who do not know him think about him ; but the good or bad opinion of those whose eyes are nearest to his life is a more serious affair.

[1] *Cf. Hudibras*, Part ii. Canto iii.
' No argument like matter of fact is :
And we are best of all led to
Men's principles, by what they do.'
[2] *On Christian Behaviour*.

It is noteworthy that here the special sin noted is drunkenness. The amazing combination of this vice with religious fluency is, alas, proverbial. It was from the life that one recent writer sketched his character, who was 'while drinking, fluent in things profane; when drunk, fluent in things religious.' [1]

So, as the intercourse goes on, we witness the general collapse of this man's character. He is one of the multitude to whom the pithy saying of a northern Scot applies—'We're war tae please wi' preaching nor we are wi' practising.' 'The works of the law' are none of Talkative's weaknesses, and he takes rank among those antinomian Ranters of whom Bunyan tells that ' they would also talk with me of their ways, and condemn me as legal and dark; pretending that they only had attained to perfection, that could do what they would and not sin.' For such Bunyan reserves his strongest language—' abominating their cursed principles.'

There is a sense in which acting enters into the religious life legitimately. It is part of the venture of faith to live and speak upon the platform of the ideal, claiming our inheritance in better life than we have yet in fact attained. To act as if we had attained, in the sense of seeking to live a life worthy of a point of faith and conduct further on than that which we have reached, is a great secret of the growing Christian life. Yet that, if it be legitimate and helpful, presupposes a real aspiration and a genuine and whole-hearted endeavour to be worthy of the inheritance claimed. But the more any one takes the position of a religious man while his heart is not in it, the more hopelessly will he ruin his soul. Talkative's talk has slain his conscience. He is a man gospel-hardened under his own preaching. Bunyan knew the danger of that when he wrote: 'All this while I was not sensible of the danger and evil of sin; I was kept from considering that sin would damn me, whatsoever religion I followed, unless I was found in Christ.'

[1] Fergus Mackenzie, *Glenbruar*.

TALKATIVE

8. *The Effect of Talkative upon the World.* He *puzzles* the world.' The world has a genuine grievance against many professing Christian men. It is all too easy for them to draw their garments close about them and regard 'the world' as a conspiracy of dark characters with whom they have nothing in common. But there remains the fact of their common humanity, and the inevitable responsibilities it entails. Now, if there be one thing clear in this connexion, it is that the world has little need of such puzzling as this. On spiritual things it is confused and dark enough already. There is, indeed, a problem which the Christian should present to the world, and which is ever insoluble to it—the problem of a 'peace that passeth all understanding,' and of a power and love to which the world has no clue. But this contradiction between high words and low deeds is a puzzle of a different sort, and one which the world will be only too ready to solve according to its own lights. When openly irreligious men see that the only point in which the Christian is superior to themselves is in high-sounding talk, they form their own conclusions. If they despise not only the hypocrite, but the Christianity he professes and the Christ he is betraying, that is an error of judgment for which he, as well as they, is responsible. If the world is proverbially wary in dealing in business with those who make a great profession of religion, it is not well for religious men to meet that slander with an angry scorn. For, however true it may be that some of the worldlings are glad to find in such an opinion an excuse for their irreligion, yet there is a deeper fact to reckon with. Every man who is not himself religious has a certain hope in religion somewhere within him. The irreligious are quite genuine in their demand that religious profession shall be true, and the religious professor faithful. It is their tribute to a life which their consciences tell them they ought to lead ; and every man who truly leads it keeps them within touch

of grace. No responsibility could be heavier than that of those whose life is such as to shake the confidence of men in that to which their own violated consciences still urge them, or to confirm in them the deadly delusion that after all there is no reality in goodness.

In these dialogues, Faithful is true to his name. His intelligence is not very wide, but his faithfulness to the principles he holds is absolute. Had he visited the Interpreter's House and the House Beautiful, his intelligence would have been a better match for his faithfulness. Nay, had he kept his eyes open for the study of his fellow-men, and his heart open to the human interest of life, he would have been a better judge of character. It is significant that Faithful knew nothing of his fellow-townsman, and that Christian knew much of him. Faithful had kept aloof from men who differed from him, a course in which exclusiveness is apt to become a subtle and unconscious form of self-indulgence with such temperaments as his. The nemesis of all self-indulgence is unpreparedness, and the case we are studying is no exception. At first he is too friendly with Talkative, and at the last he is too rude to him.

We see something of the same kind in regard to doctrine. From Faithful's speeches a very complete and satisfactory statement of Protestant Christian doctrine might be compiled. Indeed, it would seem as though the author had deliberately chosen this part for setting forth something in the nature of a manifesto regarding the dogmatic side of Christianity, while he was obviously constructing a very memorable and classical plea for its practical side.[1] All this

[1] If any reader should find these expositions of Faithful's dull or too dogmatically complete, let him compare with them Baily's *Practice of Piety*, one of the most popular books of religion in its day, and one of the books which Bunyan's first wife brought with her as her dowry. The fearless and heavy tread through so many ludicrous and impossible doctrines; the description of God, more elaborate and not less damnatory

TALKATIVE

is good, and characteristic of Faithful. Yet not less characteristic is the fantastic paragraph regarding the chewing of the cud and the parting of the hoof. It is true that Bunyan himself had at one time (as he tells us in *Grace Abounding*) been much exercised with that most unnecessary discussion. It is true that Dante takes, quite seriously, another view of the same allegorical division,[1] departing in this from the still more famous allegorising of Aquinas.[2] Yet by this time Bunyan is evidently doubtful, and he makes his Christian chary of committing himself to Faithful's interpretation. In point of fact, all such interpretation is the merest absurdity. But faithful people whose outlook on the world is narrow, are apt to take the most fanciful ideas with a great solemnity, making up by their excess of ingenuity for their want of humour.

The most interesting part of the whole passage is its description of Faithful's practical dealing with Talkative. So characteristic is this, that the word 'faithfulness' has come to bear a certain grim suggestion of reproof in the religious language of this country. At first, before he suspects Talkative, we are inclined to credit him with having learned a lesson in politeness. His first word to Faithful is 'friend,' while the word with which he first greeted Christian was 'No!' The pleasant address, however, is afterwards exchanged for a very different manner. The hectoring and rude style of these rebukes tempts us to think that Faithful, like some other good people, has a certain reserved store of the unregenerate life, which he regards as legitimate for the rebuking of unrighteousness. The distinction between a

---

than the Athanasian Creed; the dulness of the descriptions of good men and the luridness and gusto of the descriptions of death and hell;—from all these we see how much the author has left unsaid, and understand the curious reserve with which he praises Baily's book, 'wherein I also found some things that were somewhat pleasing to me.'

[1] *Purgatorio*, xvi. l. 98.   [2] *Summa*, i. 2; cii. 6.

faithful rebuke and a railing accusation is sometimes subtler than ordinary people can quite understand. There is such a thing as the abuse of faithfulness. Cheever tells a Persian legend of Abraham driving an idolater forth with blows from his tent into the wilderness. To God's question, the patriarch explains the reason of his cruelty, and receives this reply : ' Have I borne with him these ninety-and-eight years, and nourished him and clothed him, notwithstanding his rebellion against me ; and couldst not thou, who art thyself a sinner, bear with him one night ? '[1] It is difficult not to side with Talkative a little when Faithful turns upon him. The parts are reversed, and Faithful becomes Talkative now with a vengeance. And yet, after all, Talkative is fair game, and it is satisfying to see him thus paid in his own coin —evidently the only way of silencing him. Bunyan's sidenote at the close of the interview is, ' A good riddance.'

Throughout the dialogue Christian keeps back and lets Faithful manage the affair. But when he is appealed to by the bewildered Faithful, he does not hesitate to express his mind with the utmost freedom. His conversation sparkles with remarkable passages, which show at once the wisdom and thoroughness of his dealing with his own soul, and the breadth and human nature which have characterised his study of men around him. The fact that Talkative ' makes good men ashamed ' is one such saying. We are told in Proverbs that ' When righteous men do rejoice there is great glory,'[2] and he who looks for the signs of glory or of shame on the faces of righteous men has found an excellent criterion of character. Again, the picture of the man who, on the first appearance of a tender conscience in his sons, calls them fools and blockheads, is the work of a shrewd observer.

---

[1] Franklin, quoted in Cheever, *Lectures on Bunyan*, p. 81. Used by Jeremy Taylor in *Liberty of Prophesying* ; for other antecedents *cf.* Stanley's *Jewish Church*, I. i.

[2] Prov. xxviii. 12.

TALKATIVE

More than two centuries later Stevenson made Weir of Hermiston meet his son Archie's tender conscience with the retort, 'You're splairging.'

But the choicest sentence of all that passed between Faithful and Christian is that in which the former says: 'Like a Christian you make your reports of men.' This, in the midst of so tremendous a philippic, is certainly daring. That his plain words are also just ones is not in itself a justification. The sin of evil-speaking does not refer only to false accusation. There is a way of speaking the truth which is quite as unchristian as lying. If the only, or the main reason for the retailing of truths derogatory to our neighbour's character be the gratification of that unclean and morbid interest in evil which is so discouraging to all honest believers in human nature, or if it be the indirect flattery of oneself by the implied contrast with another, then truth may serve the purposes of hell as well as lies. But there is another side to this question besides these. Bishop Butler, in his sermon upon the Government of the Tongue,—perhaps the wisest discourse ever uttered on this subject,—leads up to his conclusion by the plea that 'it is in reality of as great importance to the good of society that the characters of bad men should be known as that the characters of good men should. People who are given to scandal and detraction may indeed make an ill use of this observation; but truths which are of service towards regulating our conduct are not to be disowned, or even concealed, because a bad use may be made of them.' Now it is unquestionable that there are times when society, or an individual member of it, requires to be protected from some dangerous hypocrisy which is gaining too easy credence. Mere kindliness and good humour are not enough for such occasions. A habit of universal appreciation, unstiffened by any criticism, is not only insipid: it is unreal, and therefore bangerous in a world where the only safety in all cases ultimately lies in reality. A Christian is not essentially a pleasant person, nor is fair speech the essential Christian virtue. Truth in the inward parts is *the* Christian virtue, and he is the best Christian who knows best, both in its gentleness and its severity, the art of 'speaking the truth in love.'

Nay, further, it is Christian who, on the departure of Talkative, says, 'Let him go.' It is a tragic world, in no part more tragic than in the moral and spiritual responsibility of one man for another. To such responsibility there is in every case a limit, and out of his wide experience Christian knew this limit when he crossed it.[1] With deepening awe and sadness all faithful men see a certain number of their fellows going off from more straight-spoken to more comforting preachers. Jesus Christ Himself watched with wistful eyes the departure of the young ruler whom He loved as He looked upon him, but He did nothing further to hinder his departure. After a certain point, men who have deliberately rejected the judgment of good men must be left to the judgment of God. It is about such men that John Bunyan, in his *Barren Fig-Tree*, quotes the words [2] 'I will answer him by myself,' and adds : 'Thou art too hard for the Church; she knows not how to deal with thee. Well, I will deal with that man myself.'

We do not need to be so outrageously and grotesquely unreal as this Talkative to have a share in his fault. Our greatest danger will be unconsidered speech, which will often degenerate into unkind speech, where unkindness was wholly unnecessary and could serve no ultimate end of love. There is a story of Erasmus Darwin, who was afflicted with a stammer, being asked on one occasion, 'Don't you find it very inconvenient stammering, Dr Darwin ? ' The

[1] *Cf.* p. 75. [2] Ezek. xiv. 7.

TALKATIVE

answer was, 'No, sir, because I have time to think before I speak, and don't ask impertinent questions. To which may be added the beautiful words of Mr Peyton:[1] 'You must often have thought of two silences—the silence of the stars above you, and the silence of the graves around you. And here we are, chattering, speaking, brawling between these stillnesses. Our true speech is to work well, to love much, to do great good. Be true to your home and family, loyal to your God and Saviour, friendly to all men around you. And somehow this speech blends wonderfully with the silences.'

[1] *Memorabilia of Jesus*, p. 331.

CHAPTER XXI

WILDERNESS AND CITY

WITH one of his touches of unconscious poetry, Bunyan mentions casually that ' now they went through a wilderness.' The reader comes to suspect some sort of connexion between the story and its scenery, lending even to such details as this a certain allegorical significance. There is little doubt that this wilderness was suggested to the author by the mood which his last-composed passage had induced. The effect of all this talking was that inevitable sense of dreariness that falls upon the spirit after any excess of speech. The speech had been more than ordinarily barren, and every sensitive spirit will recognise the truth of John Bunyan's instinct in making those who have been in company with Talkative find themselves in a wilderness. The trail of boredom which Talkative leaves behind him in the world is more marked when he is among spiritual men. The dreariness of his empty talk seems to take the sense of reality out of even the spiritual things which they most firmly believe.

But they are drawing near to a city, and are soon to catch their first glimpse of its towers and palaces. The city, seen from the wilderness, is always one of the most exhilarating of imaginations. To hear once again the hum and stir of life, and to mingle with our fellows in the crowded streets, seems in itself so fascinating an expectation that the eye gleams, and the blood flows quicker for it. The colour and brightness of crowds, the adventure of a thousand changing encounters, the manifold vitality and companionship, all ' call us by the ear and eye.

WILDERNESS AND CITY

Alas for the disillusion of the city! From rural simplicities where sin and goodness alike were primitive, men have, not knowing what they did, massed themselves together in cities, and created a new type of human existence. This has brought a change upon every relation between man and man, and a still subtler change upon the very consciousness of the individual self. New and desperate problems have arisen, both moral and social. The work of man's hands has mastered him, and he frankly confesses that he does not understand it. The cities which he has built have turned upon him like Frankenstein's monster, and overwhelmed him in conditions which it will take many a year to reduce to anything like rightness or beauty. The city, seen from the wilderness, has given the world most of its Utopias, which have generally been written in rough times and inspired by contrast. But as men have entered the gates, successive generations have sadly found that it was not εὐτόπος, but οὐτόπος—not the 'fair city' but the 'nowhere' of dreams from which they have wakened.

Just at this point they again meet EVANGELIST, while still feeling the dreariness of the unreality behind them, and when about to face the more formidable unrealities that awaited their approach. They recognise him emphatically as a friend, although one of them at least has had a former meeting whose bitterness he has not forgotten. These men do not judge their acquaintance by mere pleasantness. All men are to them friends or enemies, according as they help or hinder their spirit and progress. No wonder if beyond all other friends they greet him who has set them both in the way.

This meeting with Evangelist is of great significance. It is not recorded in the first edition, but the maturer thought of the author gives to Evangelist a wider and more prominent sphere of work. This expansion of Evangelism from the call to repentance and the start of pilgrimage, to the larger task of 'the cure of souls,' is well worth noting. His work is not merely initiatory, as at the City of Destruction, or negative, as at Mount Sinai. It is the pastoral and positive work of one who is ever watchful over the souls of his converts. And yet it is but occasional. Bunyan's Evangelist is not continually interfering, nor undertaking the responsibilities of the whole life of the pilgrims. He has been busy with other duties, and among other souls. A touch now and then, a meeting at critical moments and then a parting,— these are the ways of Evangelist with his friends. He hears their story, speaks his words, and vanishes. There is a word of wisdom here for those who desire their spiritual guides to do for them the whole work of pilgrimage—a desire which has made the lives of some ministers an impossible and discouraging attempt to do more than can be done, and which has been responsible for much unjust criticism of the clerical profession.

The interview with Evangelist is a heart-searching one, as all meetings with old friends are, when men review earnestly the events of the interval since last they met. Yet this is a cheerful as well as a pathetic interview. Not only are they cheered by Evangelist: he is cheered by them. It is sometimes forgotten that the director of the souls of others has also a soul of his own—a soul which may at times be very much in need of cheer. This is a lonely man, who is glad of their friendship and goes away brighter for it. In his blessing on their helpers, we see how companionable is the man's view of life, and how generous and genuine his interest in their welfare. We are brought back here to the old strain, the value of encouragement. Shortly after the death of John Ruskin, the following appeared in a South African newspaper :—' Ruskin's great defect, it has been often remarked, is that he does not encourage enough. . . . A beautiful writer on art, its meaning and its lessons, but in

WILDERNESS AND CITY

matters social and political he has hardly a word of praise. He says much that is true in the condemnation of the faults and follies of men, but it is spoiled from want of a little praise. And he himself, in later years, has admitted this. " Ah, if I had known all this when I began to write," he says, in a pathetic statement referring to multitudes of letters he had received from various correspondents, " how differently I would have written. I see now that I might have touched very different strings, and have awakened better music." '

Evangelist's exhortations remind us strongly of Bunyan's *Heavenly Footman*, part of which was quoted in a previous chapter.[1] His language savours of the Heavenly Footman —soldier and sinner both. The soldier reminds them that they are not yet out of gunshot of the devil;[2] the sinner warns them to let nothing that is on this side of the other world get within them. And, besides these two, the *man* speaks. He is right glad of this thing, for his own sake as well as for theirs. He has felt his responsibility for souls in a way that only one who has identified himself with them can feel it, and he is relieved and glad to know of their success.

Offor sees in this exchange of the wilderness for the city a possible allusion to Bunyan's being set apart for the work of the ministry in 1656, as that event is narrated in *Grace Abounding*, and reminds us that ' the second address of Evangelist peculiarly relates to the miseries endured by Nonconformist ministers in the reign of Charles II.' ' Evangelist's address,' he says, ' would make a good outline for an ordination sermon.' But this second address, warning them of *Vanity Fair*, is of wider application. Every man who has in his communicants' class prepared young men and women for their first communion, has some searching and

---

[1] P. 171.
[2] In these words we surely recognise the voice of that redoubtable old fighting man of the Parliamentary Wars, Mr John Gifford.

peculiar memories as he reads this passage. He remembers the earnest faces, that were soon to look upon a world of which they were ignorant as yet. He remembers the change from those days of sincerity and eagerness to the gradually increasing carelessness that came as the world engrossed and dazzled them. He will warn his next class with a passionate urgency which they may not comprehend at the time, but whose meaning the world will afterwards interpret for them.

The prophecy of Faithful's death is full of the sound confidence which Christ gives to believers. Among the last words of Socrates were these : ' And now it is time that we have done. I go to die, you remain to live, but which of us goeth the better way, the gods only know.' Evangelist has heard from St Paul [1] which of the two went the better way. ' He that shall die there, although his death will be unnatural, and his pain perhaps great, he will yet have the better of his fellow.' The words remind us of the famous Scottish story of the same period, which tells how Peden, at the grave of Richard Cameron, cried, ' Oh, to be wi' Ritchie ! '

One of the reasons for this preference is striking—' He will be arrived at the Celestial City soonest.' Evangelist's appearances are curiously connected with cities—the City of Destruction, the Town of Morality, Vanity Fair, and the Celestial City. He is a man of the city, though we always meet with him in the open. He knows the evils of the city, and he knows them all the better by contrast with that ideal city, the true and eternal Utopia, in which his soul has its citizenship and home.[2]

---

[1] Phil. i. 23.

[2] Those who would further pursue the suggestions of this view of Evangelist should read the poem entitled *The City*, in Dr Bonar's *Hymns of Faith and Hope*.

CHAPTER XXII

VANITY FAIR

THE adventure of Vanity Fair is one of the permanent and priceless gifts of religion to literature. The world is very sensitive, and all ordinary and direct criticisms of it are keenly resented. But in this brilliant picture it has consented to recognise itself. The genius manifest alike in the name and in the description is so irresistible, the mingled sarcasm and pathos of the passages so true to life, that no course was open for the world but to adopt the title or to change its ways; and, when frankness and repentance were the only alternatives which John Bunyan had left to it, it boldly chose the former.

Bunyan's trade had led him to know well the COUNTRY FAIRS of his time and neighbourhood, and his natural disposition had led him to love them only too well. In the reign of Henry II. the nuns of Elstow received the right of holding an annual fair on Elstow Green, where the Moot Hall still stands, in which at these Fairs and at other times John Bunyan danced in his younger days. From *Horne's Yearbook*, published in 1786, we have the following graphic account of the Fair of Sturbridge, near Bedford:—'The shops or booths are built in rows like streets, having each its name; as Garlick Row, Booksellers' Row, Book Row, etc. Here are all sorts of traders, who sell by wholesale or retail; as goldsmiths, toymen, braziers, turners, milliners, haberdashers, hatters, mercers, drapers, pewterers, china warehouses, and, in a word, most trades that can be found in London. Here also are taverns, coffee-houses, and eating-houses in great plenty. The chief diversions are puppets, rope-dancing, and music-booths. To this fair, people from Bedfordshire and the adjoining counties still resort. Similar kinds of fairs are now kept at Frankfort and Leipzig. These mercantile fairs were very injurious to morals; but not to the extent of debauchery and villainy, which reign in our present annual fairs, near the metropolis and large cities.'[1]

John Bunyan has elsewhere expounded pretty fully his views on trade. In *The Holy War* we find that Mansoul was 'a market town, much given to commerce,' and so 'cumbered with abundance that they shall be forced to make their castle a warehouse.' In *The Life and Death of Mr Badman*, we have the exposition of an extraordinary number of mean tricks in petty commerce—tricks with weights and measures, with the manipulation of accounts, with dishonest bankruptcy, with selling under cost price, and so on. The lines laid down in that treatise by Mr Wiseman for christian trading would, we fear, be regarded in many quarters as naïve to-day: 'If thou sellest do not commend; if thou buyest do not dispraise, any otherwise but to give the thing that thou hast to do with its just value and worth. Art thou a seller and do things grow cheap? set not thy hand to help or hold them up higher. Art thou a buyer and do things grows dear? use no cunning or deceitful language to pull them down. Leave things to the Providence of God, and do thou with moderation submit to His hand.'[2]

Our walk through Vanity Fair fortunately does not lay upon us the duty of settling the relations between Providence and Political Economy. The main thing which the adventure stands for in the allegory is the change from inward to external life. This is the first crowd we meet with. The introspective aspect of christian life comes more naturally to the Puritan author, and he has kept largely to that. The

---

[1] For a fuller account of Sturbridge Fair, *cf.* Brown, *John Bunyan*, chap. xi.
[2] *The Life and Death of Mr Badman*, chap. xi.

THE
MOOT HALL,
ELSTOW

public aspect, however, must also be dealt with. The allegory has to locate this, and so it comes to pass that almost all the worldliness and folly which a Christian has to meet with in a lifetime is concentrated in the streets and buildings of this Fair. As it happens, this is a city—' the City of Destruction in gala dress,' and, as we have already noticed, there is here the contrast between city life and life on the highway. The passage is thus specially intended for young people coming from the country to the town, and for all who are called forth to more public situations in shop, factory, office, or university. Yet big cities are not the only places of worldliness, temptation, and sin. Vanity Fair is a relative idea, and all its deadliness and danger may be found in many a quite humble place. It may be, and often is, a country fair.

The picture is evidently intended to represent ' European society as it existed in the days of Charles II.'—honest and dishonest, quiet and outrageous alike. The various rows represent the types of worldliness cultivated by each of the several countries at that time. Yet certainly the special reference is to England. Cheever [1] quotes a remarkable passage from Hume, in which that historian sympathetically describes the relaxation of Puritan strictness at the Restoration: and in the figures of these two pilgrims austerely walking through the noisy streets of Vanity, we can see the forms of such men as Owen, Baxter, Goodwin, and Howe, walking apart amidst the dance of contemporary English life.[2] These plainly-clad men have long ago entered among the splendours of the Celestial City, and as we look back into the past, the sadness gathers not on them, but on the faded colours and quenched lights of the world from which they kept aloof. There is no pathos more tragic than that of an

---

[1] *Lectures on Bunyan,* p. 10.
[2] *Cf.* the Pilgrims' March sounding through the Venus-music in *Tannhäuser*

ancient Vanity Fair. As we walk through the streets of Pompeii or Herculaneum, as we pore over an old wood-engraving of the Villa of Mæcenas, or read such a poem as Browning's *Toccata of Galuppi's* we feel the full force of this. They were so intensely alive, those 'dear dead women' and men—and now they are so dead. More common than this sentiment of the Vanity Fairs of the past, is the habit of bringing Vanity Fair up to date, and describing it as it may be seen to-day. Thackeray's great classic is, of course, the supreme example of this.[1] But Hawthorne has done it in a few masterly touches which form the cleverest part of his Celestial Railroad. Cheever does it, allegorising on his own account in some striking pages; and indeed, the idea is too obvious to have been omitted by any commentator. It is noteworthy that in these modern versions the *religion* of Vanity Fair is usually marked out for special attention. Thackeray's worldly clergymen, Hawthorne's, and Cheever's, are all of the same school, to which belongs also Meredith's 'Rev. Groseman Buttermore.'[2]

Ancient and modern, Vanity Fair is to some a place of infinite boredom, and presents to them no temptation. To others it is so tempting as to utterly intoxicate them until they openly ask, 'If this be vanity, who'd be wise? Vanity let it be.' But the solemn lesson which Bunyan proclaims at the beginning in his 'lighter than vanity,' must be learned sooner or later. There is a tale of a great Italian lawyer, who had staked his fortune and career on a famous case he was to plead. In the pleading he surpassed himself, and all seemed secure. But in the progress of the case it became clear that he had based his whole argument on the mistaken reading of a statute. At first he resisted the conviction, but eventually he saw that it was so indeed. In bitterness he

---

[1] *Cf.* an amusing anecdote told by Dr Brown, *John Bunyan*, chap. xix.
[2] *One of our Conquerors*

turned to leave the court, and as he passed they heard him say, 'World, I've found thee out!' To which may be added the words of Thackeray, in which he describes Miss Crawley's illness: 'Picture to yourself, O fair young reader, a worldly, selfish, graceless, thankless, religionless old woman, writhing in pain and fear, and without her wig. Picture her to yourself, and, ere you be old, learn to love and pray.'[1]

THE LORD OF THIS FAIR is the fiend Beelzebub. It is characteristic of Bunyan that, in spite of his abnormally developed imagination and the literary fashion of his day, his demonology is so restrained. We have already pointed out, that while Milton's Satan, sometimes indeed represented as a toad or reptile, is sometimes a really great and magnificently princely figure, no devil of John Bunyan's is ever admirable. His Beelzebub is purposely kept out of sight. We see his works, and hear his laughter from the empty air or behind the wall, but himself we do not see. But he is always loathsome, despicable, and hated with a deadly hate. He is liker Luther's devil than Milton's—not a literary creation, but a terrifying memory of experience. Bunyan could never have drawn Mephistopheles, that 'familiarly devilish' creation of Goethe's. His Beelzebub is indeed a monarch of vast power. Yet the emphasis is always laid not so much on the power as on the malignancy of it, and on the despicable meanness of its exercise. He is coarse and scoundrelly, nearer Milton's toad than his archfiend. The weird conception of the city owned by a devil reminds us of Victor Hugo's *Notre Dame,* and of one especially of the carved demons whose stony leer, as he looks down upon the city, seems still to say, 'It is mine, and I shall claim my own.'

The bitter words of Tacitus come to mind as we read the list of wares exposed for sale, that 'at Rome anything might be bought for money.' There is the same combination of solid

Vanity Fair, chap. xiv.

material reality and meretricious brilliance, which always characterises 'the picture of the Pursuit of Pleasure. It needs some strength of moral fibre to resist the power of that combination, and in Part III. it is a stroke almost of genius that makes Yielding mistake this Fair for the Celestial City, and forthwith enter a tavern, where he gets drunk and dies in the night.

Beelzebub 'governs by amusing' like a sort of infernal music-hall manager. It is a secret that can always be made profitable. It was the policy of the later Roman Empire, as the ruined amphitheatres that lie on the hillsides of many lands still attest. In every age when the disease of pleasure-loving has become epidemic in certain sections of the community, Beelzebub and his representatives find that he who can amuse can rule. The appeal to the lust of pleasure is a potent force in politics as well as elsewhere, and Vanity Fair stands for great and terrible facts in public life. 'There was a sort of stock or scrip called Conscience,' says the author of the *Celestial Railroad*, ' which seemed to be in great demand and would purchase almost anything. Indeed, few rich commodities were to be obtained without paying a heavy sum in this particular stock, and a man's business was seldom very lucrative unless he knew precisely when and how to throw his hoard of Conscience into the market. . . . Occasionally a member of Congress recruited his pocket by the sale of his constituents, and I was assured that public officers have often sold their country at very moderate prices. . . . Tracts of land and golden mansions situate in the Celestial City were often exchanged at very disadvantageous rates for a few years' lease of small, dismal, inconvenient tenements in Vanity Fair. . . . I once had the pleasure to see him [Beelzebub] bargaining with a miser for his soul, which, after much ingenious skirmishing on both sides, His Highness succeeded in obtaining at about the value of sixpence. The prince remarked, with a smile, that he was a loser by the transaction.'

Every word of Bunyan's strange CATALOGUE OF SALE has public or private history behind it. One has not to seek long among the records of European diplomacy to find the names of countries that have been bought and sold. As to wives and husbands, the story of Buonaparte and Josephine is but a conspicuous instance of much that is done in humbler places. Richter, in his *Levana*, describes the tricks of the matrimonial market not too bitterly when he speaks of fashionable mothers and daughters who sacrifice hearts to gain a fashionable alliance as 'shooting wildfowl with diamonds.' As to the 'souls' that were for sale, that is the ghastliest touch of all, and the most patent fact.

One article of commerce is omitted, and yet it is implicit in all the rest. In *Grace Abounding* we read that John Bunyan's great temptation at one time was 'To sell and part with this most blessed Christ, to exchange Him for the things of this life, for anything.' It was this suggestion that became for a whole year almost an insanity with Bunyan, so that 'I could neither eat my food, stoop for a pin, chop a stick, or cast mine eyes to look on this or that, but still the temptation would come, "Sell Christ for this, or sell Christ for that; sell Him, sell Him."' There is no word of this in the present passage, yet this is what it all implies. The men were very poor. Their one possession was Christ. Would they play the part of Judas? Put thus, the temptation seems so disproportionate and monstrously unreasonable that one would think it must cease to be a temptation at all. Yet many men do actually sell Christ for trifles offered in their own Vanity Fair, and that is often a pitiable market enough.

The rows are national in their names, every country having its own form of Vanity. But Rome receives special notice, in view of the struggles of the time between the fashionable ritualism and the unfashionable Protestant worship. Perhaps there may be an allusion to the sale of indulgences, but more probably the reference is to sensuous as opposed to spiritual ways of religion. If the sneer at Rome seem to some uncalled for, it is to be remembered that this was written during the reign of that King of England who ' was crowned in his youth with the Covenant in his hand, and died with the Host sticking in his throat.'

Their way lay just through this town of Vanity. Not that there were not other ways, as in the case of the Hill Difficulty, which would have led them round the walls. Every religious faith has found it necessary to provide for the unsocial and ascetic moods of its professors. The Roman faith has done this by its conventual and hermitage life ; the Protestant by such hymns as Cowper's—

> ' Far from the world, O Lord, I flee
> From strife and tumult far,
> From scenes where Satan wages still
> His most successful war.'

These ways of evading the world are tempting enough at times. As occasional luxuries, they are not only legitimate but very helpful, as one of these Pilgrims had already found in the House Beautiful. But in the main, the way lies up the face of Hill Difficulty and just through Vanity Fair. If it were not so, Satan would always and everywhere ' wage his most successful war.' As Bunyan reminds us, Jesus Christ Himself had found His course to lie that way ; and tempted men may well tremble to think what would have been the consequence to them if He had avoided the danger of the direct path. When, however, we try to translate our allegory into plain terms, and inquire into the meaning of this walk just through the Fair, we find ourselves at once among subtle questions of casuistry. If it be the mark of a Christian to be obviously and violently different from the world, the easy expedient of nonconformity in every detail of speech, manner, and conduct is open to him. So we have at once that fantastic and exaggerated mannerism which advertises a peculiar people. The solution of the problem seems to be that nonconformity, as well as conformity, may be a snare to Christian men. Either, when it becomes an end in itself, is a means of 'taking the eye off the object.' Looking to Jesus, and to the straight path of His will, one learns to disregard the conventionalities either of the world or of its enemies, to judge each detail of conduct by one's own light, and so to be original in the sense of direct dealing with conscience and with God. While this is so upon essential matters, one finds, as a rule, that in things non-essential the most profitable and worthy course is that which is the least conspicuous. There is no virtue in my painting my front door black because my godless neighbour happens to have painted his door red.

THESE MEN, however, walking through the street with no parade of protest or of difference, soon attracted the notice of the natives. It is surely an insecure condition of affairs in which men raise a hubbub because somebody they have met is unlike themselves. There is not so much to break the monotony of life for most of us that we should so resent an innovation *a priori*. It is to be feared that a restless conscience must have been at work here to account for the attack. Three points of difference had attracted their attention.

1. *Their raiment.* 'You, sir, I entertain for one of my Hundred; only, I do not like the fashion of your garments: you will say, they are Persian; but let them be changed.'[1] It is curious that after the fight with Apollyon, we never again hear of Christian's armour. The exigencies of the allegory are sufficient to explain this, and we may conceive of the two

[1] *King Lear*, quoted in Robert Browning's *Ferishtah's Fancies*.

in Vanity Fair clad in those robes of righteousness which the shining one gives to pilgrims at the Cross.

There is nothing in which, then and now, there has been less freedom of action than in the wearing of clothes. Men are accustomed to imagine that the bondage of fashion in dress is a weakness exclusively cultivated by the other sex. Let any man to-day dress himself in the Early Victorian garments of John Leech's pictures, and venture but once down the quietest street in his district, and he will find himself less emancipated than he thought. In his *Foundations of Belief*, Mr A. J. Balfour has a clever and instructive passage upon fashions in dress,[1] which is not without its bearing upon this part of the *Pilgrim's Progress*. In Bunyan's day the Puritan was a marked man by his dress, and no doubt this picture is drawn directly from the life.

Yet it was not merely the cut of the Pilgrims' garments which disgusted these well-dressed people. They wore old and tattered garments—a thing inexcusable in the streets of any self-respecting community. Yet old and tattered flags are hung in cathedrals, and if the uniform of a soldier returning from the wars excites the ridicule of dandies who have been hanging about the ante-chambers of the Court while he was fighting for them—well, so much the worse for the dandies. There is many a lad and many a girl whose clothes are worn till they are shabby, that they may help their parents, or contribute towards the scanty income of the amily. And there is many a life that is intellectually and artistically threadbare because it has spent itself in ministries that left no time for self-culture.

But besides all this, which, after all, is accidental, the very act of the robe of righteousness is an offence to the men of the world. With all its tinsel, their clothing is not keeping out the rain or the wind from them, and they know well enough

---

[1] Part i. chap. ii.; *cf.* also Carlyle's *Sartor Resartus*.

which is the better cloth when they see men protected by it from the weather.

All these things offended the men of the Fair, and so they called the Pilgrims ' Bedlams.' It is an easy taunt, this name of lunatic. In most men's mouths it means simply ' different from myself,' or at most ' unlike other people.' The Pharisees used it of the Master Himself; and their descendants, and the populace who echo their words, still use it of His followers. It is a taunt very hard to bear. A man who can be indifferent to scurrility and immune to the vilest slanders, may yet feel it almost intolerable to find himself not taken seriously at all. Those are wise who remember that this accusation of lunacy is double-edged. Either they or their accusers are beside themselves. And the taunt often expresses nothing more than a shrewd suspicion on the part of those who use it, that their own judgment is not too securely seated. God has, after all, set Eternity in the hearts of men, and people who live for the things of time, in those few years that are so obviously hastening into the unknown, can hardly escape such doubts in their bad quarters of an hour.

2. The pilgrims' *speech* also irritated them. The men of the fair doubtless said that it was their Puritan drawl which got upon their nerves, and that they disliked men who talked sanctimoniously. But it was such speech as that which he had heard the poor women of Bedford use that Bunyan meant, of which he says that ' they were to me as if they had found a new world.'[1] That was the real trouble of it—the feel of a new world. Vanity Fair is above all things provincial, a place of the narrowest outlook and the most intensely local spirit. In its littleness and vulgarity it resents and despises everything foreign, and those who know something of the true breadth of the world of human interests are sure to offend its insularity.

[1] *Cf.* p. 97.

3. *The pilgrims set light by their wares.* There is a touch from real life, for we are told that Holy Hunt of Hitchin, a friend of Bunyan's, passing the market-place where mountebanks were performing, one cried after him, ' Look there, Mr Hunt!' Turning his head another way, he replied, 'Turn away mine eyes from beholding vanity.' If it be replied that Holy Hunt of Hitchin was perhaps an unlikely person to judge fairly of such things as Art, or Literature, or Science, and that these also are good gifts of God, and may be looked on as the inheritance of His saints, Bunyan's reply is in his Pilgrims' words, ' We buy the Truth.' The finest gifts of the world may or may not be part of the Truth. It is easy for the inhabitants to speak of them in lofty and solemn terms as the true gifts of Heaven. But all depends upon whether they are seen and sought after in the light of time or in the light of Eternity. ' Truth,' as has been memorably said, ' is the cry of all, but the game of only a few.' Vanity Fair, seeking eagerly after many good things as well as many bad ones, seeks them only for the enrichment and pleasure of this earthly life. That motive turns them at best into half-truths, which for practical purposes, and in their effect on the spirit, become the most dangerous kinds of lies.

It is no wonder that this retort angered the townsmen. Had the Pilgrims called their ideals wicked, they would have cared less. But to call them false—empty and passing shows, which none but deluded men would follow as they were doing —that touched their vanity and struck home.

Very striking and far-reaching in its suggestiveness is this conception of the Christian's course as a lifelong purchase of truth. It reminds us of the pilgrimage of Piers the Plowman, and the Castle of Truth to which it led. Half-truths and lies, which can pass the hour pleasantly, are always cheap: truth is dear, and may be had only at a great price. The searcher for truth, whether it be scientific or religious, always finds it costly. The poem, *A Grammarian's Funeral*, is Browning's great statement of its price. It costs prejudice, self-will, and habits of thought that have to be surrendered; pleasures and much time that have to be sacrificed; health perhaps, and inclination certainly, if study is to be efficient. Those who buy the truth are a standing conscience to all intellectual, moral, and spiritual dilettantes.

CHAPTER XXIII

VANITY FAIR—THE PERSECUTION

'THEY that were appointed to examine' the pilgrims began their examination by beating them and besmearing them with dirt. This auspicious beginning was an excellent prophecy of the end. Evidently such an examination would not largely contribute to the world's information upon any subject except the state of the examiners' minds. An ancient Board of Examiners began their investigation into a case of reported resurrection from the dead by a resolution ' to put Lazarus to death.' Dr Dods has compared that resolution to the conduct of a Hindoo pundit who smashed the microscope which had showed him that his theory of the universe was absurd. For the eliciting of truth, it is a senseless method. From the examiners' point of view, even in Vanity Fair, the beating was a mistake. The besmearing of them with mud was a much more clever line of action. To impute motives, to raise slanders without authentication, to mingle the names of the men with the general idea of hypocrisy, was an effective policy. The populace soon tires of the spectacle of strangers being flogged; but mud-throwing saves it the trouble of thinking, relieves it from the responsibility of judging upon evidence, and, by rendering the victims contemptible, sets it free to enjoy the lust of cruelty.

THE CAGE into which the prisoners were next thrust brings us back to one of the primitive methods which were fashionable in the ' good old days' for dealing with crime. Victor Hugo, in his *Notre Dame*,[1] vividly describes the rat-hole and

---
[1] Book vi., chap. ii. *Cf. Hudibras*, Part i. canto ii.

VANITY FAIR—THE PERSECUTION

the pillory of a still earlier century. Such a cage is still to be seen at Wootton, a village about three miles from Elstow.[1] Dr Whyte, identifying the cage in modern times with the newspapers, gives us a very suggestive and convincing reminder that it is the forms rather than the essences of things that have changed in these enlightened days. The mingled impertinence and indecency of this method of dealing with persons or views which happen to be obnoxious to us, is sufficiently evident. Emphasise the fact that your victim is in your power, and quench pity by rendering his situation ridiculous, and you may go great lengths in gratifying your thirst for revenge. There are still such cages, set up in homes, workshops, churches, theatres, and, indeed, in all public and private places. David Scott, in his picture of this scene, has reminded us of the variety of types of human nature to which such an opportunity for malice as the cage affords may appeal. The philosopher is there—a modern Diogenes in his tub—the fop, the monk, the mother with her child. It is a sad account of poor human nature! One thing, however, must be added. There are cages like this which man constructs for his brother man, and there are other cages which a man constructs for himself. The man in the iron cage was a still more pitiable spectacle than those two. But he had put himself on exhibition.

The essential element in the punishment of the cage is enforced publicity. But that is always a dangerous weapon to use against a man. By degrees, the good as well as the evil in him will become conspicuous and impressive, and if there be much good evident there will certainly be a reaction of public feeling against those who encaged him. Daniel Defoe, in the pillory, found himself a hero enthroned rather than a martyr or a victim—so thoroughly had he won the favour of the English public.[2] These pilgrims, whose crime

[1] Foster, *Bunyan's Country*, p. 112.
[2] Mrs Oliphant, *The Reign of Queen Anne*, p. 307.

was actually their innocence of crime, were bound to win in the end. They were a standing testimony to the fact that evil may be overcome with good. If a persecuted and slandered man will be brave enough to keep on his way, and to preserve his magnanimity, and watch for chances of helping his maligners, he is sure to have the best of it when truth comes to its own.

So it happened here, and, without meaning to do it, the prisoners won in Vanity Fair a party of men who began to reflect that there were some in the Fair more worthy to be put in the cage than these. The silent testimony of consistent character is bound to have its effect. The conscience of such as have a conscience is on the side of character, and the intelligence of such as have intelligence. From the days of Nicodemus and Gamaliel until now, Christianity has had in the Sanhedrim friends to protest against persecution.

The paragraph beginning ' Here, therefore, they called again to mind what they had heard from their faithful friend Evangelist,' does not occur in the first edition. With time, the importance of Evangelist and his interventions increased in the view of John Bunyan, and with time also there seems to have come a greater tendency to dwell more upon the advantages of death over life for those who believe, for in this paragraph we also read that ' each man secretly wished that he might have that preferment '—*i.e.* of martyrdom.

This is touching, although it is neither a very safe nor wholesome line of thought. In *Grace Abounding*, we find sometimes the expression of Bunyan's longing to die at once, that he might be out of danger. In other Christian lives it has run to a far greater extreme, and if any one is repelled by morbidness here, let him read the Epistles of Ignatius that he may see how much reserve Bunyan has after all been exercising. These epistles, in which the craving for martyrdom has come to be of the nature of a monomania, show us noble courage degenerating into sentimentality, and even threatening to become a kind of inhuman and unclean passion. It is never safe for the spiritual balance of any man to go out of his way to meet an enemy, a trouble, or a temptation. Bunyan, however, was saved from such excess by his natural sanity and his fine instinctive sense of proportion. And this touch, in which the shadow of death falls so unmistakably upon the story before the beginning of the trial, has the power of a great unconscious artistry in it. The story is one of heroic courage and faithfulness unto death, and we hear it with the laughter of Vanity Fair in our ears. It reminds us of the famous English story of Captain Douglas going down in the Thames with the ship which the Dutch had set on fire, while at Whitehall King Charles II. was chasing butterflies with his ladies.[1] It reminds us of an older scene, where Jesus fasted and fought out His battle against the world and its ideals on the mountain of Quarantana, while below, almost within earshot, the Court of Herod feasted with wild revelries at Jericho.

THE TRIAL.—How far John Bunyan was writing his account of this imprisonment and trial with his own experiences of English law and justice in his mind, it would be difficult to say. Opinion is divided as to what these experiences actually were, and Mr Froude takes a much less serious view of his sufferings than Bunyan himself took. This, however, is not very convincing, as Mr Froude's views on many things are so much less serious than John Bunyan's. Readers will decide for themselves, but it is certainly worth while to compare chapter vi. of Mr Froude's *Bunyan* with Bunyan's own accounts of the events narrated in that chapter.

It would not be easy to show that this trial is point by point modelled on Bunyan's own examinations. One of

[1] R. L. Stevenson, *The English Admirals: cf.* Pepys' *Diary.*

Bunyan's judges, Sir John Keelynge, has been supposed to stand for Hate-good, and it is interesting to note that even the dispassionate Pepys speaks of one of his judgments as 'a horrid shame.' There is, indeed, the same freedom of repartee between examiner and prisoner, and there is the same boldness of statement in dangerous circumstances. But the model for the passage is almost certainly that of Judge Jeffreys' courts, and parts of this account are almost literal reproductions of the trial of Algernon Sidney.[2] The outburst of the judge, ' Sirrah, sirrah, thou deservest to live no longer,' etc., is exactly in the manner of Jeffreys.

In the history of persecution[3] there have been two kinds of trial. Some prisoners have been (as in the ancient days of 'Diana or Christ') urged to recant, and unwillingly condemned. Others have been, as in this case, tried ' in order to their condemnation.' Witches used to be thrown into deep water by way of ordeal, and the ingenious mind of the times decided that if they were innocent they would sink and be drowned, while if they floated they were guilty and must be hanged. Faithful's trial was one of this kind. His condemnation was a foregone conclusion, and this must be remembered in judging of his answers to the charges brought against him. His blunt outspokenness, which we have already noticed in his dealings with Talkative, has already the crackle of the faggots in it.[4] It has been argued that ' a prisoner who admits that he has taught the people that their Prince ought to be in hell, and has called the judge an ungodly villain, cannot complain if he is accused of preaching rebellion.'[5]

[1] Pepys' *Diary*, 23rd October 1667-8.
[2] *Cf.* Macaulay's *History*.
[3] *Cf.* Lecky, *The Rise and Influence of Rationalism*, chap. iv.
[4] *Cf.* Mrs Oliphant's saying of William Penn, ' Not much wonder if they sent him to Newgate; for the pestilent fellow was generally in the right.' *The Reign of Queen Anne*, p. 163.
[5] Froude, *Bunyan*, chap. ix.

That is true, but besides the fact of Faithful's constitutional directness of speech, it should be remembered that whatever he had said, the end would have been his burning, and that he knew it.

This trial stands in interesting contrast with that reported in the *Holy War*, where the prisoners are the aldermen of Diabolus, Mr Atheism, Mr Incredulity, Mr Lustings, Mr Forget-good, Mr Hardheart, Mr False-peace, etc. That trial is careful in its detail, dignified and constitutional. This one is rushed with indecent haste, the judge being so eager to get to the condemnation that he forgets to administer the oath to a witness, and is only reminded of the omission by the witness's eagerness to ruin the prisoner, leading him to strengthen his assertion by making it ' on oath ' without being asked to do so.

The indictment [1] here bears a curious resemblance to two others. John Bunyan's own indictment in 1661 was that ' he hath devilishly and perniciously abstained from coming to church to hear divine service, and is a common upholder of several unlawful meetings and conventicles, to the great disturbance and distraction of the good subjects of this kingdom, contrary to the laws of our sovereign lord the King,' etc. The indictment in the *Holy War* is: ' Thou art here indicted by the name of Haughty, an intruder upon the town of Mansoul, for that thou didst most traitorously and devilishly teach the town of Mansoul to carry it loftily and stoutly against the summons that was given them by the captain of the King,' etc. There is one noteworthy omission from the present indictment—that of the word ' devilishly.' The reason for it is obvious. In Vanity Fair the prince and the devil are one.

[1] The indictment might have been more frivolous than it was, and still have been true to contemporary facts. Dr Brown (*John Bunyan*, chap. i.) mentions the case of a woman who was excommunicated for having attended the funeral of her own husband.

The first count in this indictment was that Faithful had disturbed trade. This is an old story. From the earliest days of Christianity, persecution has grown acute when commerce felt the touch of the new doctrines. It is said that among the first opponents of Christianity were the sellers of hay for the beasts of sacrifice in Ephesus. The image-makers of Ephesus, and the men whose hope of gains lay in the Philippian damsel with the spirit of divination, were those who first framed this charge against Faithful.[1] Bunyan's lawyers have certainly not been the last to frame it.

The second charge was that of stirring up commotion. The placid life of the Fair, where men lived on such particularly easy terms with one another and with themselves, was now no longer possible. It is a serious thing to stir up strife, and in itself it is certainly no sign of grace. Some dispositions have a positive genius for it, and their religious principles are firebrands in the community, or home, or workshop, until the place is habitable only when they have been got rid of. Enemies may indeed be a sign of righteousness, but they may also be a sign of rudeness, unpleasantness, and conceit. But there is a difference to be observed here between the various qualities of peace which may be thus disturbed. If the peace is that of honest and companionable men, each in his own fashion striving to follow God and righteousness in friendship with his neighbours, then the disturbance of it is a crime, even if it be in the name of Christ. But if the peace be, as in this case it was, nothing better than drugged conscience, both in individuals and in the community, then the sooner it is disturbed the better for all concerned.

The third charge was that of having won a party to their opinions—not so much a new charge as a new aspect of

[1] Acts xvi. 19; xix. 24.

the second. To win a party is to confirm that state of commotion and strife which they had made, and to perpetuate it. But whether this be a virtue or a crime depends simply on the rightness or wrongness of the views they hold. There is all the difference in the world between the case of proselytisers winning a party for self-will, and truth winning a party for itself.

The main note of this trial is that all the personages introduced in it, except the prisoners, are bad. When such men as these are in the places of responsibility, ' the post of honour is a private station.' ' Such a verdict from such a jury,' is indeed itself an honour and a testimonial to any good man. But the whole malice and wickedness of the court is summed up in the name of the judge—*Hate-good*. A whole theology, a whole psychology and ethical philosophy, as well as a deep and thorough knowledge of the Scriptures, are wrapped up in that name. The judge, indeed, had his human models —Judge Jeffreys beyond all, whose savage cruelty, bullying, and undisguised injustice have branded not himself only, but the age in which he was possible, for all time to come. Yet that ferocity, which is said to have kindled a light in his eyes while he was condemning, that lust for railing which found in the enforced deference of a court of justice an opportunity for its atrocious and filthy gratification, seem to be phenomena that recur. Every now and then history produces a man whom a little brief authority affects in this fashion. Stevenson's picture of Lord Braxfield and his ' hanging face,' and his taunting of his victims, will recur to the minds of many.[1] Fortunately for our country, such cases owe something of their conspicuousness, and the mark they have made upon the imagination of the land, to their rarity. Such a judge is here fitly chosen as the type and pattern of the Master-Sin. Hatred of good—that is sin at the black

[1] *Weir of Hermiston.*

THE ROAD

heart and essence of it. Stripped of excuses and explanations, seen directly and with the severe eyes of conscience, the moral problem is a simple one. Good is set before us, and we have to say whether it shall be loved and chosen, or hated and rejected. To see the alternative clearly, and to say, with Milton's Satan, 'Evil be thou my good,' is to have expressed the supreme and lordly sin, to have deliberately adopted a sin against the Holy Ghost. We have already overheard Apollyon's frank profession of such sin—'I am an enemy to this prince: I hate his person, his laws, and his people.'[1] Judge Hate-good has been an excellent learner in that school of the devil. This judge is a type which stands for the evil element that is in us all. In every court of judgment of the soul, where we pronounce upon the character of men or things, there are two voices that may be heard from the bench. Hate-good and Love-good both are there. Hate-good has the richer ermine and the louder voice; Love-good speaks too often inaudibly, like one who apologises. Yet where there is a mind open for the truth, the gentle speaker will have most authority. Behind these two are the protagonists whom they love and hate—Good and Evil. He is wise who looks beyond the appearances of their representatives to these supreme facts of this world and the next, who boldly commits himself to the side of Good, and dares to make Evil his enemy.[2]

The three witnesses may possibly be portraits also. John Bunyan had had wide experience of misrepresentation, and could write on such a subject with authority. 'Therefore,' he says, 'I bind these lies and slanders to me as an ornament; it belongs to my Christian profession to be vilified, slandered, reproached, and reviled; and since all this is nothing else, as my God and conscience do bear me witness, I rejoice in reproaches for Christ's sake.' The most trying element in

[1] *Cf.* p. 136. [2] *Cf.* p. 131.

such witness, however, is the subtle fashion in which truth and falsehood are interwoven in it. It is true that—

> 'A lie which is all of a lie may be met and fought with outright,
> But a lie which is part a truth is a harder matter to fight.' [1]

The words of the three witnesses are little more than a paraphrase of Faithful's own confessions. Yet they have the subtle power of putting every detail into a base instead of a heroic light. This is the fine art of lying.

Envy [2] is the first of them, and he is so eager to speak that he is already in the full swing of his address (for such it is) before the judge remembers that the oath has not been administered. The name is suggestive. Whom did this man envy? There can be no question as to the answer. He envied Faithful. He envied him those 'principles of faith and holiness' at which he was sneering. He envied the man who, he swore, was 'one of the vilest men in our country.' He said these things because he envied him. His tongue was bitter because his heart was sore. In fact, men often envy Christians, although they refuse to have that for which they envy them. To know that another has the best of it, and yet to love that which you know to be worse, is a state of mind in which all that is false and bitter in human nature comes to its strength. Yet, if we could but remember it, that strength is but labour and sorrow, and no one deserves a man's pity so deeply as he who thus envies him. All who have had much experience in dealing with men must remember case after case in which the first bitterness and defiance has broken down suddenly into the confession of a heart miserably sore and empty. Poor Envy! he will envy Faithful more even than to-day, when he sees the faggots kindled for his burning.

The next witness was *Superstition*. They had a religion

---

[1] Tennyson, *The Grandmother*.
[2] *Cf. John Bunyan*, by the author of *Mark Rutherford*, p. 184

in Vanity Fair, and Superstition was its representative supporter. It was a religion of observances, whose demands were ceremonial, and which made no claim either on the conscience, the heart, or the intellect. It would have been interesting to overhear that reported conversation between Faithful and Superstition. Men talking two different languages could not have been more unintelligible to one another. The ritualist, with his mingled haughtiness and fear, is proud of his assertion that he neither knew, nor desired to know, the man he is helping to condemn. He does not like to think out problems, and his accusation amounts to little more than a general impression that Faithful had been attacking his religion. The sketch is drawn with Bunyan's usual insight.

Pickthank is the last witness. It is always painful to hear the words of good men reported by the bad. The report seems to rob them of their dignity, and give to them an evil infection. An old author has said of this passage that what Pickthank had heard Faithful say was, ' Other lords besides thee have had dominion over us, but by thee only will we make mention of thy name.' Pickthank, unlike Superstition, has known the prisoner a long time. And all that long time he has been watching for opportunities of stirring up personal animosities against Faithful, for ends of his own. ' It was his practice,' says Stevenson of one of his characters, ' to approach any one person at the expense of some one else. He offered you an alliance against the some one else; he flattered you by slighting him; you were drawn into a small intrigue against him before you knew how. Wonderful are the virtues of this process generally.' [1] True, no doubt, so far; and yet this way of making friends of the mammon of unrighteousness is not without its dangers. He who retails cutting words against another, associates himself with these

[1] *Weir of Hermiston,* chap. vii.

words and with the resentment they waken, and seldom is better loved for it in the end.

As we read over the atrocious list of impartial fellow-citizens who constitute the jury, we feel that all hope for Faithful may now be abandoned. It is like a man about to be tried by the verdict of a lunatic asylum. Carlyle's words come to mind, when he says in *Past and Present*, 'Do but contrast this Oliver with my right honourable friend Sir Jabesh Windbag, Mr Facing-Both-Ways, Viscount Mealy-mouth, Earl of Windlestraw.'[1] This jury is but a repetition, in other personalities, of the combined characters of the judge and witnesses. It is peculiarly interesting to remember that, 'These words and this trial were quoted (January 25, 1848) by the Attorney-General, in Westminster Hall, in answer to the manner in which Dr Hampden was then charged with heresy by the Puseyites.'[2]

The jurymen have their little remarks to make, each characteristic of the speaker, like Mr Blindman's 'I see clearly.' Mr No-good is of the family of the judge; Messrs Love-lust and Live-loose remind us of Faithful's early temptations. Mr Highmind, whose satisfactory and final opinion is embodied in the words 'a sorry scrub,' has caught the ear of Robert Browning for one of the pleasantries in his *Andrea del Sarto*.

THE END OF THE TRIAL was inevitable, and Faithful, as has been already indicated, may have felt the freer in his replies from the consideration that his death was already resolved on. The detailed circumstances of the execution may all be found in Foxe. But the chariot and horses come from an older book. To Bunyan, as he looked on at that judicial murder,

[1] *Past and Present*, p. 191.
[2] Offor, *sub loco*. The reference is to the saying of Mr Blindman, 'I see clearly that this man is a heretic.'

was given the power of seeing the invisible, with which Elisha's servant had been gifted long ago.[1] It was the martyrs' secret also, and nothing short of it could have explained the long story of their courage and endurance. The late Bishop Paget has a memorable passage in which he describes the Christian martyr waiting under the scowl of a hostile sea of faces, for the coming in of the lions.[2] In no words could the impression be better conveyed of a soul that saw beyond and above the world. A very striking poem, recently published, is applicable here :—

> 'They wore their wounds like roses
> Who died at morningtide.
> From Youth's enchanted closes,
> From loves that did adore them,
> With perfumes broken o'er them
> As bridegroom goes to bride,
> They rode the Flaming Ride.
> They wore their wounds like roses
> Who in their morning died.'[3]

So ended the earthly pilgrimage of Faithful. There are words in Bunyan's *House of Lebanon* which have been aptly applied to him : ' Was not this man, think you, a giant ? Did he not behave himself valiantly ? Was not his mind elevated a thousand degrees beyond sense, carnal reason, fleshly love, and the desires of embracing temporal things ? This man had got *that* by the end that pleased him ; neither could all the flatteries, promises, threats, reproaches make him once listen to or inquire after what the world or the glory of it could afford. His mind was captivated with delights invisible. He coveted to show his love to his Lord by laying down his life for His sake. He longed to be where there

[1] 2 Kings vi. 17. Contrast this with Bunyan's confession of his fear of execution, or rather of his fear as to his power to face it bravely, in which occurs the great sentence, 'I was ashamed to die with a pale Face and tottering Knees for such a cause as this.' *Grace Abounding.*
[2] *Faculties and Difficulties of Belief and Disbelief*, pp. 41, 42.
[3] Rachel Annand Taylor, *Rose and Vine*, p. 115.

shall be no more pain, nor sorrow, nor sighing, nor tears, nor troubles. He was a man of a thousand.' . . . 'These men had the faces of lions, they have triumphed in the flames.'

Christian was spared for further pilgrimage. The close of persecutions is generally as unaccountable as their origin.[1] Political motives enter, the reaction and disgust of public opinion, and the actual advantage to the cause which is attacked, all contribute to this result. Yet Christian felt that Faithful had the best of it. At least his was the easier part. While he had mounted up with wings as eagles, Christian must yet for a long while walk and not faint.

[1] *Cf.* Brown, *John Bunyan*, chap. ix.

END OF VOL. I.

INDEX

INDEX

ABBOTT, Dr, 105.
Accidia, 142, 174.
Adam the First, 169.
Allegory, 38, 160, 161.
Amusement, 208.
Angels, 71, 97, 189.
Aquinas, Thomas, 193.
Arbour, the, 89.
Armour, Chaps. xiv., xv.
Arnold, Matthew, 16, 18, 57, 99, 168, 173, 185.
Arthur, King, Chaps. xiv., xv.
Asceticism, 210.
Assurance (*cf.* Roll), 73.
Aurelius, Marcus, 21.
Austerity, 38, 168.
Authority, 35 f., 80 f., 115.
Ayala, 1.

BACON, Sir Francis, 97, 213.
Bain, Dr Kerr, 5, 26, 42, 100, 118, 128, 129, 136, 154, 156, 161, 175, 179.
Balfour, A. J., 212.
Beautiful, the House, Chap. xix. ff.
Bedford, 20, 56, 75, 93, 96.
Bedford, poor women of, 96, 213.
Bengel, 35.
Benson, A. C., 164.
Beowulf, 130, 162.
Bevis of Hampton, 124 ff., 154, 157.
Bible, the, 3, 22, 29 f., 56 f., 113 f., 120, 168, 169, 185.
Bismarck, 140.
Bonar, Dr H., 71, 202.
Book of Sports, 109.
Borrow, George, 142.
Bradford, John, 45.
Brontë, Charlotte, 146.
Brown, Dr John (Life of Bunyan), 40, 56, 86, 88, 94, 113, 114, 129, 131, 153, 155, 206, 221, 229.
Browne, Sir Thomas, 124.
Browning, E. B., 24, 65.
Browning, Robert, 5, 8, 10, 15, 21, 24, 36, 52, 64, 67, 72, 76, 84, 85, 88, 91, 112, 116, 134, 146, 163, 174, 182, 206, 211, 215, 227.
Bruce, Dr A. B., 150.
Bunyan, John, as poet, 54, 112, 151, 176.
—— as soldier, 114, 118, 201.
—— examination of, 30, 88, 107, 216 ff., 221.

Bunyan, John, other works (*cf.* Holy War) 94, 96, 110, 116, 118, 125, 129, 131, 155, 167, 171, 187, 189, 196, 201, 204, 228.
Burden, Christian's, 3, 4, 27, 47.
Burke, Edmund, 187.
Burns, Robert, 4, 73, 100.
Butler, Bishop, 36, 164, 195.
Butterworth, John, 37.

CAGE, the, 216 f.
Carlyle, Thomas, 9, 79, 114, 143, 149 150, 227.
Catechism, The Larger, 95.
Catechism, The Shorter, 41.
Certainty, 17, 18, 29, 30.
Cervantes, 1.
Charity, 107.
Charles II., 219.
Chaucer, 2, 14, 60, 103, 123, 124, 151, 174.
Cheever (*Lectures on Bunyan*), 2, 22, 36, 40, 49, 58, 65, 110, 112, 155, 174, 194, 205, 206.
Children, 22, 108, 109.
Christoferus, 33.
Church, the, Chaps. xii., xiii., xiv., 115, 118, 165.
Cities, Chap. xxi.
City, the Celestial, 117.
City of Destruction, Chap. i., 162, 165, 182, 205.
Clothes, 2, 72, 82, 175, 212.
Commerce, 29, 204, 222.
Companionship, 150, 159.
Confession, 104.
Conversation, 97 ff., 164 f., 181.
Cowper, William, 27, 55, 127, 210.
Cranford, 97.
Creech, William, 77.
Criticism, 195 f.
Cromwell, Oliver, 114.
Cross, the, 36, 41, Chap. ix., 77, 84, 102, 106, 149.
Crusades, the, 157, 160.
Cynewulf, 70.

DANTE, 2, 69, 70, 77, 80, 83, 84, 85, 122, 147, 148, 174, 193.
Darwin, Erasmus, 196.
Death, 7 ff.
Decadents, 144.
Defoe, Daniel, 217.
Delectable Mountains, 117.

233

Denominations, 34, 56.
Despair, 64.
Despond, Slough of, Chap. iii.
Devils, 43 f., 61, 65 f., 119, Chap. xv., 207.
Dickens, Charles, 79, 100.
Difficulty, Hill of, 77, Chap. xi.
Discontent, 172 f.
Discouragers, 21, 61, 87.
Discretion, 99.
Disraeli, Benjamin, 33.
Doctrine, Christian, statement of, 192.
Doddridge, 90.
Dods, Dr Marcus, 81, 216.
Door, the, 44 f., 63, 71.
Double personality, 132.
Doughty (*Arabia Deserta*), 3.
Dreams, 1, 67.
Drummond, Prof. H., 13, 16, 61, 65.
Drunkenness, 189 f.
Du Chaillu, 97.

EFFICIENCY, 37.
Election, Doctrine of, 164.
Eliot, George, 28, 118, 186
Elstow, 20, 40, 43, 62, 70, 93, 96, 177, 203, 217.
Emerson, R. W., 16, 161.
Enemies, 222.
Envy, 225.
Erskine, R., 17.
Euripides, 24.
Evangelist, 5 ff., 29, 34 ff., Chap. v., 55, 199 f.
Everyman, 2.
Ezekiel and other Poems, 43.

FABER, 48.
Fairs, Chap. xxii.
Faith, 120, 162.
Faithful, Chaps. xviii., xix.
Family and wife of Christian, 4, 27, 37, 107 ff.
Faust, 26, 66, 131, 133, 149, 207.
Fear, 24, 86 f., 105, 145.
Fence, 69.
Fire of London, 4.
Firth, Professor, 114.
Flesh, the, 169 ff.
Formalist, 73, Chap. x.   [96, 217.
Foster (*Bunyan's Country*), 62, 70, 94,
Foxe (*Book of Martyrs*), 153, 227.
Francis of Assisi, 73, 127.
Frithjof's Saga, 121, 130.
Froude, J. A., 1, 2, 114, 123, 124 f., 135, 169, 185, 219, 220.

GENTLEMANLINESS, 14, 26 f., 175.
Gifford, John, 34, 56, 82, 201.
Goethe (*cf*. Faust), 26, 66.
Goodwill, Chap. vi., 99.
Goodwin, 14.
Gordon, A. L., 65.
Grail, the Holy, 49, 108

Gravity, 43, 55.
Gregory, Saint, 53.

HALL, Fielding, 46.
Hampden, Dr, 227.
Hardy, Thomas, 8.
Hatch (*Hibbert Lectures*), 154.
Hawthorne, Nathaniel, 21, 41, 51, 55, 56, 57, 83, 95, 146, 148, 155, 206, 208.
Healthy-mindedness, 143.
Heaven, 15, 117.
Heine, 37.
Hell, 147.
Help, 23 ff., 38.
Herakles, 23.
Herbert, George, 14, 49, 55, 139.
Heroism, 5.
Herrick, 88.
Hole, W., 42.
Holy Spirit, 49 ff.
Holy War, 74, 127, 135, 153, 164, 204, 221.
Honour, 133.
Horton, Dr, 57.
Houghton House, 93 f.
Hudibras, 82, 176, 177, 181, 189, 213, 216.
Hugo, Victor, 97, 201, 216.
Humiliation, Humility, Chap. xv., 127, 193.
Hunt, Holy, 214.
Hypocrisy, Chap. x., 188 ff.

IGNATIUS, 218.
Imagination, 15, 87, 107, 150, Chap xiv.
Indifference, 73.
Interpreter's House, Chap. vii., 101.

JEFFREYS, Judge, 220, 223.
Jerome K. Jerome, 24.
Jones, Sam, 63.
Jowett, Dr J. H., 184.

KEBLE, 55.
Keelynge, Sir John, 220.
Kempis, T. à, 172.
Kernahan, Coulson, 111.
Kingsley, Charles, 24.
Kipling, Rudyard, 64, 87, 88, 132, 147, 171.
Knox, John, 35, 46, 103 f.

LANGLAND, William, 2, 72, 214.
Lasalle, 173.
Law, William, 11.
Law, the, 58 f., 171.
Lecky (*History of Rationalism*), 154, 220.
Leech, John, 212.
Leighton, Archbishop, 28.
Leonardo da Vinci, 58.
Lessing, 67.
Lions, 74, 86 ff., 95, 125, 154.
Longfellow, 9, 23.
Luther, 1, 128, 161, 172, 184, 207.
Lyall, Edna, 56.

INDEX

Lytton, Bulwer, 139.

MACAULAY, Lord, 114, 220.
MacCunn, Mrs, 83.
Macdonald, George, 28.
MacGregor, Professor James, 174.
MacKenzie, Fergus, 190.
Maclaren, Ian, 143.
Macleod, Fiona, 157, 171.
Maguire, Bishop, 27, 139.
Mark, Christian's, 72.
Martyrdom, 218 f.
Masson, Professor David, 91, 128.
Matheson, Duncan, 78.
Maundevile, Sir John, 129.
Melancholy, Chap. xv. [206.
Meredith, George, 58, 63, 98, 110, 131,
Milton, John, 42, 48, 72, 112, 127, 128, 130, 131, 133, 138, 207, 224.
Ministry, The Christian (*cf*. Evangelist), 39, 50, 53, 55 ff., 99, 200.
Montaigne, 183.
Montgomery, 47.
Morality, 30 ff., Chap. v.
Morality Plays, 2, 96, 147.
Moses, 171.

NAMES, 100.
Nansen, 4, 150.
Napoleon Buonaparte, 92, 163.
Natural Man, 169 ff.
Newman, Dr J. H., 16.

OBSTINATE, Chap. ii., 26, 28.
Offor, 122, 176, 182, 201, 227.
Oliphant, Mrs, 217, 220.
Omar Kayyám, 158.

PAGANISM, 153.
Paget, Bishop, 228.
Parasitism, 16.
Passion, 58 f.
Pater, Walter, 51, 52, 57, 58, 59.
Patience, 59 f.
Patmore, Coventry, 49.
Peabody, Dr, 75.
Peace, 72, 112, 121, 222.
Peden, 202.
Pèlerinage de l'Homme, 2.
Penn, William, 220.
Pepys, Samuel, 176, 219, 220.
Persecution, Chap. xxiii.
Petrarch, 18, 62.
Peyton, W. W., 62, 197.
Pickthank, 226.
Piety, 100 f.
Pilgrim's Progress, Editions of, 6, 34, 199.
—— Part II., 42, 51, 72, 76, 87, 127, 137, 139.
—— Part III., 38, 50, 73, 85, 94, 100, 152, 156, 167, 180, 208.
Plain Man's Pathway to Heaven, The, 110, 124, 169, 175.
Pliable, Chap. ii., 26, 45, 163, 164.

Poe, E. A., 66.
Porter, The, 91, Chap. xii., 98 f., 122, 165.
Practice of Piety, The, 110, 192.
Praed, 156.
Prayer, 42 f., 121, 148.
Prison, John Bunyan's, 1.
Prison, books written in, 1.
Promises, 22.
Prophecy, 115.
Prudence, 103 f.
Pulpit (John Bunyan's), 177.
Puritanism, 71, 177, 181, 204, 205, Chap. xxxii.

QUESTIONING, The art of, 7, 34, 100.
Quorm, Dan'l, 21.

RAGS, 2, 72.
Ramsay, Sir W., 10.
Ranters, 190.
Reality, 77, 83, 84, 187.
Reason, 6 16.
Renan, 38, 168.
Responsibility, limited, 75, 196.
Reticence, 182.
Richter, J. P., 209.
Ridicule, 176, 213.
Robertson, F. W., 20, 75.
Roll, Christian's, 73, Chap. xi.
Roman Catholic Church, 70, 104, 115, Chap. xiii., 209 f.
Romances of Chivalry, 2, 62, 93, 121, 124.
Romanes, J. G., 9, 62, 138.
Rosetti, Christina, 90, 94, 172.
Rosetti, D. G., 2, 51, 108.
Ruskin, John, 14, 18, 24, 200, 201.
Russia, 119.
Rutherford, Samuel, 1, 118.
"Rutherford, Mark," *John Bunyan*, 1, 56, 98, 128, 147, 153, 155, 225.

SALVATION, Chap. ix., 121.
Scott, Sir Walter, 94, 146.
Scott, Dr., 151, 175.
Scott, David, 24, 74, 86, 87, 217.
Second chances, 137.
Self-denial, 46.
Servants, 189.
Shakespeare, 8, 14, 24, 27, 49, 64, 112, 118, 121, 136, 148, 162, 180, 211.
Shame, 137, 174 ff.
Shaw, Bernard, 31.
Sheridan, 14, 30.
Silence of God, 134.
Simple, Sloth, and Presumption, 73 ff., 85.
Sin, 3.
Sinai, 33 ff., 37 ff.
Sirens, 169.
Smith, Sidney, 39, 57.
Snell (*The Fourteenth Century*), 1, 2, 62.
Socrates, 202.
Southwell, 153.

235

Spectacular, the, 15, 19, 68, 107.
Spenser, Edmund, 4, 151.
Spira, Francis, 35, 64 ff., 185.
Stanley, Dean, 113, 194.
Stead, W. T., 41.
Stevenson (*Text-Book*), 49, 55, 73, 74, 85.
Stevenson, R. L., 14, 26, 35, 38, 84, 93, 94, 132, 137, 174, 195, 219, 223, 226.
Stewart of Aberdeen, 184.
Stoics, 83.
Strenuousness, 62, 63, 83.
Study, 113 ff.
Sunrise, 151.
Superstition, 226.
Swinburne, Algernon, 171.

TACITUS, 207.
Talkative, Chap. xx.
Tannhaüser, 205.
Tasso, 136.
Taylor, Jeremy, 102, 194.
Taylor, Rachel Annand, 228.
Temptation, Chaps. xv., xix.
Tennyson, 13, 22, 38, 170, 225.
Thackeray, W. M., 60, 206, 207.
Thompson, Francis, 5.
Timorous and *Mistrust*, 86 ff.
Toleration, 153.
Tolstoi, 183, 186.
Trimmers, 17.
Truth, 196, 214.
Turning back, 23, 35, 37, 45, 65 f., 74.
Twain, Mark, 118.

UTOPIA 199.

VALLEY of the Shadow of Death, Chap. xvi.
Vanity Fair, Chaps. xxi.-xxiii.
Vicars, Hedley, 86.
Virgil, 101, 117.
Vision, Spiritual, 116 f.

WANTON, 167.
Ward, Mrs H., 76.
Watts, Isaac, 86.
Way, The, 46, Chap. ix., 136.
Webster, Augusta, 36.
Weltschmerz, 21, 26, 144,
Weyman, Stanley, 138.
Whittier, J. G., 18, 147, 148.
Whittington, Sir Richard, 26.
Whitman, Walt, 51.
Whymper, E., 75.
Whyte, Dr, 14, 21, 36, 47, 59, 91, 109, 175, 182, 217.
Wicket Gate, 8, Chap. vi.
Wilde, Oscar, 30.
Wilkins, Mary, 119.
Wolfram's *Parsifal*, 108.
Woman, 24.
Wonder, 184.
Wordsworth, 117.
World, the, 57 f., 177, Chap. xxii.
Worldly Wiseman, Chaps iv., v., 49.

ZOLA, Emile, 121.